Lecture Notes in Computer Science 3792

Commenced Publication in 1973
Founding and Former Series Editors:
Gerhard Goos, Juris Hartmanis, and Jan van Leeuwen

T0223607

Ita Richardson   Pekka Abrahamsson
Richard Messnarz (Eds.)

Software Process Improvement

12th European Conference, EuroSPI 2005
Budapest, Hungary, November 9-11, 2005
Proceedings

 Springer

Volume Editors

Ita Richardson
University of Limerick, Department of Computer Science and Information Systems
National Technological Park Castletroy, Limerick, Ireland
E-mail: ita.richardson@ul.ie

Pekka Abrahamsson
VTT Technical Research Centre of Finland
PO Box 1100, Kaitoväylä 1, 90571 Oulu, Finland
E-mail: pekka.abrahamsson@vtt.fi

Richard Messnarz
International Software Consulting Network GmbH Research Office
Schieszstattgasse 4, 8010 Graz, Austria
E-mail: rmess@iscn.com

Library of Congress Control Number: 2005935531

CR Subject Classification (1998): D.2, K.6, K.4.2

ISSN   0302-9743
ISBN-10   3-540-30286-7 Springer Berlin Heidelberg New York
ISBN-13   978-3-540-30286-5 Springer Berlin Heidelberg New York

Springer is a part of Springer Science+Business Media

springeronline.com

© Springer-Verlag Berlin Heidelberg 2005
Printed in Germany

Typesetting: Camera-ready by author, data conversion by Scientific Publishing Services, Chennai, India
Printed on acid-free paper   SPIN: 11586012   06/3142   5 4 3 2 1 0

Preface

This volume is intended for SPI (software process improvement) managers and researchers, quality managers, and experienced project and research managers. The papers constitute the research proceedings of the 12th EuroSPI (European Software Process Improvement, www.eurospi.net) conference held in Budapest, 9–11 November 2005, Hungary. Conferences have been held in 1994 in Dublin, 1995 in Vienna (Austria), 1997 in Budapest (Hungary), 1998 in Gothenburg (Sweden), 1999 in Pori (Finland), 2000 in Copenhagen (Denmark), 2001 in Limerick (Ireland), 2002 in Nuremberg (Germany), 2003 in Graz (Austria), and 2004 in Trondheim (Norway). EuroSPI established an experience library (library.eurospi.net) which will be continuously extended over the next years and will be made available to all attendees. EuroSPI also created an umbrella initiative for establishing a European Qualification Network in which different SPINs and national initiatives join mutually beneficial collaborations.

From 2005, through EuroSPI partners and networks, in collaboration with the European Union (supported by the EU Leonardo da Vinci Programme), a certification body will be created for the IT and services sector so as to offer SPI knowledge and certificates to industry, establishing close knowledge transfer links between research and industry. The biggest value of EuroSPI lies in its function as a European knowledge and experience exchange mechanism between SPI research institutions and industry.

September 2005

Dr. Richard Messnarz
General Chair EuroSPI
www.eurospi.net

Organization Committee

EuroSPI 2005 is organized by the EuroSPI partnership (www.eurospi.net), internationally coordinated by ISCN, and locally supported by the John von Neumann Computer Society.

Program Committee

Conference Chair	Richard Messnarz (ISCN, Ireland)
Scientific Program Chair	Ita Richardson (University of Limerick, Ireland)
Scientific Program Chair	Pekka Abrahamsson (VTT, Finland)
Industrial Program Chair	Nils Brede Moe (SINTEF, Norway)
Industrial Program Chair	Risto Nevalainen (STTF, Finland)
Tutorial Chair	Richard Messnarz (ISCN, Ireland)
Exhibition Chair	Stephan Goericke (ISQI, Germany)
Organizing Chair	Miklos Biro (Corvinus University, Hungary)
Organizing Chair	Adrienne Clarke (ISCN, Ireland)

Local Committee

Local Organizer	John von Neumann Computer Society, www.njszt.hu

Additional Scientific Reviewers

V. Ambriola	T. Dyba	E. Ostolaza
A. Aurum	J. Pries-Heje	K. Molokken-Ostvold
A. Beriozko	S. Hope	G. Ruhe
S. Biffl	K. H. Kautz	P. Runeson
M. Biro	D. Landes	M. Shepperd
C. Bunse	M. Lindvall	K. Siakas
M. Ciolkowski	P. McQuaid	K. Schneider
K. Cox	M. Mueller	T. Stalhane
K.C. Desouza	J. Muench	T. Varkoi
H. Duncan	J. Niere	C. Wohlin
T. Daughtrey	M. Oivo	

Table of Contents

Quality and Knowledge Management

Engineering and Development

Software Process Improvement – EuroSPI 2005 Conference

R. Messnarz, P. Abrahamsson, and I. Richardson

EuroSPI , c/o ISCN LTD, Bray, Co. Wicklow, Ireland
http://www.eurospi.net

Abstract. This book constitutes the refereed research proceeding of the 12th European Software Process Improvement Conference, EuroSPI 2005, held in Budapest, Hungary in November 2005. The 18 revised full papers presented were carefully reviewed and selected from 40 submissions. The papers are organized in topical sections on agile methods, SPI studies, improvement methods, engineering and development, and quality and knowledge concepts.

1 EuroSPI

EuroSPI is a partnership of large Scandinavian research companies and experience networks (SINTEF, DELTA,STTF), the ASQF as a large German quality association, the American Society for Quality, and ISCN as the co-coordinating partner. EuroSPI collaborates with a large number of SPINs (Software Process Improvement Network) in Europe.

EuroSPI conferences present and discuss results from improvement projects in industry and research, focusing on the benefits gained and the criteria for success. Leading European universities, research centers, and industry are contributing to and participating in this event. This year's event is the 12th of a series of conferences to which international researchers contribute their lessons learned and share their knowledge as they work towards the next higher level of software management professionalism.

The biggest value of EuroSPI lies in its function as a European knowledge and experience exchange mechanism where researchers, industrial managers and professionals meet to exchange experiences and ideas and fertilize the grounds for new developments and improvements.

1.1 Board Members

ASQ, http://www.asq.org
ASQF, http://www.asqf.de
DELTA, http://www.delta.dk
ISCN, http://www.iscn.com
SINTEF, http://www.sintef.no
STTF, http://www.sttf.fi

I. Richardson et al. (Eds.): EuroSPI 2005, LNCS 3792, pp. 1–3, 2005.
© Springer-Verlag Berlin Heidelberg 2005

1.2   EuroSPI Scientific Programme Committee

Pekka Abrahamsson, VTT Electronics, Finland
Vincenzo Ambriola, University of Pisa , Italy
Aybuke Aurum, University of New South Wales, Australia
Alexander Beriozko, Russian Academy of Sciences, RU
Stefan Biffl, TU Wien , Austria
Miklos Biro, University of Budapest, Hungary
Christian Bunse, Fraunhofer IESE, Germany
Marcus Ciolkowski, University of Kaiserslautern, Germany
Karl Cox, NICTA, Australia
Kevin C. Desouza, University of Illinois, USA
Howard Duncan, Dublin City University, Ireland
Taz Daughtrey, James MADISON University, USA
Tore Dybå, SINTEF, Norway
Jan Pries-Heje, ITU, Denmark
Sian Hope, University of Wales, Bangor,UK
Karl Heinz Kautz, Copenhagen Business School, Denmark
Dieter Landes, Coburg University of Applied Sciences, Germany
Mikael Lindvall, Fraunhofer Center, USA
Patricia McQuaid, California Polytechnic University, USA
Matthias Mueller, University of Karlsruhe, Germany
Juergen Muench, Fraunhofer IESE, Germany
Joerg Niere, University of Siegen, Germany
Markku Oivo, University of Oulu, Finland
Elixabete Ostolaza, European Software Institute, Spain
Kjetil Molokken-Ostvold , Simula Research Laboratory, Norway
Vincent Ribaud, University of Brest, France
Ita Richardson, University of Limerick, Ireland
Gunther Ruhe, University of Calgary, Canada
Per Runeson, University of Lund, Sweden
Martin Shepperd, Bornemouth University, England
Kerstin Siakas, Technological Education Institute of Thessaloniki, Greece
Kurt Schneider, University of Hannover, Germany
Tor Stålhane, Norwegian University of Science and Technology, Norway
Colin Tully, University of Middlesex, UK
Timo Varkoi, Tampere University of Technology, Finland
Claes Wohlin, Blekinge Institute of Technology, Sweden

1.3   EuroSPI Scientific Chairs

 Dr Richard Messnarz
General Chair of EuroSPI
ISCN, Ireland and Austria
rmess@iscn.com

Dr Ita Richardson
EuroSPI Scientific Programme Committee Chair
University of Limerick , Ireland
Ita.Richardson@ul.ie

Dr Pekka Abrahamsson
EuroSPI Scientific Programme Committee Chair
VTT Technical Research Centre of Finland
Pekka.Abrahamsson@vtt.fi

2　How to Read the Proceedings

Since its beginning in 1994 in Dublin, the EuroSPI initiative outlines that there is not a single silver bullet to solve SPI issues but you need to understand a combination of different SPI methods and approaches to achieve real benefits. Therefore each proceeding covers a variety of different topics and at the conference we discuss potential synergies and combined use of such methods and approaches. This proceeding contains selected research papers for 5 topics:

SPI and Agile Methods & Soft Issues (3 papers)
SPI and Improvement Methods (3 papers)
SPI Studies (3 papers)
SPI and Quality & Knowledge Concepts (3 papers)
SPI in Engineering and Development (6 papers)

2.1　Recommended Further Reading

In [1] we integrated the proceedings of 3 EuroSPI conferences into one book which was edited by 30 experts in Europe. In [2] you find the most recent EuroSPI research proceeding published by Springer andbased on EuroSPI 2004.

References

1.　Messnarz R., Tully C. (eds.), Better Software Practice for Business Benefit - Principles and Experience, IEEE Computer Society Press, ISBN: 0-7695-0049-8, paperback, 409 pages, Wiley-IEEE Computer Society Press, September 1999
2.　Dingsøyr, T. (Ed.) , Software Process Improvement 11th European Conference, EuroSPI 2004, Trondheim, Norway, November 10-12, 2004. Proceedings, 2004, X, 207 p., Softcover, ISBN: 3-540-23725-9, in: Lecture Notes in Computer Science, Vol. 3281 , Springer Verlag, November 2004

Framework of Agile Patterns

Teodora Bozheva and Maria Elisa Gallo

European Software Institute, Parque Tecnológico Edif. 204,
48170 Zamudio (Bizkaia), Spain
{Teodora.Bozheva, MariaElisa.Gallo}@esi.es
http://www.esi.es

Abstract. The variety of agile methods and their similarity could be a problem for software engineers to select a single or a number of methods and to properly execute them in a project. A pattern describes a problem, which typically occurs under certain circumstances and a basic approach to solve it providing opportunities to adapt the solution to the problem. The agile patterns, described herein, are based on the principles and practices of the best known agile methodologies. While individual practices included in any of these methods vary, they all have particular objectives and related to them activities. Therefore, every pattern is described as to show the core solution to a particular problem. Special attention is paid to the rationale for applying the agile patterns: what are the business drivers to adopting them; in what cases do they bring benefits; how could they be introduced in an organization.

1 Introduction

Nowadays lots of organizations face the need to adapt quickly to modifications requested by their customers, changes on the market or challenges from competitors. This happens in small as well as in large organizations, in ones following standard (ISO 9001:2000, CMMI) or their own processes. These business needs force the companies evaluate how the agile methods could address their necessities.

Agile methods recognize that any project, team and organization has its unique peculiarities and respond to the specific needs via business value based prioritization, short feedback cycles and quality-focused development. When appropriately applied the agile practices bring a number of business benefits as better project adaptability and reaction to changes, reduced production costs, improved product quality and increased user satisfaction with the final solution.

The agile methods differ in the approaches to software development and management they propose. Some focus more heavily on project management and collaboration practices. These include Adaptive Software Development (ASD) [6], Scrum [7], Lean Development (LD) [10] and DSDM [8]. Others, such as eXtreme Programming (XP) [3], Feature-driven Development (FDD) [9] and Agile Modeling (AM) [5], focus more extensively on software implementation practices. Nevertheless, all the methods stick to the principles of maintaining good understanding of the project

I. Richardson et al. (Eds.): EuroSPI 2005, LNCS 3792, pp. 4 – 15, 2005.

objectives, scope and constraints, developing software in short, feature-drive iterations, receiving constant feedback from the customer and the developers, and focusing on the delivery of business value.

An important issue in defining an organizational process is that all the elements it consists of reflect properly the specifics of the environment, in which the process will be implemented. When selecting an agile method, the business and organizational context, in which it will be applied, determines the benefits that could be achieved for a project and for an organization. In their book [1] B. Boehm and R. Turner have defined the "home grounds" in which agile and disciplined methods are most successful. Additionally, they define five factors, which help the organization determine whether they are in either the agile or disciplined area, or somewhere in between. These are size, criticality, personnel, dynamism, and culture.

Our work on applying agile practices in different organizational contexts inspired the development of the framework of agile patterns, presented in this paper. The idea is instead of providing a complete method, which might not be fully applicable in any situation, to provide a set of patterns addressing different aspects of the software development process, which could be combined in such a way as to fit to the peculiarity of a project. The patterns are derived from the most widely known lightweight methods XP, Scrum, FDD, AM, LD, and ASD.

Implementing a software development process based on patterns has several advantages:

- The patterns address activities performed by software engineers and project managers who are accustomed to using well structured information like pattern definitions.
- Patterns describe individual practices in a general enough way to be applied in different situations. Therefore they can be easily tried out and included in definitions of new processes. Adopting a small set of new practices gives a more profound understanding of the practices themselves and of the benefits from applying them together, which facilitates the continuous process improvement.
- As each pattern is selected and adapted as to best fit a project and organizational context, the whole process will be more suitable for that context than any general one.

We describe the framework of agile patterns in section 2 and in section 3 we present lessons learnt from applying the patterns in the industry.

2 Framework of Agile Patterns

A pattern describes a problem, which typically occurs under certain circumstances. It also describes a basic approach to solve the problem providing opportunities to adapt the solution to the particular problem context. In general, a pattern has three essential elements: problem, solution and consequences. Each solution consists of activities that, when collectively applied, resolve the problem. The solution is abstract enough to make it possible to apply it in different situations. The consequences are results and trade-offs of applying the pattern.

Three key terms take part in the agile methods: *practices*, *concepts* and *principles*. *Practices* describe specific actions that are performed in the whole process of software development, e.g. create product backlog (SCRUM). *Concepts* describe the attributes of an item, e.g. a project plan. *Principles* are fundamental guidelines concerning software development activities, e.g. empower the team (LD).

To be coherent with the agile methodologies the framework of agile patterns (FAP) includes definitions of three types of patterns: practice patterns, concepts and principles.

2.1 Practice Patterns

In the FAP each agile pattern is described by means of the following attributes:

- **Intent:** a short description of what the objective is;
- **Origin:** methodologies, from which the pattern originates;
- **Category** to which the pattern belongs. With respect to the type of issues addressed, the patterns are grouped in the following categories: *Project and Requirements Management, Design, Implementation and Testing, Resource Management, Contract Management* and *Software Process Improvement*.
- **Application scenario:** context, in which the pattern is to be applied;
- **Roles:** people involved in carrying out the pattern and their responsibilities;
- Main and alternative **Activities** that constitute the pattern. Activities can invoke other patterns;
- **Tools** that support the pattern execution;
- **Guidelines** for performing the activities including suggestions for making a decision about which alternative solution to choose when.

This structure is closest to the one proposed by E. Gamma in [2]. Compared to the classic pattern definition (problem-solution-consequences), Intent and Application scenario correspond to the problem attribute. Activities matches to solution. Some patterns provide alternative solutions to the same problem. This typically happens when the problem is addressed by more than one agile method and different solutions to it are proposed. Guidelines include hints for performing the activities and the consequences from them. An example of a pattern is:

CodeIntegrator

Intent: To have working code at the end of every day. In a software development environment with collective code ownership, the idea is to build the system every day, after a very small batch of work has been done by each of the developers.

Origin: LD: Synch and Stabilise (Daily build and smoke test); XP: Integrate often

Category: Implementation & Testing

Application scenario: After implementing a piece of code

Roles: Developers

Activities

- Check out source code from the configuration management system.
- Put together the newly implemented and the existing code.

- Check to see, if anyone else has made changes to the same code, and if so, resolve the conflicts by applying <u>CodeImplementer.</u>
- Apply <u>AcceptanceTester.</u>
- Check in the new code.

Tools: Version control tools support this activity.
Guidelines:

- Continuous integration avoids or detects compatibility problems early. If changes are integrated in small batches, it will be infinitely easier to detect and fix problems.
- A single integration point (computer) has to be defined.
- Every developer is responsible for integrating his/her own code always when there is a reasonable break. This could be when all the unit tests run at 100% or some smaller portion of the planned functionality is finished. Only one developer integrates at a given moment and after only a few hours of coding.
- All the tests have to pass successfully after integrating the system. Each integration results in a running system. Integration happens every 1-5 hours, at least once a day.

Apart from the natural language description of the patterns, every category is graphically illustrated showing which patterns, concepts and principles it includes, and the relationships between them.

On the graphics the following symbols are used:

Symbol	Meaning
⬭	Principle
▭	Pattern
▱	Concept
⟶	*"invokes"*
A ------▶ B	Pattern A supports B, but it is optional to use A when implementing B

As an example, let's consider the *Implementation and Testing* category (Fig.1).

The patterns and their intents, which belong to this category, are the following ones.

Code Implementer: Implement code

FDDCoder: Implement defect-free code following FDD

XPCoder: Implement defect-free code following XP

SoftwareInspector; Find out defects in project work products

UnitTester: Define and execute in an automated way unit tests for a module of code.

AcceptanceTester: Define and execute in an automated way tests written by the customer to show that her requirements have been implemented correctly

CodeIntegrator: To have working code at the end of every day. In a software development environment with collective code ownership, the idea is to build the system every day, after a very small batch of work has been done by each of the developers

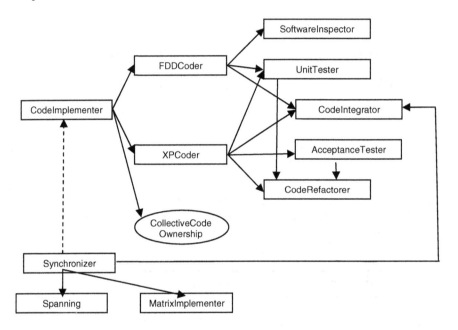

Fig. 1. Implementation & Testing category

CodeRefactorer: Maintain good quality of the code

Syncronizer: Maintain the code developed and owned by several people synchronised

Spanning: Synchronize the work of several teams using a simple spanning application that allows getting a real understanding of the strengths and weakness of alternative solutions.

MatrixImplementer: Synchronize the work of several teams by letting them sketch out an overall architecture, and then develop separate components or subsystems.

The *CollectiveCodeOwnership* principle belongs to this category, and there are no concepts in it.

A brief description of the other pattern categories is provided in the Annex.

2.2 Concepts

Concept is a definition of a class of items that consists of characteristics or essential features of the class. For consistency reason the concepts in the FAP are described by a subset of the attributes of a practice pattern. The principal distinction of a concept from a practice is that there are no activities associated with the concept.

For instance, *ProjectPlan* is a concept describing the attributes of a good project plan in accordance with the philosophy of the agile methodologies.

ProjectPlan
Intent: Serves as a focal point and quick reminder of the most important elements about the project.

Origin: ASD: Project Data Sheet; XP: Release plan; FDD: Development plan

Application scenario: Project planning

Roles: Customer: makes business decision (scope, priorities, release planning)
Developers: make technical decisions (effort estimations, risks)
Project Leader: makes the planning

Definition: The Project Plan is one-page summary of the key information about the project. The Project Plan includes the following details:

- Project objectives statement
- Overall Architecture
- Major project milestones
- Core team members

The project objectives statement should be specific and short (25 words or less), and it should include important scope, schedule, and resource information.

Guidelines: In FDD the development plan consists of:

- Feature sets with completion dates
- Major feature sets with completion dates derived from the last completion date of their respective feature sets
- Chief Programmers assigned to feature sets
- The list of classes and the developers that own them

Eleven concepts are defined and used in the FAP.

Mission describes what constitutes a software development project. It consists of *Vision, ProductSpecificationOutline* and *ProjectPlan*.

Vision provides a short definition of key business objectives, product specifications, and market positioning.

ProductSpecificationOutline describes the features of a product in enough detail so that developers can understand the project scope, create a more detailed adaptive iteration plan, and estimate the general magnitude of the development effort.

ProjectPlan serves as a focal point and quick reminder of the most important elements of a project.

IterationPlan describes the requirements to be implemented within an iteration.

DesignDocument is a sufficient enough description of a software product design, which facilitates the verification of the output of the design activities.

DailyMeeting is a short meeting of a project team, which purpose is to communicate the current status of the project and problems encountered.

FixedPart indicates the content of a fixed part of an agile contract.

VariablePart indicates the content of a variable part of an agile contract.

Team is the software development team.

Waste in software development is everything that does not deliver business value to the customer (development of not explicitly required features, partially done work, paperwork not directly needed for the development processes, handoffs, defects, switching between different projects, waiting for a project/task to start).

2.3 Principles

Principle is a set of fundamental guidelines concerning the software development activities. The principles are people-oriented and flexible, offering generative rules. Again for consistency reason the principles in FAP are described by a subset of practice pattern attributes: Intent, Origin and Guidelines. An example of a principle is

CollectiveCodeOwnership
Intent: The code is collectively owned by the developers. Anyone change it. The programmers use a coding standard to enforce a common style.
Origin: XP: Collective Code Ownership
Guidelines: Collective code ownership is more reliable than putting a single person in charge of watching specific pieces of code, especially because, if a person leaves the project at some time, the other project team members will know the code he has implemented and will be ready to continue his work.

We consider seven principles most important among the ones defined in the investigated methods. *Collective code ownership* is from XP and the rest of the principles originate from Lean Development.

Avoid sub-optimization. Instead of optimizing the performance of small project parts, optimize the complete system, i.e. focus developers on what's important, namely meeting the customer's business needs, not on building a product with the excellent characteristics from technology point of view only.

Decide Late. Take decisions as late as possible, reducing in this way the risk of making mistakes due to insufficient information.

Deliver Fast. Provide rapid delivery to customers. This often translates to increased business flexibility.

Empower the Team. Move decision-making to the lowest possible level in an organization, while developing the capacity of those people to make decisions wisely.

Queuing Theory. Optimize resource management as to reduce the time spent for waiting for a resource to start working on a task.

Simple Rules. Chose a small number of strategically significant processes and craft a few simple rules to guide them.

2.4 FAP and Other Related Approaches

The patterns approach is not new in the software development area. However, most of its applications address object-oriented design and implementation of software. [2] defines design patterns. Wiki (http://www.c2.com) provides a catalog of object-oriented patterns. There are plenty of books on this subject and the Pattern Languages of Programs conferences (http://hillside.net) dedicated to it too.

These are valuable sources of knowledge for the software developers. Nevertheless, it proves that being able to implement good software is not enough in the e-era, which demands additional capabilities to perform in a flexible and rapid manner. Therefore the focus of our work is on the agile practices for software development and management. At the time being the repository of the agile patterns is being developed and piloted within the ITEA AGILE project (ITEA IP030003; http://www.agile-itea.org).

3 Guidelines for Applying the Framework of Agile Patterns

From software developer's perspective the key benefits of the patterns are the experience-based guidelines and the rationale for patterns implementation, which complement the definitions derived from the literature. Concerning practical experience with the agile practices we gathered valuable information from seven projects performed in different organizations within the *e*Xpert project (IST-2001-34488; http://www.esi.es/Expert). The trials were focused on applying XP practices in e-commerce and e-business application development. The main objectives for the projects were to evaluate how the agile practices contribute to increasing the productivity and the efficiency of the software engineers, and to improving the quality of the products they develop[1]. Other relevant experience has been coming from companies to which we provide consultancy services on software process improvement. Currently the patterns are being experimented in the ITEA AGILE project.

3.1 Who Should Apply the Agile Patterns

Similarly to all lightweight methodologies the agile patterns are most appropriate for highly dynamic projects. In all the cases, mentioned above, the business needs forced the companies evaluate how agile practices could address their necessities. Out of 13 companies 7 wanted to increase their responsiveness to the changing customer's or market needs; 6 were looking for ways to decrease their time-to-market. Two companies had to follow the rigorous Metrica-3 methodology, and were looking for a way to perform some activities more flexibly, remaining compliant with the basic methodology. Three companies were applying ISO or CMMI standard. The other ones had their own processes established.

Among the specific problems, the organizations had, were provision of unclear requirements and frequent changes to them; incorrect effort estimation, which later caused difficulties to deliver the product on time without working extra hours or adding more resources; inefficient project management. One of the project teams said that they were feeling like a fire brigade, because whenever their customer needed to quickly release a product, he contacted them and expected their professional solution on time and within budget. Although all this sounds trivial, the companies did not believe that the traditional approaches would help them and started investigating more lightweight ones.

The agile patterns are successfully adopted by small teams having development experience and motivation to maintain good communication with the customer and to deliver software with low defect rate in a short time. It is easier to introduce the

---

[1] For the sake of completeness, the results from the experiments are as follows: Productivity increased up to 73%. One company decreased its productivity; Schedule deviation reduced between 7% and 38%; Cost deviation decreased up to 31%. Only one company increased its cost deviation; Defect rates reduced between 10% and 83%.

patterns in organizations with a relatively flat hierarchy, because the direct communication to the management is important for the success of the projects.

With respect to CMMI and ISO-certified organizations the agility of their processes can be increased by means of agile patterns and the typical work products could be developed in a more flexible and efficient manner.

3.2 When Should Be Agile Patterns Applied

Our experience shows that agile patterns are successfully applicable in the following cases:

- Projects, in which the client only has a broad-brush picture of the envisioned system without knowing its detailed frames and final features. Using patterns from the category of *Project & Requirements Management* reduces the time and effort spent on initial customer requirements analysis and involves the client in the implementation of the system features.
- Projects, which development includes exploration and application of new or less known technologies. In such cases the *Iterative&IncrementalModeller*, *InTeamModeller* and *CodeImplementer* patterns, applied in short iterations, are of particular use.
- Projects, which outcome is a critical success factor for the organization's business. This implies close tracking of the results, the schedule and budget.
- The client and the development team have established high confidence relationship and mutual trust, which brings additional success factor for the implementation of a new process. Constant awareness on the project status increases the client's confidence in the final result and in the agile practices.
- Teams applying CMMI or ISO who are interested in increasing the agility of their processes. In such cases the developers should select patterns to appropriately substitute practices they currently perform and to adapt the patterns to the other process activities.

3.3 How to Adopt the Agile Patterns

The adoption of agile patterns has to be done gradually, and it has to be taken into account that the better the philosophy of the agile methodologies is accepted and applied in an organization, the higher the benefit from the practices used.
These are typically the steps to start applying agile patterns:

1) Identify Changes to be Made
Apply the *WasteEliminator* to identify processes or parts of processes, which agility has to be increased. Identify agile patterns that could be used to improve the current activities. Define how the selected agile patterns will be adjusted to the practices, which are already in place.

2) Customize a patterns-based process to a project and the team
Building a process from patterns is like using a Lego construction set. First, one should have an idea of what he wants to build up and afterwards to start constructing it combining different pieces. In the context of software development it translates to identifying which activities should be made more lightweight and applying respective patterns to achieve them. Since the approach is very much dependent on the team

culture and on the specifics of the projects, the application of the patterns has to be analyzed and adapted to a particular context.

    3)   Introduce selected patterns

Explain to or train all the team members how to apply the selected patterns. A gradual transition from a heavyweight to an agile process make the changes easier for the development team. We have supported several projects in applying the agile patterns and the most important lessons learned by the development teams are as follows:

- FAP should not be adopted using the "Big Bang" approach. That is the team should not try to apply at once all the patterns covering a complete development process because some of the practices are very different from what most of the developers are used to do, e.g. write test cases before the code. Instead, the team should try to adopt the patterns sequentially, following the natural project lifecycle. However, the patterns are dependent on each other; therefore all selected ones have to be put in place at some point.
- The good communication with the customer is a key factor. The foundation of an agile approach is in the close customer involvement into the project creation from the first steps to the last test performed. It is not so important to have the customer really on-site. An alternative is Customer on-demand (by phone, mail, meetings). The important thing is that if the customer gives the team rapid feedback when required. If the customer does not provide prompt feedback on project issues then the project is in trouble. It can spoil all other efforts, no matter how hard the team tries, because there will be no way they can be sure that the product they build is the product the customer wants.
- Automate! Use tools wherever possible. They save a lot of manual effort and increase the productivity a lot. There are lots of tools that aid the unit testing, acceptance testing, refactoring, requirements management, defects tracking, effort tracking, etc. Lots of them are open source or free, so they will not compromise the project budget. The effort needed to start using them is usually very small compared to the benefits they provide.

4 Conclusions

Today's enterprise solutions are complex, time critical and developed against rapidly changing business needs. The framework of agile patterns helps software engineers and practitioners to optimize the software development by selecting and putting together practices that fit the peculiarities of their projects and teams better than whole methods.

    This approach provides a superior synchronization throughout a project and an organization, because the positive results are quickly seen and motivate people to go in the direction of flexibility, adaptability and responsiveness.

References

1. Boehm B., Turner R.: Balancing Agility and Discipline: A Guide for the Perplexed, Addison Wesley (2003)
2. Gamma E., et al: Design Patterns, Addison-Wesley (1995)

3. Beck K: Extreme Programming Explained: Embrace Change, Addison-Wesley (2000)
4. Poppendieck M., Poppendieck T.: Lean Software Development: An Agile Toolkit for Software Development Managers, Addison-Wesley (2003)
5. Scott W. Ambler: Agile Modelling, John Wiley&Sons, Inc. (2002)
6. Highsmith J.A: Adaptive Software Development: A Collaborative Approach to Managing Complex Systems, Dorset House Publishing (2000)
7. Schwaber K., Beedle M.: Agile Software development with Scrum, Prentice Hall (2002)
8. http://www.dsdm.org
9. Palmer S., Felsing J., A Practical Guide to Feature-Driven Development, Prentice Hall (2002)
10. Poppendieck M., Poppendieck T.: Lean Software Development: An Agile Toolkit for Software Development Managers, Addison-Wesley (2002)

Appendix: Patterns Catalog

The patterns from the Implementation and Testing category (discussed in the paper) and the Communication category diagram are not included in this appendix for the sake of space limits.

AgileContractCreator. Define a contract that provides a software provider some degree of flexibility in any development parameter: schedule, cost, scope or quality.

AgileDocumenter. Create and maintain models and design documentation.

Communicator. Maintain good communication between project stakeholders

CustomerFeedbackIncreaser. Increase the feedback from the customers to development teams by holding a customer focus group at the end of each iteration

Designer. Design a software product in an iterative and incremental way.

DesignRefactorer. Improve the design of a software product.

DevelopmentFeedbackIncreaser. Increase the feedback from the development team to the management.

FeatureDesigner. Identify and specify classes to be involved in the design of a feature

FeedbackIncreaser. Increase feedback from developers and customers

IterationReviewer. Review an application, find, record and document customer changes requested to be implemented in the next iteration.

Iterative & Incremental Modeller. Perform iterative and incremental modeling.

Iteration Planner. Make a plan of the requirements to be implemented in one iteration

InTeamModeller. Enable effective teamwork and communication within the development team and with the project stakeholders.

Mission Creator Create and document project mission. The related artifacts need to answer three questions: What is this project about? Why should we do this project? How should we do this project?

MissionValuesSharer. Building a shared vision and responsibility for achieving the project mission.

ModellingMotivator. Better understand and communicate the models. Compare design alternatives to identify the simplest solution that meets the requirements.

ModelValidator. Validate the design work by considering how it will be tested and proving it by code.

ProductFeedbackIncreaser. Increase development team's feedback about the product

ProductivityIncreaser. Optimise the work of a team as to increase its productivity.

ProjectCloser. Help people learn from experience and anticipate the future.

Project Planner. Make a plan of the requirements to be implemented in a project

SimplicityModeller. Enable simplicity within the modeling effort. That means keeping the actual content of the models (requirements, architecture, design) as simple as possible, depicting models simply, using simple tools.

SoftwareInspector. Find defects and accelerate team learning

StandardApplicator. Model and code according to agreed standards. This ensures that the models and the code communicate as clearly as possible.

TeamFeedbackIncreaser. Increase the feedback within the team.

ValueMapper. Create a flow diagram of an activity granulating it to atomic tasks and specifying the time /effort/expenses spend for the performance of each atomic task.

ValueTracker. Identify the points in a process or activity, where effort is spent without generating value for the customer.

WasteEliminator. Reduce the activities, which take part in a process, but do not generate value for the customer, i.e. do not contribute to the final result.

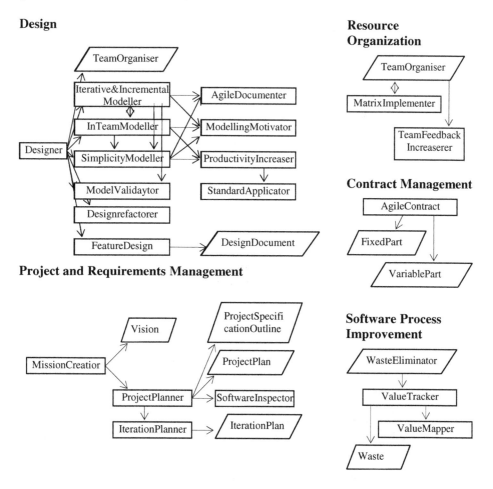

Design

Resource Organization

Contract Management

Project and Requirements Management

Software Process Improvement

Deploying Agile Practices in Organizations: A Case Study

Minna Pikkarainen[1], Outi Salo[1], and Jari Still[2]

[1] VTT Technical Research Centre of Finland, P.O. Box 1100, FIN-90571 Oulu, Finland
Minna.Pikkarainen@vtt.fi, Outi.Salo@vtt.fi
[2] F-Secure Corporation, Elektroniikkatie 3, 90570 Oulu, Finland
Jari.Still@f-secure.com

Abstract. Currently, software development organizations are increasingly interested in adopting agile processes and practices. The organizations, however, need procedures and methods for supporting a systematic selection and deployment of new agile practices and for tailoring them to suit the organizational context. In this paper, an agile deployment framework is proposed. It is compatible with the ideology of continuous improvement of organizational practices (QIP), while it also integrates it with the opportunities provided by short iterations of agile process model. The suggested framework includes the procedures and methods needed for selecting suitable new agile practices in an organization. It also embodies the means for iteratively tailoring and validating the deployed practices within agile projects and gaining feedback rapidly from projects to the organization. The paper presents the empirical experiences of a case study where the F-Secure Corporation deployed a new agile software development process (Mobile-D) in a pilot project in order to utilize its experiences in developing an organization specific agile process model alongside their traditional F-Secure product realization process.

1 Introduction

Over the past years, there has been increasing interest towards agile software development methods and practices. Agile software development attaches weight to, for example, rapid responding to constant changes and increasing customer collaboration (agilemanifesto.org). In spite of the promising experience reports of applying agile practices [1, 2], their deployment is a challenging task demanding a great deal of adjustment from all the stakeholders involved in the software development process (e.g., software developers, testers, management, and customers) [1, 2]. Thus, organizations need agile specific guidelines and methods to support systematic selection, deployment and tailoring of agile practices to fit the organization's software development context. In this paper, an agile deployment framework is proposed in order to provide organizations with procedures for adopting and improving practices in the agile software development context. The suggested framework and its steps are designed to comply with the continuous improvement ideology of the Quality Improvement Paradigm (QIP) [3]. However, since the existing

I. Richardson et al. (Eds.): EuroSPI 2005, LNCS 3792, pp. 16 – 27, 2005.

software process improvement (SPI) approaches, such as QIP, have originally been developed for the context of the traditional software development, they do not necessarily include all the elements and possibilities provided for the deployment by the agile software development process. For example, the iterative process adaptation within agile project teams is addressed in the principles of agile software development (www.agilemanifesto.org/principles.html). This provides project teams with a means of iterative tailoring the deployed practices in a validated manner and offers organizations rapid feedback from the deployment [14].

The traditional SPI methods can be utilized in the deployment of agile practices, e.g. the Goal-Question-Metric method for identifying feedback metrics [4]. However, the agile deployment framework identifies the agile specific methods that support the various tasks of deploying agile practices (i.e., agile assessment [5] used for setting goals and identifying suitable agile practices, and post-iteration workshops [6] for iteratively improving, validating and packaging feedback in projects).

This paper presents the empirical experiences of a case study where the F-Secure Corporation adopted an entire agile software development process (i.e., Mobile-D [7]) in order to evolve a agile approach alongside the traditional F-Secure product realization process. Thus, the aim of this study is to evaluate the proposed framework and to present how the steps of the agile deployment framework provide a loop for continuously improving organizational software development practices. The paper is composed as follows: Section 2 presents the agile deployment framework; Section 3 contains the research goals and context; and Section 4 the empirical evidence from the case study. The last section concludes the paper with final remarks.

2   The Agile Deployment Framework

There are many different SPI approaches addressing continuous and systematical improvement of software development processes in organizations, such as the QIP [8]. The existing approaches include the aspect of deploying new practices if these are required to meet the organizational improvement goals. In QIP, two cycles of improvement are identified: 1) the organizational learning cycle in which, for example, the improvement goals and improvements are executed, and 2) project learning cycle which is used, for example, for piloting and for collecting feedback needed for finding problems and validating improvements. Many of the existing SPI approaches are goal-oriented and address the utilization of metrics data from software development projects in selecting and evaluating process improvements.

In this paper, an agile deployment framework is proposed. It is designed to integrate the iterative cycles of agile software development with the continuous improvement of organizational practices. Its focus is on deploying agile practices in organizations and it addresses the importance of utilizing the experiences of the software developers an important source of input to SPI. In 0, the original cycle of QIP (white) is mapped with the steps of the Agile Deployment Framework (grey): select agile practices, plan deployment, execute deployment, analyze and package results, and improve. The main difference of the proposed approach compared to traditional approaches is in its iterative execution of deployment, which provides feedback from the iterative improvement and from the validation of the deployed practices in software development projects.

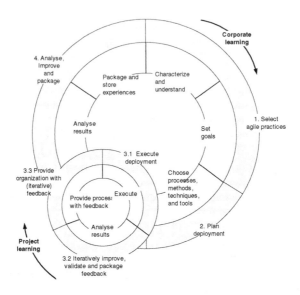

Fig. 1. QIP cycle (from [9]) and Agile Deployment Framework

Table 1. defines the steps of the QIP approach [8] and maps them with the steps of the agile deployment framework. The main activities of the deployment steps as well as the suggested agile specific methods to support deployment (i.e., agile assessment [5] and post-iteration workshops [10] (hereafter referred as PIWs)) are also included. The PIW method was evolved based on two existing agile reflection techniques, namely the reflection workshop technique by Cockburn [11] and the postmortem reviews by Dingsøyr et al., [12]. The PIW method, however, has been complemented with systematic planning, follow-up, and validation of SPI actions [10].

Table 1. Mapping the Agile Deployment Framework with QIP

QIP Steps	Main Activities	Agile Deployment Steps	Main Activities	Agile Methods
1.Characterize and understand	Gather knowledge of projects	1.Select agile practices	Set goals for deployment	Agile assessment
2.Set goals	Set goals for improvement		Identify suitable practices	Agile assessment
			Select practices to deploy	-
3.Choose processes, methods, techniques, tools	Define models needed by a project to achieve the goals	2.Plan deployment	Plan deployment	-
			Prepare deployment	-
4.Execute	Implement the plans, collect measurement data and provide feedback to project	3.Execute deployment	Execute deployment	-
			Iteratively improve, validate and package feedback in projects	PIW
5.Analyze results	Analyze project practices, problems, findings and recommendations	4.Analyse, improve and package	Analyze project feedback to identify improvements	Agile Assessment
6.Package	Package experiences and ensure their use in future projects		Improve the organizational processes	-
			Package	PIW

In the following, the agile deployment steps are defined in more detail.

2.1 Select Agile Practices

An organization should first *set goals for deployment* and consequently, *identify* the potential agile practices. The existing ways to discover the agile methods to deploy are unstructured; for example, one may study the current agile literature or gain knowledge from partners who have already applied certain agile practices. The agile assessment [5], however, provides systematic and goal-driven mechanisms for *identifying* and *selecting* suitable agile practices for the organization specific context.

The steps of agile assessment are: 1) focus definition, 2) agility evaluation, 3) data collection planning, 4) data collection, 5) analysis and 6) final workshops. In the first step, the goals are set for adopting agile methods. The second step provides a better understanding on how suitable and effective the various agile methods would be in specific projects. The agile assessment data can be collected using interviews, agile assessment workshops, and from the recorded iterative SPI actions (from PIWs) and improvement opportunities (from project postmortems). In addition, various metrics data can be utilized in the analysis. Agile assessment workshops are conducted in order to identify the strengths and weaknesses of the software development process and to discuss the possibilities of increasing the agility of the development process together with the project stakeholders. The assessment workshops support project and organizational learning between different projects and also the development of an organizational level agile software development model. The agile assessor should be well aware of the available agile methods as well as the agile assessment method.

2.2 Plan Deployment

Organizations have different approaches to the deployment of new practices. An organization can, for example, select a pilot project or even embody the new practices directly in its organizational software development processes. Whether an organization plans to experiment with the new practices in a pilot project or to deploy the new practices in a larger scale, it should also *plan* how empirical feedback is provided for a continuous improvement of organizational practices. For example, it should be defined how the suitability of each adopted method will be evaluated during the piloting, and how the feedback from the (pilot) projects is stored and analyzed. Thus, in this step of agile deployment, it should be ensured that there are mechanisms available for the project teams to collect and store the relevant feedback in an appropriate format from projects to the organizational level.

The deployment phase also includes the *preparation* of projects involving changes to the daily software development practices. The preparation includes, for example, training, tailoring the deployed practices to fit the existing process, and preparing the tools considering the used practices. The deployment, thus, includes all the preparations needed for using the selected new practices in the selected projects.

2.3 Execute Deployment

Unlike the other steps of the agile deployment model, the execute step is conducted at the project level. Its focus, from the organizational viewpoint, is to gain feedback from the deployed practices in order to enhance the organizational processes. The execution of deployment consists of three steps: 1) execute deployment, 2) iteratively improve, validate, package feedback, and 3) provide the feedback to an organization. In the QIP, the execute step is defined as the project learning cycle (0).

The projects selected for deploying agile practices can be regarded as pilot projects providing the organizational level with feedback on applying new agile practices. The short development cycles of agile software development provide rapid loops, which allow project teams to *iteratively improve* and adapt their daily working practices in a validated manner [13] based on their own experiences and domain knowledge. From the viewpoint of deploying new practices in an organization, this kind of iterative adaptation and *improvement* also provides a means for organizations to gain on-time feedback on how the project teams have adapted and improved their practices.

In agile deployment, the PIW method can be used for two purposes: 1) to provide project teams with a mechanism to tailor the deployed and the existing software development practices during the ongoing project in a validated manner, and 2) to provide the organizational level with mechanisms for gaining systematic and rapid feedback from the process improvement of (pilot) projects. The validation is done by implementing process improvements in the ongoing project and iteratively evaluating their usefulness with available metrics and experience data.

At the end of the software development project, the last PIW can be conducted as a traditional project postmortem [14]. As the project team will no longer be able to implement or validate the improvements at this point, the goal of the project postmortem is to harvest process knowledge from the stakeholders of the project teams solely for organizational improvement purposes. The postmortems, thus, provide another experience based feedback mechanism from projects to organization.

The PIW method offers mechanisms to *provide the organization with iterative feedback* from individual projects. A structured action point list [13] suggests how the SPI actions may be iteratively documented in a project in order to support SPI in an ongoing project and to provide validated SPI knowledge from projects to organizational improvement activities. Thus, the action point list includes the identification of the following issues for each improvement action: 1) the exact problem that the action point aims at solving, 2) the specific action to be taken, 3) the responsibilities for implementing the action and schedule, 4) the means to validate the usefulness of an action point, and 5) the results (qualitative or quantitative) of validation (updated in the following PIW after piloting). Another output of PIWs are the flap-sheets containing grouped experiences of the project team, which form the basis for the improvement actions of the project team (see more in [6, 15]).

2.4 Analyze, Improve, and Package

The key purpose of the *analyze, improve and package* step is to make sure that the deployed practices that have been found useful in the pilot projects are identified and employed in the organization. In the agile deployment framework, the organizational level can gain process knowledge from two sources: 1) agile assessments and 2) individual projects. More specifically, the projects can provide the organizational level with experience based process knowledge (validated improvements from PIW's and improvement opportunities from project postmortems). As suggested in QIP, the projects may have collected metrics data defined at the organizational level. The feedback from projects is analyzed, the improvement actions planned and implemented, and the results stored and packaged for later SPI purposes.

3   Research Context

In this section, the goals, context, and methods of this research are presented.

3.1   Research Goals and Methods

The goal of this research is to evaluate the proposed agile deployment framework in an industrial context. In particular, the usefulness of the agile specific methods integrated in the agile deployment framework is assessed, i.e., agile assessment [5] for *selecting* suitable agile practices in individual projects and within an organization and PIWs [6] for a continuous *adaptation and improvement* of these practices. In other words, the goal of this study is to evaluate if iterative software development model provides added value to the deployment of new practices and how it bonds with the loop of continuous improvement of organizational software development.

This research can be characterized as constructive research, in which a case study forms the basis for further development and evaluation of the proposed agile deployment model and the methods integrated in it. As a researcher was acting as a facilitator in the PIWs and project postmortem, an action research approach (e.g., [16]) was applied especially in activities concerning project level SPI. Both the agile assessor and the facilitator participated in the improvement activities at the end of the project. An participative approach enabled an effective way to "integrate theory with practice through an iterative process of problem diagnosis, action intervention, and reflective learning" [17] throughout the case study. Both quantitative and qualitative data was collected from project and organizational SPI activities. In addition, a questionnaire was prepared to collect the developers' perceptions of the PIWs.

3.2   Research Context

The case study of this research was conducted at F-Secure Corporation, an organization developing products to protect individuals and businesses against computer viruses and other threats spreading through the Internet and mobile networks. At F-Secure, a project named Phantom was set up to pilot an agile software development process (i.e., Mobile-D [7]) that had earlier been developed at VTT.

The goal of the Phantom project was to develop a mobile security application. The core of the case project team consisted of four software developers and one tester who were working in an open office space. The Phantom team conducted five software development iterations in all (1x1 week, 3x2 weeks, 1x1 week) and completed a total of 7.2 person months of effort. The team leader of the project provided by the research organization was an expert in the Mobile-D process. Thus, the team had constant support and coaching available on adopting the new agile practices. Other stakeholders of the project were the organizational management, a project manager, two customers and quality engineers, and an exterior facilitator. The customers were available on-site in the same department, but not constantly working in the Phantom office-space as suggested in Extreme Programming (XP) [18].

4   Case Study

In this section, the most important empirical results are presented concerning how the case organization conducted the deployment of Mobile-D in the Phantom project.

4.1   Select Agile Practices

The goal at F-Secure was to deploy an agile software development model (i.e., Mobile-D) in a pilot project in order to utilize its experiences in evolving an organization specific agile process model. Prior to launching the Phantom project, the Scrum method had already been introduced in a few projects. The Mobile-D process itself contained the methods for gaining feedback from projects to the organization (i.e. PIWs, project postmortem, and defined metrics). These methods were systematically used in the case organization for iterative adaptation of the used practices in the project and in order to provide the organization with validated improvements and improvement opportunities from the case project.

4.2   Plan the Deployment

At F-Secure, various activities were needed for setting up the pilot. Firstly, in order to ensure a successful deployment of Mobile-D, the project team of F-Secure was complemented by developers from VTT, who were experts in Mobile-D and could thus provide on-line coaching for the in-house developers. Many of the agile practices and tools included in the Mobile-D process were new at F-Secure. Thus, a software development (e.g., unit testing tools) and working environment (e.g., open-office space) was set-up, and the project team was trained to use the new procedures. In the case project, however, no tailoring of the deployed practices to the existing organizational processes was needed as Mobile-D was adopted as such.

4.3   Execute Deployment

The iterative *improvement, validation and packaging* tasks were ensured by adopting the PIW method and by conducting a project postmortem. The Phantom project team collected a fair amount of metrics data, as suggested by Mobile-D. The data was used, for example, for validating the iterative process improvements in PIW's.

In Phantom, a total of three PIWs where held after the first three iterations. The workshops were attended by the project team and also by one of the customers and some quality assurance team members. The participants first collected positive and then negative experiences from the previous iteration on a flap-sheet. The facilitator (expert in the Mobile-D process) led the discussion using the negative experiences as a basis to define process improvements for the next iteration.

Fig. 2 illustrates the number of positive and negative experiences, as well as the implemented improvements resulting from the three subsequent PIWs. It should be noted that there were five participants in the 1st PIW and seven in the last two. Thus, the declining trends in all the categories presented in Fig. 2 would be even more distinct if relative numbers were presented for the findings of the 1st PIW.

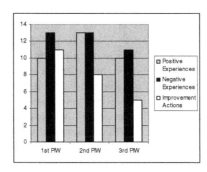

Fig. 2. Quantity of Phantom Post-Iteration Workshop Results

Each PIW resulted in a structured action point list (see more in [13]), which was put on the wall of the open-office space and also iteratively e-mailed to project management for monitoring and organizational improvement purposes. Thus, the PIW data was iteratively packaged in the project and delivered to the organizational level. For each process improvement, the specific improvement action, the reasons for it, the means of validation and its effectiveness were documented. After the validation (i.e., after the improvement had been experimented in project iteration) the proven usefulness or non-usefulness of the process enhancement was also documented.

Table 2. Most Important Improvement Categories in the Phantom Project

Improvement Category	Improvement Actions	Negative Experiences
Quality Assurance	8	3
Pair-Programming	4	7
Project Monitoring & Management	4	1

The PIWs revealed several problems and produced a number of improvement solutions. The top three improvement categories are illustrated in Table 2 along with the number of resulting improvement actions and the amount of negative experiences on each topic. As it can be seen in Table 1, several improvements were needed on the Quality Assurance (QA) category, which includes issues related to unit testing, verification of tasks, and system testing. The Pair-Programming (PP) practice was also found highly controversial throughout the project. Some project members (4/7 of negative experiences) wished to increase the use of PP in the project, whereas the others (3/7 experiences) found it mostly unnecessary. For solving this problem, the team agreed to iteratively identify the tasks that would require PP. However, due to the resistance of a proportion of the project team, none of the tasks were identified as such and in the second iteration, for example, only two out of a total of 12 tasks were partially implemented using PP. Thus, the team failed to reach an agreement during the project on how extensively the PP practice should be adopted. The third most active improvement category was project management, which was mainly concerned with the improvement of the templates used for defining tasks and improving the usefulness of the information radiator [11] for project monitoring.

In addition, a project postmortem was held after the Phantom project together with the Phantom project team and its stakeholders. The aim was to distinguish the most suitable and unsuitable agile practices for the F-Secure specific agile process. Because of the Agile Assessment purposes, the Phantom postmortem was organized together with the PIW facilitator and the agile assessor. In the postmortem, the project stakeholders identified the most suitable and unsuitable practices of Mobile-D process. The best practices identified were unit testing, the incremental process model, and iterative planning of tasks with the customer. The most unsuitable practices were the PP practice, open office space, and the procedures of QA. In the postmortem, improvements for the three top unsuitable agile practices and the key benefits of the best agile practices compared to their traditional plan driven software development approach were also identified. On the basis of the project experiences, a number of problems and solutions were revealed. These were summarized by the facilitators and reported to the F-Secure management for further analysis.

At F-Secure, the PIWs were found a useful method of improving the practices at project and organizational levels. In the Phantom postmortem, the management and the customer reported PIWs as one of the positive practices of Mobile-D. Likewise, the questionnaire filled in by the project stakeholders revealed that they either strongly or somewhat agreed (other options being neutral, somewhat disagree, and strongly disagree) on the claim that "PIWs were useful in finding improvements in software development practices during the project". They also strongly or somewhat agreed that "it would be useful to carry out PIWs also in future agile projects". However, both the project team and the management requested that in future PIWs the project team would need to be able to suggest action points iteratively directly to the organizational level also as some of the action points could not be implemented by the project team on its own. They might have required, for example, organizational participation or decision making. The management was willing to consider and implement such process changes already during the pilot project.

4.4 Analyse, Improve and Package

At F-Secure, the *organizational improvement* of the used agile practices was done immediately after the Phantom postmortem. The F-Secure management, Phantom project team and its stakeholders participated in the organizational improvement workshop, which focused on elaborating the used agile practices for the organizational agile software development process. The external facilitator (of PIWs and the Phantom postmortem) was present to provide information on the SPI actions during the project as well as on the Mobile-D when needed. The agile assessor observed the workshop and gathered information for the ongoing agile assessment.

In the organizational improvement workshop, the recommendations of project stakeholders were collected and discussed on each Mobile-D phase. Prior to the workshop, the F-Secure management had made the necessary preparations and provided feedback from the PIWs and the Phantom postmortem. Thus, the sheet that was used for collecting the opinions of the workshop participants was pre-filled by the management to include the evident improvements that had already been identified (e.g. separated office space, and exclusion of the PP practice). Table 3 illustrates the organizational SPI decisions on QA practices made in the improvement workshop.

Table 3. Organizational Improvements on the QA Practices

Practice	Improvement	Cause	Origin
QA	Established collaboration of test and development teams	Lack of external test team activities in the used process	PIWs
	Iteratively updated documentation to support an external testing team	Unclear test focus due to lack of design documentation	Organization Improvement Workshop
	Daily wrap-up meetings	Development team in separate rooms	Postmortem
	Defined code review practices	PP excluded from the process	Postmortem

The *agile assessment* [5] was held after the first organizational improvement workshop. It was conducted by assessors who were familiar with the existing agile software development practices and with the agile assessment method. The goal was to *analyse* the suitability of the agile practices based on the feedback from the agile pilot projects and also from more traditional software development projects in order to evolve an F-Secure specific agile software development process. Two earlier projects had piloted the Scrum method while only the Phantom project used Mobile-D that included PIWs and postmortems providing agile assessments with validated process knowledge and improvement opportunities. In addition to the action points lists, reports and flapsheets of PIWs and postmortem, assessment data was collected using interviews, agile assessment workshops, and by observing the organizational improvement workshop. The available metrics (e.g. effort data) were utilized.

In the Scrum projects, agile assessment workshops where conducted to analyse the used agile practices together with the development team. The key problem, however, was the validity of the workshop results. The team members could not necessarily remember exactly what had happened in the project two or three months earlier during the project iterations. Instead, the validated PIW data (flap sheets, action point lists) provided new opportunities to analyse the advancement of the used agile practices (i.e., different solutions that had been experimented and evaluated) between the project iterations and to compare experiences of the different projects for finding the relevant agile based solutions for improving future software development processes. As an example, PP was one of the most problematic practices used in all the projects. In the Scrum projects, PP had been used in an unsystematic manner in complex coding situations. PP was also one of the most controversial practices in the Phantom project. The validated PIW data proved that PP was problematic throughout the project. It was defined in the first PIW that PP should be used but only in complex tasks and for knowledge dissemination purposes. In spite of this, one of the key negative findings in the second and third PIWs was the use of PP in the project. Due to the resistance of a few persons, a decision was made not to use PP systematically in organizational practices at that point. The analysis of the postmortem data in the agile assessment, however, revealed that dropping PP from the software development process would demand additional QA practices such as code reviews.

5   Conclusions and Further Work

Currently, the agile software development methods provide an attractive alternative to the traditional plan-driven software development approaches. Specific procedures are, however, needed to support a systematic selection and deployment of new agile practices as well as for tailoring them to suit individual organizations. Thus, this paper proposes an agile deployment framework for software development organizations, designed for deploying and adapting agile practices in an iterative and agile specific manner. The framework puts emphasis on how the deployment can be carried out in the iterative life cycle of agile software development and how it integrates with the continuous improvement of organizational practices.

In this paper, the empirical results from a case study are presented in order to illustrate how an agile development method (Mobile-D) was deployed in a pilot project in F-Secure Corporation. The organizational goal was to utilize the experiences from the pilot project in establishing organizational agile process. The pilot project applied a post-iteration workshop method [6] (i.e. PIWs) for iterative *adaptation and improvement* of agile practices. Some more traditional mechanisms were also used for collecting the experience based feedback from the project for the needs of the organization (i.e., project postmortems). In addition, agile assessment [5] was conducted, utilizing the validated knowledge from PIWs.

The key point of this paper is to empirically evaluate the efficiency of PIWs in agile SPI, and the usefulness of systematically collected and validated PIW results in agile assessments. Furthermore, it is defined how these two agile specific SPI methods can be used to build an agile deployment framework, i.e. compatible and appropriate mechanisms for adopting and adapting agile methods, which also provide for continuous SPI in software development organizations. The qualitative results of deploying the different agile methods and practices of Mobile-D in the case project, however, are organization specific and not generalizable without further empirical evidence. Thus, the focus of this paper is on describing how the agile deployment was conducted in an industrial environment as suggested by the agile deployment framework and not so much on any detailed analysis of the qualitative findings of different agile practices adopted in the case organization.

The empirical evidence from the case study illustrates how the case organization was able to employ and benefit from the deployment mechanisms suggested in the agile deployment framework. Both the customer and the project team found the PIW method a useful mechanism in iteratively improving the daily working practices. The management also found the iterative and validated feedback from PIWs as well as the results of agile assessment useful in monitoring the deployment process and evolving an organization specific agile process model alongside with their plan-driven product development process. However, in future projects both the software developers and the management would like to increase the on-time collaboration of project team and management already during the ongoing projects. This would allow the process improvements that the project team finds useful but can not implement all by itself to be experimented already in the ongoing project.

The agile deployment framework, as a whole, is primarily designed for the *iterative* software development model. Thus, it does not directly support the changing of process model type from traditional to agile. Yet, some of its individual methods, such as agile assessment, can also be applied in the traditional mode of development.

Acknowledgement. To all the employees of VTT and the F-Secure Corporation who have participated in the Phantom project. The research was conducted within the Agile ITEA project funded by the National Technology Agency of Finland (TEKES).

References

1. M. Cohn and D. Ford, "Introducing an Agile Process to an Organization," *IEEE Computer Society*, pp. 74-78, 2003.
2. H. Svensson and M. Höst, "Introducing an Agile Process in a Sotware Maintenance and Evolution Organization," 9th European Conference on Software Maintenance and Reengineering, 2005.
3. V. R. Basili, "Software Development: A Paradigm for the Future," COMPSAC '89, Orlando, 1989.
4. V. R. Basili, "The Goal Question Metric Approach," in *Encyclopedia of Software Engineering*, vol. 2: John Wiley & Sons, Inc., 1994, pp. 528-532.
5. M. Pikkarainen and U. Passoja, "An Approach for Assessing Suitability of Agile Solutions:A Case Study," 6th International Conference on Extreme Programming and Agile Processes in Software Engineering, Sheffield University, UK, 2005.
6. O. Salo, "Improving Software Process in Agile Software Development Projects: Results from Two XP Case Studies," EUROMICRO 2004, Rennes, France, 2004.
7. P. Abrahamsson, A. Hanhineva, et al., "Mobile-D: An Agile Approach for Mobile Application Development," 19th Annual ACM Conference on Object-Oriented Programming, Systems, Languages, and Applications (OOPSLA'04), Vancouver, British Columbia, Canada, 2004.
8. V. R. Basili and D. Weiss, "A Methodology for Collecting Valid Software Engineering Data," *IEEE Transactions on Software Engineering*, vol. SE-10, pp. 728-738, 1984.
9. V. R. Basili and G. Caldiera, "Improve Software Quality by Reusing Knowledge and Experience," *Sloan Management Review*, pp. 55-64, 1995.
10. O. Salo and P. Abrahamsson, "A Post-Iteration Workshop Approach for Agile Software Process Improvement: Implications from a Multiple Case Study," *Under Review*, 2005.
11. A. Cockburn, *Crystal Clear: a Human-Powered Methodology for Small Teams*: Addison-Wesley, 2005.
12. T. Dingsøyr, Moe, N.B., Nytrø, Ø. "Augmenting Experience Reports with Lightweight Postmortem Reviews," 3rd Int'l Conference on Product Focused Software Improvement (Profes 01), Kaiserslautern, Germany, 2001.
13. O. Salo, "Systematical Validation of Learning in Agile Software Development Environment," 7th International Workshop on Learning Software Organizations, Kaiserslautern, Germany, 2005.
14. N. L. Kerth, *Project Retrospectives: A Handbook for Team Reviews*: Dorset House Publishing, 2001.
15. O. Salo, K. Kolehmainen, et al., "Self-Adaptability of Agile Software Processes: A Case Study on Post-Iteration Workshops," 5th International Conference on Extreme Programming and Agile Processes in Software Engineering (XP 2004), Garmisch-Partenkirchen, Germany, 2004.
16. J. B. Cunningham, "Case study principles for different types of cases," *Quality and quantity*, vol. 31, pp. 401-423, 1997.
17. F. Lau, "Toward a framework for action research in information systems studies," *Information, Technology & People*, vol. 12, pp. 148-175, 1999.
18. K. Beck, Extreme Programming Explained: Embrace Change: Addison Wesley Longman, Inc., 2000.

Pair Programming vs. Side-by-Side Programming*

Jerzy R. Nawrocki, Michał Jasiński, Łukasz Olek, and Barbara Lange

Poznan University of Technology, ul. Piotrowo 3a, 60-965 Poznan, Poland
{Jerzy.Nawrocki, Michal.Jasinski, Lukasz.Olek,
Barbara.Lange}@cs.put.poznan.pl
http://www.cs.put.poznan.pl

Abstract. In agile methodologies communication between programmers is very important. Some of them (e.g. XP or Crystal Clear) recommend pair programming. There are two styles of pair programming: XP-like and side-by-side (the latter comes from Crystal Clear). In the paper an experiment is described that aimed at comparison of those two styles. The subjects were 25 students of Computer Science of 4th and 5th year of study. They worked for 6 days at the university (in a controlled environment) programming web-based applications with Java, Eclipse, MySQL, and Tomcat. The results obtained indicate that side-by-side programming is a very interesting alternative to XP-like pair programming mainly due to less effort overhead (in the experiment the effort overhead for side-by-side programming was as small as 20%, while for XP it was about 50%).

1 Introduction

In classical approach to software development, a programming task (e.g. writing a software module to a given specification) is assigned to one programmer (see e.g. [9]). To assure quality all the production code should go through a peer-review process (it can be inspection, walkthrough, formal technical review etc. [16]).

Kent Beck, the creator of Extreme Programming (XP for short), has introduced to his methodology a different approach called pair programming [2]. In pair programming, as the name suggests, a task is assigned to a pair of programmers who are equipped with one computer. While one programmer is writing a piece of code, the other is watching, asking some questions, and proposing test cases (that provides so-called continuous review).

The efficiency of pair programming has been studied by many researchers. The first experiment concerning pair programming has been described by John Nosek [14]. He reported that pairs required about 30% less time than individuals but effort associated with pair programming was by 40% greater. Perhaps the most optimistic results have been obtained by Laurie Williams [21, 22]. According to her experiments the speedup accomplished by pair programming was at the level of 40% and the effort overhead was as small as 20%. The results of first experiments with pair

---

* This work has been financially supported by the State Committee for Scientific Research as a research grant 4 T11F 001 23 (years 2002-2005).

I. Richardson et al. (Eds.): EuroSPI 2005, LNCS 3792, pp. 28–38, 2005.

programming performed at the Poznan University of Technology [13] were more pessimistic. The speedup gained by pair programming was at the level of 20% and the effort was about 60% higher than for individuals.

Just recently another version of "programming in pairs" has been proposed by Alistair Cockburn [7]. It is called side-by-side programming (SbS). In SbS a task is assigned to a pair of programmers, and each programmer has his own computer. That allows them to split the task into subtasks and work on each subtask individually (similarly to the classical approach). The main difference between SbS and the classical approach is physical proximity of the pair members (which enhances communication) and unity of the goal (SbS programmers are working on the same task and they both are responsible for it). Unfortunately, so far there are no experiments comparing efficiency of SbS and pair programming.

The objective of the paper is to present an experiment aiming at comparison of SbS and pair programming. In Sec. 2 methodological aspects concerning programming experiments are discussed. Next the experiment is described (Sec. 3) and its results are presented (Sec. 4). An important issue concerning pair programming experiments is involvement of pair members in the development process (there is a danger that actually only one person will write and understand the code while the other person will be only a spectator). This aspect is discussed in Sec. 5. We have also asked our programmers a few questions concerning their impression and the results are presented in Sec. 6.

2 Methodological Aspects of Programming Experiments

In the software engineering community there is an increasing understanding that experimental research is needed in order to explain and improve software development processes [20, 1]. An experiment tests theoretical predictions against reality and is defined as a form of empirical study where the researcher has control over the independent variables being studied. It is carried out under controlled conditions in order to test a hypothesis against observation [1].

Experimentation in software engineering is difficult, because the process of developing software involves both technical aspects and human factors. Especially, psychological factors, which are less predictable, are a challenge for experimenters. For that reason, software engineering experimentalists should adopt well developed and elaborated methodological techniques used in the behavioural disciplines. Some issues concerning studying programmer behaviour experimentally has been discussed as long as 20 years ago [3, 19]. It was pointed out, that behavioural researchers in computer science must pay close attention to methodological issues. Some aspects of a programming experiment are presented in the next paragraphs.

Representative Sample
One of main problems in such empirical studies is *selection of appropriate subjects* for the experiment. To make a statement about the behaviour which will be true for the whole population, the experimenter must ensue that the subjects are representative. That means that subjects should be chosen randomly from the whole population of programmers. If this condition is not fulfilled, then such a type of

research is called by behavioural scientists a *quasi-experiment*. Unfortunately, the results of a quasi-experiment cannot be extended to the whole population [4]. Every experiment we know about in the area of pair programming is in fact a quasi-experiment [21, 14]. First, because it is difficult to characterize the population of programmers. We do not know of any research that would aim at characterizing distribution of programmers' age, sex, experience in software development, technology used at work (including programming languages) etc. Secondly, conducting sensibly long experiments (a week or longer) on a large enough and diverse group of professionals (according to standards used in sociology and political sciences it should be hundreds of people) would be very expensive and difficult (we have observed a 'contest syndrome': it is easier to attract fast programmers than slow ones, so there is a danger that the sample will not be representative).

Due to these limits many experimentalists decide to conduct experimental research using Computer Science students as the subjects [13, 21]. Obviously, *students are not professionals*, but their way of thinking and their academic background is similar to professional programmers. Due to our observations most of programmers are young people (below 35). Moreover, many 4th and 5th year students have part-time jobs at software companies. Therefore, using Computer Science students, especially students of the 4th and 5th year, seems acceptable.

Another issue is *selection of programming assignments* for an experiment. Programming tasks should be a representative sample of some wider class of programs similar to those written by professionals at work. Especially, they should be of an appropriate level of difficulty and length to produce data with desirable statistical characteristics [3]. For instance, very short assignments or difficult algorithmic 'puzzles' used in the ACM programming contests (although very interesting) seem not representative.

Statistical Significance

An important methodological aspect of experimentation is statistical analysis of collected data. Usually a null hypothesis H_0 along with an alternative hypothesis H_1 is formed and an appropriate test statistic is computed. An obtained value of the test statistic is compared with a 'threshold' and H_0 is rejected or not. The probability of rejecting H_0 when H_0 is true is called a level of significance. The lower the level of significance is, the greater the confidence in statistical analysis. In behavioural sciences the standard value of level of significance is 0.05. In the case of programming studies the level of significance is sometimes as big as 0.20 [19]. A good approach is to present a *P-value* which is the smallest level of significance that would lead to rejection of the null hypothesis H_0 [12].

When performing statistical analysis, it is necessary to check if distribution of a dependent variable is *normal*. If the distribution is not normal another (much more difficult) statistical analysis should be conducted. Unfortunately, many reports from programming experiments do not mention this (see e.g. [21, 14]).

Fairness

Human factor in programming experiments is very important. Programmers can differ in programming speed as 1:10 or even more (see e.g. [8, 17]). When comparing two (or more) different programming techniques one has to ensure that average programming speed (and variance) in each group are similar. A good solution is to make a pre-test before an experiment, to estimate a programming speed for each subject. That is not easy and sometimes other simpler methods (e.g. questionnaires about years of experience [15]) are used.

Documentation of an Experiment
A scientific experiment should be replicable. Thus, a good documentation of the process is necessary. It should describe used materials, design, procedure and scoring [4]. In the case of research on programmer behaviour, a description of programming tasks and test cases should also be included. In addition, a measurement procedure (e.g. how the finish time is defined) should be presented. Unfortunately, some reports lack this information [11].

Controlled Conditions
To ensure credibility of a programming experiment one has to carry it out in a controlled environment to minimise the influence of external factors that could impact the results. However, some researchers conduct experiments in an uncontrolled environment, e.g. they let the subjects to do their programming assignments at home.

3 Experiment Description

3.1 Subjects and Environment

The experiment was run at the Poznan University of Technology from February till April 2005. The subjects were 30 volunteers: students of master degree programs in Software Engineering, and in Database Systems (4th and 5th year of study). They had completed various programming courses (including Java and web-based applications) amounting to over 400 hours. They have also participated in a 1-year-long university project playing the roles of programmers.

The subjects worked in a few open-space laboratory rooms under supervision of research assistants. They were equipped with PCs (Pentium IV, 512 MB RAM). The programming environment consisted of Java J2SDK 1.4.2_06, Tomcat 5.0.18, Eclipse 3.1, MySQL 4.0.21 database server, and a CVS code repository server.

3.2 Process

The process consisted of five phases: Homework, Preparation, Selection, Warming-up and Run. Each time the subjects were to solve one or more programming assignments.

In the *Homework* phase the subjects were given a programming assignment concerning the technology and tools used in the subsequent phases (Java, Tomcat, Eclipse etc.). They worked individually at home. The aim of the phase was to allow them to learn (or re-call) the technology and tools.

During the *Preparation* phase the subjects worked individually at the university in the actual experimental environment. They were supervised by research assistants who also did the quality assurance: acceptance testing. The subjects worked until successful completion of the assignment (all the acceptance tests passed). There were no additional quality factors introduced, but the acceptance tests. The main aim was to make sure that the subjects know the tools and technology. Moreover, it gave the subjects a chance to get familiar with the process (acceptance testing, time measureement etc.). The preparation phase took one day. On the average the assignment completion time was 522minutes.

The *Selection* phase took another day. The subjects worked individually at the university on programming assignments. We have measured the time that elapsed from beginning of the experiment till successful completion of the task (all acceptance tests passed). In this case, average completion time was 370 minutes. We used the collected data to split the subjects into three groups: Pairs1, Pairs2, and Individuals. In the next phases of the experiment the Pairs1 and Pairs2 groups were to do pair programming (using different programming styles) and the Individuals group contained individual programmers serving as a reference group. It is well known that people differ in programming speed significantly (see e.g. [8, 17]). Therefore, to be able compare results concerning different programming styles we had to ensure that all the groups will be (on average) equally fast. Thus, the following problem arose: how to partition $5n$ subjects of known completion time into Pairs1 subset ($2n$ elements), Pairs2 subset ($2n$ elements) and Individuals subset (n elements) in such a way that average completion time of each subset is (almost) the same. Of the 30 initial volunteers 25 passed successfully the Selection phase and we split them into three abovementioned groups with $n=5$ (we have used three different heuristics and chosen the best result).

We wanted to compare XP-like pair programming (1 computer per pair) to side-by-side (SbS) programming (2 computers per pair). The aim of the *Warming-up* phase was to make sure that the subjects know how to do XP or SbS pair programming. The phase took two days. Each day started with a 20-minutes-long training based on a process miniature [6] (the subjects were solving programming puzzles). After the training session the subjects were developing a web application (that took the rest of the day). On the first day of Warming-up one group of pairs was following XP-like pair programming and the other one SbS-like pair programming. On the second day the groups switched. The average assignment completion time was 323 and 370 minutes respectively.

The most important was the *Run* phase. It took last two days. The aim was to collect data that would allow to compare XP-like and SbS-like pair programming from the point of view of development time and effort (meaning completion time for individuals and double completion time in case of pairs).The subjects worked like in the Warming-up phase but without training sessions. Again on the first day the Pairs1 group was doing XP-like pair programming and on the second day they switched to SbS (Pairs2 did the opposite). That way we have mitigated the risk of unbalanced groups of pairs (we did our best during the Selection phase to have balanced groups but development time is a random variable and you never can be sure). During the *Run* phase, the average assignment completion time was 335 minutes on the first, and 491 minutes on the second day of the experiment.

3.3 Programming Assignments

More and more programmers are working on web applications. For that reason we have decided that our subjects will be working on Java-based web applications in JSP and Java servlet technology.

During the Preparation phase the subjects were to implement a password protected web site with security data stored on a database server. They had to implement the login procedure together with basic user management services (displaying list of users, adding and removing a user).

The Selection phase was based on two assignments. The first one was a simple document management application. Documents could be public or internal. Everybody could browse a public document, but only registered users could access internal documents (after passing the authorization control). The second assignment was a web application that would collect submitted abstracts and papers.

During the Warming-up and Run phases (4 days) the subjects incrementally developed a conference management system called Papers-Online (it was an extension of the second assignment from the Selection phase). Papers-Online has the following actors: authors, reviewers and a conference chairman. Authors can submit abstracts and papers. The chairman can register reviewers and assign papers to them. Reviewers can submit their reviews. Authors can view status of their papers. The chairman can set a conference program.

Each assignment contained use-cases [5] describing required functionality and a number of acceptance test-cases derived from them. More information can be found in [10].

4 Completion Time and Effort Analysis

Completion Time Analysis

The programming assignments were accompanied by acceptance tests. Each day we have measured *completion time* i.e. the time that elapsed from the beginning of programming session till successful completion (all the acceptance tests passed). We subtracted from that amount the duration of lunch break.

The Run phase took two days. As we have already mentioned, to mitigate the risk of unbalanced assignment of subjects to groups Pairs1 and Pairs2 (although we did it as carefully as possible – see Sec. 3.2) we decided that both Pairs1 and Pairs2 will do XP-like and SbS-like pair programming. A simple solution would be to have both groups do XP-like programming on the first day and SbS-like programming on the second day. But there would be a problem with a programming assignment. If the programming assignment was the same, then on the second day they would have just to repeat what they did on the first day and that would give fault results (SbS would seem more effective than it really is). If the programming assignments were different and, for instance, the first one was somehow easier than the second one, than XP would be privileged and one would come to false conclusions. To overcome that difficulty we decided that on the first day Pairs1 will be doing XP-like pair programming and Pairs2 will follow SbS. On the second day we gave them new assignments and Pairs1 was doing SbS while Pairs2 was following XP. Since the assignment used on the first day was different from that one used on the second day, we decided to use in our calculations *relative completion time*, i.e. the ratio of time used by pairs to the average time used by individuals (if the assignment used on the first day was by 30% more time consuming than the assignment used on the second day , than the average completion time for individuals was also by 30% greater for the first day than for the second day and that would compensate longer completion times for the first day).

The average values of relative completion times for SbS, XP, and individuals are shown in **Fig. 1** (obviously, the average relative completion time for individuals is 1). As the chart suggests, SbS is faster than XP and this observation is statistically significant with significance level equal to 0.15 (i.e. the probability of accepting the hypothesis that SbS is faster while it is not equals 0.15). Another observation saying that SbS and XP are faster than individual programming is statistically significant with significance level 0.05.

The above statistical analysis is based on the assumption that analyzed data are normally distributed (or reasonably close to normal distribution). Thus, one has to check if the collected data satisfy that condition. For that purpose we used the Shapiro-Wilk (SW) test [18]. The test confirmed that both raw completion times and relative completion times are normally distributed for all the programming styles, i.e. XP, SbS and individual (the confidence level is 0.05).

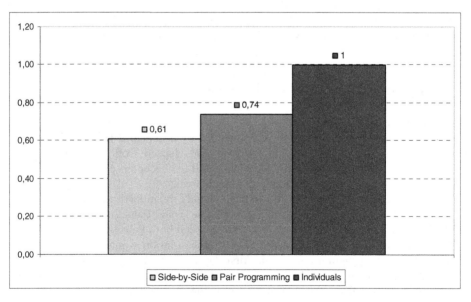

Fig. 1. Average relative completion time for individuals, XP pairs, and side-by-side pairs

Effort Analysis

For individuals *effort* equals completion time. In case of pairs the effort equals double completion time. For the sake of the reasons described in the first part of this section we are using *relative effort*, i.e. the ratio of effort for a given programming style to the average effort of individuals. The average relative effort for XP, SbS and individuals

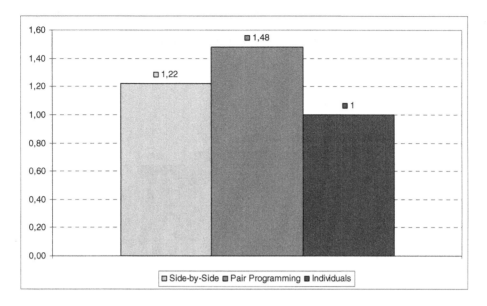

Fig. 2. Average relative effort for individual programmers, SbS and XP pairs

is shown in Fig. 2. As the figure suggests, the effort for XP is greater than for SbS and this is statistically significant with significance level 0.15.

5 Familiarity-with-Code Analysis

In XP two programmers work all the time together: while one is writing code the other is doing continuous (on-the-fly) inspection. In SbS a pair has two computers and the partners can work on different tasks. Thus, a question arises how it does influence familiarity of the partners with all the code. To check it we decided to introduce a postmortem step which was performed at the end of each day. During postmortem step all the subjects were given a micro-assignment: they had to implement (individually) a small change request (the change request was the same for all the subjects). We measured the time required to complete the task. Relative completion time is the ratio of individual completion time (also for members of Pairs1 and Pairs2 – in the postmortem step they worked individually) to the average completion time for members of the Ind group. In Fig. 3 average value of relative completion time for XP, SbS and individual programming is presented (here "individual programming" refers to programming of the main assignment, not post-mortem). As the figure suggests, for SbS the code understanding is worse than for XP (in terms of average time required to implement a change). However, the smallest significance level at which one can assume this hypothesis is 0.25 (it is relatively high, so the hypothesis is rather weak). Figure 3 suggests that completion time for XP is greater than for individuals – that means that familiarity with code for XP is less than for individual programming. However, this hypothesis is not statistically significant.

We have also checked normality of the distribution of completion time for all the programmers performing postmortem step (we used the Shapiro-Wilk test). The completion time data are normally distributed with significance level equal to 0.10.

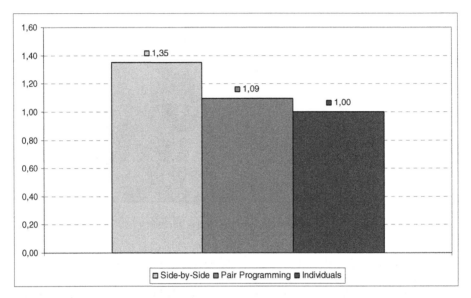

Fig. 3. Average relative completion time of the postmortem task (small change request) for individuals using different styles (XP, SbS or individual programming) for the main task

6 Participants Impression

After the experiment we have conducted a survey and asked the subjects a few questions about their impression on the programming styles. 55% of the subjects preferred collaborative programming (SbS or XP approach) to individual; while 40% had the opposite opinion (5% had mixed feelings). Of those 55% the Side-by-Side approach was preferred by 70% of the subjects, and XP by 30%.

The communication in SbS pairs was considered positive (very good or good enough) by 95% of the subjects.

48% of the subjects working in pairs were satisfied with their own code and 36% was unsatisfied. As regards partner's code, 45% were satisfied and another 45% had the opposite opinion. Since all the pair members were using both XP and SbS we do not know if this confidence (or lack of confidence) in code was greater for XP or for SbS.

7 Conclusions

From the described experiment it follows that side-by-side programming (SbS) is an interesting alternative to XP-like pair programming. Completion time for SbS was at the level of 60% compared with individual programming, what means that the effort overhead for SbS is as small as 20% (in some earlier experiments the effort overhead associated with XP-like pair programming was as big as 60% and in this experiment it was at the level of 50%). However, the effort of individual code maintenance for SbS was about 20% greater than for XP what indicates that knowledge about code is spreading slower for SbS than for XP. As regards personal impression, only 55% of the subjects preferred pair programming (SbS or XP) to individual one. Among them 70% was for SbS and only 30% for XP-like pair programming.

In further studies we shall focus on guidelines for applying particular software development approach. The goal is to deliver a framework for project managers and software developers helping to choose the right team organization the right software project, depending on importance of such factors like: completion time, effort or solution's quality.

References

1. Basili, V. E., Lanubile, F.: Building Knowledge through Families of Experiments. IEEE Transactions on Software Engineering, Volume 25, No. 4 (1999) 456–473.
2. Beck, K.: Extreme Programming Explained: Embrace Change. Addison-Wesley Professional (1999).
3. Brooks, R. E.: Studying programmer behavior experimentally: the problems of proper methodology. Communications of the ACM, Volume 23, No. 4 (1980) 207–213.
4. Brzeziński, J.: Metodologia badań psychologicznych. Wydawnictwo Naukowe PWN (2004).
5. Cockburn, A.: Writing Effective Use Cases. Addison-Wesley (2000).
6. Cockburn, A.: Agile Software Development. Addison-Wesley (2002).
7. Cockburn, A.: Crystal Clear. A Human-Powered Methodology for Small Teams. Addison-Wesley (2005).
8. Dickey, T. F. Programmer variability. Proceedings of the IEEE, Volume 69, No. 7 (1981) 844–845.
9. Humphrey, W.: A Discipline for Software Engineering. Addison-Wesley, Reading MA (1995).
10. Laboratory of Software Engineering. http://www.se.cs.put.poznan.pl/en/content/research/experiments/experiments.html (2005).
11. Lui, K. M., Chan, K. C. C.: When Does a Pair Outperform Two Individuals? Lecture Notes in Computer Science , Volume 2675 (2003) 225–233.
12. Montgomery, D. C.: Introduction to Statistical Quality Control. Third Edition. John Wiley & Sons, Inc. (1997).
13. Nawrocki, J., Wojciechowski A. : Experimental Evaluation of Pair Programming. In: Maxwell, K., Oligny, S., Kusters, R., van Veenedaal E. (eds.): Project Control: Satisfying the Customer. Proceedings of the 12th European Software Control and Metrics Conference. Shaker Publishing, London (2001) 269–276.
14. Nosek J. T.: The Case for Collaborative Programming. Communications of the ACM, Volume 41, No. 3 (1998) 105–108.
15. Padberg, F., Mueller, M.: An Empirical study about the Feelgood Factor in Pair Programming. In: Proceedings of the 10th International Symposium on Software Metrics METRICS 2004, IEEE Press (2004).
16. Pressman, R. S.: Software Engineering: A Practitioner's Approach. Fifth Edition. McGraw-Hill (2001).

17. Sackman, H., Erikson, W. J., Grant, E. E.: Exploratory Experimental Studies Comparing Online and Offline Programming Performance. Communications of ACM, Volume 11, No. 1 (1968) 3–11.
18. Shapiro, S.S., Wilk, M.B. An analysis of variance test for normality (complete samples). Biometrika. 52, 3 and 4 (1965) 591– 611.
19. Sheil, B. A.: The Psychological Study of Programming. ACM Computing Surveys, Volume 13, No. 1 (1981) 101–120.
20. Tichy, W.F.: Should Computer Scientists Experiment More? IEEE Computer, Volume 31, No. 5 (1998) 32–40.
21. Williams, L.: The Collaborative Software Process. PhD Dissertation at Department of Computer Science, University of Utah, Salt Lake City (2000).
22. Williams, L. at al.: Strengthening the Case for Pair Programming. IEEE Software, Volume 17, No. 4 (2000) 19–25.

Finding and Ranking Research Directions for Software Testing

Ossi Taipale[1], Kari Smolander[1,2], and Heikki Kälviäinen[1]

[1] Laboratory of Information Processing, Department of Information Technology,
Lappeenranta University of Technology, P.O.Box 20, Lappeenranta, Finland
Ossi.Taipale@lut.fi, Heikki.Kalviainen@lut.fi
http://www.lut.fi
[2] South Carelia Polytechnic, Koulukatu 5 B, 55120 Imatra, Finland
Kari.Smolander@scp.fi

Abstract. The percentage of software testing in software development is high; 50 % is often mentioned in the literature. Moreover, the amount of testing is increasing because of the demand for better quality. A survey was carried out to find out where software testing research should be directed. The experts of the participating industry and the research institutes evaluated the issues of testing research. The research method was a derivative of the Delphi method. The most prominent research issues in ranking included process improvement, testing automation with testing tools, and standardization of testing. The process and results of the survey are presented and the need for further research is discussed. This study also shows an example how project steering groups can be used in resolving research priorities.

1 Introduction

Complicated systems and the demand for better software quality together require efficient software quality assurance and, generally, more efforts on software testing. The amount of software testing continues to grow. Literature related to software testing gives various estimates of the testing proportion: Osterweil et al. [18] estimate that the software testing effort is 50-60 % of the total development effort. Kit [13] states that the systems we build are even more complex and critical, and more than 50 % of the development effort is frequently spent on testing.

According to researchers, testing research should be increased in many areas: Osterweil et al. [18] pay attention on the chasm between research and industry. They suggest industry direction for the testing research. Whittaker [23] says that the demand for more practical work is strong and the time to tie academic work to real industry products is now. Jones [10] states that although testing accounts for 50 % of the costs of software it receives little treatment in most curricula. He calls for a holistic approach. Jones and Chatmon [11] present that software testing receives very little attention in undergraduate curricula.

All in all, software testing contains a wide array of research issues. In this paper the priorities of testing research is asked from industry experts and researchers. The priorities are ranked and the focus of testing research is determined using the rank-

I. Richardson et al. (Eds.): EuroSPI 2005, LNCS 3792, pp. 39 – 48, 2005.

ings. This survey is the first phase in a three year testing research project. The objective of this survey is to reveal important testing research issues and to target future testing research to those issues. To find important issues, a Delphi derivative industry survey [3, 4, 20] was conducted.

The paper is structured as follows: First, in Section 2 related research is shortly discussed. A description of the research process and method including the informants is presented in Section 3. Then the results are presented in Section 4. Finally, discussion and conclusions are given in Section 5.

2 Software Testing and Related Research

Researchers have different views of the improvement and priorities of software testing. In the following, several approaches to testing research are listed as examples of different emphasis.

Osterweil et al. [18] highlight many issues related to testing, including formal methods, testing guided by a set of program measures, analysis and testing technology integration, building the software in such a way as to assure that quality is present at the end of development, testing automation, process-based integration of testing and analysis, effective integration of the various quality tools and technologies, and how to assure software quality by building it into precode artefacts such as designs, requirements, and architecture specifications. As a summary Osterweil et al. emphasize improvement and integration of testing and development processes.

Voas [24] discusses themes like process improvement and maturity, formal methods, languages and object-oriented design (OOD), metrics and measurement, software standards, testing, computer-aided software engineering, and total quality management. Voas describes distinct issues how to raise the quality of the software, but states at the same time that none of the major challenges of creating quality software have been conquered.

Groves et al. [8] emphasize formality of process and/or notation, standards, testing and tools, and languages used. Groves et al. state that larger software development groups have more well-defined software development processes and follow more rigorous testing regimes. Dybå [6] describes different results. He states that small organizations implement process improvement elements as effectively as large organizations. The degree of process implementation seems to be more important than the size of the organization. Torkar and Mankefors [21] discuss about testing and reuse. They state that 60 % of the developers claimed that verification and validation were the first things that were neglected in cases of time shortage during a project. This finding on reuse is important because reuse is increasing.

Graham [7] discusses that testers should be involved in testing requirements. Harrold [9] underlines development of techniques and tools that support component users, use of precode artefacts, and development of techniques and tools for testing evolving systems. Both Graham and Harrold emphasize the need to integrate earlier phases of the development process to the testing process.

Our literature review and interviews yielded a long list of software testing issues that might have potential as research issues. The literature review shows that important issues of software testing are widely discussed in the academia, but a comparable industry ranking was not available.

3 Research Process

The phases of the survey are adopted from the Delphi derivative survey method developed by Schmidt [20]. The Delphi method [3, 4] was originally developed as a group decision support method. Its object is to obtain the most reliable consensus of opinions of an expert group. It is used in forecasting and in strategic decision making.

Currently, the Delphi method is used more in finding good arguments about an ongoing process. Collecting arguments was the motivation to use the Delphi method in this study. Also the method generated insights into why respondents view certain issues as being more important than others. For example, Keil et al. [12] used Delphi method in identifying software project risks. The Delphi method was selected to this study because it is suitable for group decisions and the objective here is to identify important issues in software testing from experts working together in group meetings.

The research process and the phases of the research are described in Figure 1. The process consisted of a series of expert meetings and panels, their preparations, and processing of the meeting and panel results. These tasks were organized in four phases, during which the software testing research issues were discovered, consolidated, and ranked. In the following, the phases will be explained in detail.

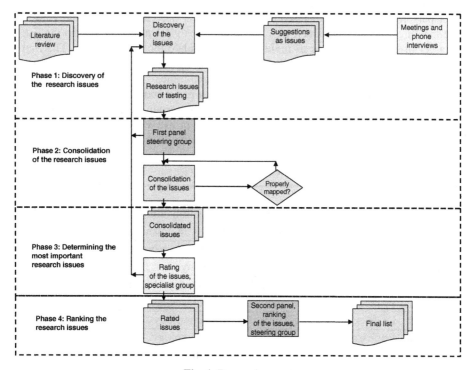

Fig. 1. Research process

3.1 Phase 1: Discovery of the Research Issues

The collection of the research issues started with a literature review and in parallel experts were interviewed either face-to-face or by phone. Notes were written and issues were collected from the expert meetings and the phone conversations. The experts were encouraged to suggest issues they felt important. Based on the interviews and literature survey, a list consisting of a broad set of testing issues was formed. This list served as the starting point in the first panel during Phase 2.

3.2 Phase 2: Consolidation of the Research Issues

The consolidation of the list consisting of issues of testing happened in three steps. Firstly, the issues of the list were consolidated to bigger entities by researchers. The consolidation was based either on a generalization-specialization structure (similar attributes and function, e.g. testing tools are a generalization of tools for test planning) or on a whole-part structure where the whole consists of parts (e.g. testing methods contain, for example, white box testing and white box testing contains branch testing).

Secondly, the list was introduced to the first panel, which was a steering group meeting. The steering group of the project consisted of 10 members. The representatives of industry were either R&D directors or persons responsible for development and testing projects, and the representatives of research institutes were either professors or persons responsible for research projects (Table 1). The issues were reviewed in the meeting. During this panel, new research issues were also accepted to the list. The target of the meeting was to review and consolidate the list of issues. The first panel was a part of the consolidation process. It both generated new research issues and reviewed and consolidated already found research issues.

Thirdly, the consolidation continued after the first panel and corrections were made based on the feedback from the members of the steering group. The consolidation was made in three steps to be sure that all the issues were properly mapped. After the first panel and the consolidation the list of 22 issues was compressed to 9 issues.

Table 1. Steering group

Member / Company
M. Sc. Tech., R&D Manager / Very large automation company
B. Sc. Tech., BA Manager / Medium sized telecommunication company
M. Sc. Tech., Project Engineer / Medium sized engineering company
M. Sc. Tech., Director / Large automation company
M. SC. Tech., Programme Man. / Technology Agency of Finland
Dr. Tech., Professor / Lappeenranta University of Technology
Dr. Tech., Professor / Helsinki University of Technology
Dr. Tech., Professor / Tampere University of Technology
Dr. Tech., Senior Scientist / VTT, Research Centre of Finland
Dr. Tech., Programme Man. / VTT, Research Centre of Finland

3.3   Phase 3: Determining the Most Important Research Issues

The consolidated list of testing issues with their explanation was given to an expert group for rating. The members of the expert group that rated the issues are listed in Table 2.

Table 2. Expert group

Member / Company
M. Sc. Tech., R&D Manager / Very large automation company
B. Sc. Tech., BA Manager / Medium sized telecommunication company
M. Sc. Tech., Project Engineer / Medium sized engineering company
M. Sc. Tech., Testing Manager / Large automation company
M. Sc. Tech., Testing Lab. Man. / Very large telecommunication company
M. Sc. Tech., Director / Small testing company
M. Sc. Tech., Director / Small testing company
M. Sc. Tech., Programme Man. / Technology Agency of Finland
Dr. Tech., Testing Researcher / Tampere University of Technology
Lic. Tech., Senior Scientist / VTT, Research Centre of Finland

The reason for assembling an expert group was that the group represents a wider cross-section of the software engineering industry than the steering group. When forming the expert group, the steering group was supplemented by two representatives from the telecommunication cluster and one independent representative from a small testing company. The expert group was balanced in a way that it contained three members from the telecommunication cluster, three members from the automation cluster, and four independent members. The members also represented different sizes of firms. Another reason for using an expert group was that we wanted to hear the opinion of experts who deal with concrete problems related to testing daily.

The experts were asked to rate the research issues. In addition, a short open-ended reasoning for each issue was requested. In the rating, we basically used a similar process as the one described by Morris et al. [15]. Priorities were determined by the experts. Each expert was able to assign one to five tokens to each issue according to their views on the importance of the issue (Likert scale 1-5). The list was sent by e-mail to the experts, and the answers also came by e-mail.

When the results were available the tokens were summed up. The information was brought to the next panel in Phase 4.

3.4   Phase 4: Ranking the Research Issues

The second panel was also a steering group meeting. First, the results of the expert group were introduced to the steering group. Second, the steering group evaluated the list issue by issue. In the evaluation the priority rating, advantages, disadvantages, and conclusions were discussed. Issues rated an average of 3 (30 tokens or more) or higher on our 5-point scale were ranked in the steering group by voting (three issues). Issues rated below 3 (less than 30 tokens) were eliminated (6 issues). This paring method was adopted from [12]. With regard to these three issues the steering group also evaluated problems with the issue and the competence to start researching the issue. To help the ranking, a short research plan was outlined for each issue.

4   Results

Table 3 presents the titles describing the issues collected from the literature review and the expert interviews in Phase 1. Only the titles of the list are expressed here because of the extensive length of the formed list of issues. The comprehensive list is available at www.it.lut.fi/project/anti.

Table 3. Research issues of testing

1.	Major documents of development and testing.
2.	Development process and test process improvement.
3.	Testing as a part of quality system.
4.	Testing and capability-maturity models.
5.	Metrics and testing.
6.	Standardization and testing.
7.	Risk analysis and testing.
8.	Timing and testing.
9.	Testing as a part of software quality assurance.
10.	Configuration management and testing.
11.	Software testing strategies.
12.	Testing methods.
13.	Unit testing, integration testing, usability testing, function testing, system testing and acceptance testing.
14.	Testing object-oriented analysis, object-oriented design and object-oriented programming.
15.	Testing and formal methods.
16.	Testing and cleanroom in software engineering.
17.	Reuse of components and testing.
18.	Software engineering and testing tools (automation).
19.	Testing tools (automation).
20.	Organization for testing.
21.	Testing systems.
22.	Testing and maintenance.

4.1   Rated Research Issues

The results of the rating are presented in Table 4 in decreasing order of priority (priority ratings in parenthesis). For example, 39 for testing automation and testing tools mean that this issue has got 39 tokens from the experts. There were in total 10 experts, so the mean is 3.9. Only the shortened table is expressed here because the table of rating results is long. The comprehensive table is also available at www.it.lut.fi/project/anti.

Descriptions of the research issues are listed in Table 4 including also literature references.

Table 4. Rating results

1. Testing automation and testing tools. (sum 39, mean 3.9)
This issue covers the methods and tools for automated software testing. Dustin, Rashka, and Paul [5] discuss the issue extensively. Poston [19] discusses how specification-based testing can be automated.
2. Standardization. (sum 37, mean 3.7)
This issue covers, for example, applying standardization, standardization of the interfaces, testing standards, and time schedule problems when standardization, development and testing slide to the parallel phases. Moore [14] discusses standardization.
3. Process improvement. (sum 30, mean 3.0)
This issue covers, for example, coupling of the development process to the testing process, artefacts and interaction between the processes, and measurements. Osterweil et al. [18] deals with this issue. One of the models is the Software Development Technologies U model [13].
4. Formal methods. (sum 28, mean 2.8)
This issue covers, for example, the development and implementation of methods that generate less faults (e.g. formal methods and the cleanroom in software engineering or extensive reuse of software components), and methods that minimize testing by producing higher quality code. Voas [24] discusses the issue.
5. Testing methods and strategies. (sum 28, mean 2.8)
This issue covers testing methods, techniques, and strategies. Beizer [1] deals with this issue widely.
6. Testing systems. (sum 27, mean 2.7)
This issue covers, for example, the development of testing systems, more extensive utilisation of testing equipment or replacement with cheaper devices, configuration and integration of measuring equipment, simulation, and analysis. The problems of testing laboratories are combined in this issue. Testing systems are expensive or testing can be done only with the customer's equipment (e.g. paper machine or telecommunication network). This issue is taken from the interviews with the personnel of testing laboratories.
7. Distinct issues (UML, TTCN, etc.). (sum 26, mean 2.6)
The distinct sectors of testing are combined in this issue, for example, test generation from the UML description, the TTCN testing language, configuration management etc. Research related to this issue includes testing with the Unified Modelling Language (UML) [2] and Testing and Test Control Notation (TTCN) language [22].
8. Test results processing. (sum 24, mean 2.4)
This issue combines the problems of the results processing. The test results processing system helps to avoid unnecessary testing and to reuse existing results. This issue is taken from the interviews with personnel of the serial production industry.
9. Finding faults that pass testing. (sum 16, mean 1.6)
This issue combines the questions of the maintenance phase. Complete testing is impossible; Myers [16] discusses the issue.

4.2   Ranked Research Issues

The panel rankings were made by voting the three issues with the highest ratings (testing automation and testing tools, standardization, and process improvement). As the result, the panel selected process improvement as the most important issue in software testing research. The second issue became testing automation and testing tools and the third was standardization.

Because the priority rating for the winning issue was only the third highest, the panel made also a justification of its selection. According to the panel, process improvement increases information flow and interaction between software development and testing. Problems in the information flow between software development and testing increase both development work and testing work. The software engineering process is under a continuous change and this change creates problems in information flows. Informants explained in the interviews that this on-going change means, for example, minimizing new programming in a company by extensive reuse of software components and by the use of commercial off-the-self software (COTS) or third party software. Further, changes in testing mean, for example, testing of software components, COTS, and third party software. Opposite opinions against the selection of process improvement as the issue with the highest priority were mainly against measuring people, which may be required when improving processes and some informants seemed not to trust on software measurements that would also be required.

The second in ranking was testing automation and testing tools. The panel justified its ranking by stating that testing automation is efficient in the repetitive situations (e.g. regression testing) and automation makes it possible to adapt to the demand for the testing capacity. The problem is that automation does not solve the problems of earlier phases in the development process. Also, quite a deal of research exists in this area and there is not much potential for novel ideas. Mature applications exist.

Standardization was ranked third. Informants emphasized that standardization is a precondition for testing automation and it raises the quality of the software, but the investment is really big for a company and the repayment period is long.

The most successful issue, process improvement, was further specified in the steering group. Process improvement was divided into subtasks (e.g. improving information flow and interaction between development and testing processes). These subtasks will be evaluated in the following phases of this research project.

5 Discussion and Conclusions

The objective of this research was to find and rank research issues of software testing. Process improvement was ranked as the most important research issue, the second was testing automation and testing tools, and the third was standardization.

Comparing the results to related research is difficult because comparable rankings are not available. Ng et al. describe in an Australian software testing survey [17] issues like software testing methodologies and techniques, automated software testing tools, software testing metrics, software testing standards, and software testing training, and education. They noticed that 58.5% of the 65 survey respondents used testing metrics (a category in our study - process improvement, the coupling of the development process to the testing process and its measurements – resembled this one). Automated software testing tools were used by 67.7% of the respondents (in our study we had a similar issue - testing automation and testing tools), and software testing standards were being adopted by 72.3% of the respondents (in our study - standardization). As already noted in parentheses, the issues are not exactly the same as in our study. Therefore, the results are not directly comparable, but high percentages in the

Australian survey suggest that our list of the top three categories indeed contains important issues of software testing.

The next phases of our research project will be based on this survey. The analysis of the answers yielded a hypothesis for continuing the research. This study revealed that according to experts, problems in the information flow between software development and testing processes may increase both development work and testing. An analysis of the information flow between the processes can reveal important information that can be used in improving total efficiency of both software testing and development.

A possible limitation of this survey is that the results can be applied only to similar environments. The informants of this survey represented organizations that produce technically highly advanced products and applications in telecommunication and automation domains. The criticality of their products is above average and the products are used in real time environments. It is possible that the rankings in other kinds of applications (for example distributed database intensive applications in public internet) may have different order and selection of issues.

The survey revealed the need to clarify the cross-sectional situation between software development and testing. To get a deeper insight into the problems we have proposed a further survey. We propose theory testing survey-research as the research method for the next phase of the project. The focus of the survey would be in the information flow and the interaction between the development process and the testing process.

References

1. Beizer, B.: Software testing techniques. Van Nostrand Reinhold, New York (1990)
2. Dai, Z. R., Grabowski, J., Neukirchen, H., Pals, H.: From Design to Test with UML. In: Proc. 16th IFIP International Conference, TestCom 2004, Testing of Communicating Systems (2004) 33-49
3. Dalkey, N. C.: The Delphi method: An experimental study of group opinion. RAND Corporation, Santa Monica, CA (1969)
4. Dalkey, N. C., Helmer, O.: An experimental application of the Delphi method to the use of experts. Management Science 9 (1963) 458-467
5. Dustin, E., Rashka, J., Paul, J.: Automated software testing: introduction, management, and performance. Addison-Wesley, Boston (1999)
6. Dybå, T.: Factors of software process improvement success in small and large organizations: an empirical study in the Scandinavian context. In: Proc. Foundations of Software Engineering. Proceedings of the 9th European software engineering conference held jointly with 10th ACM SIGSOFT international symposium on Foundations of software engineering (2003) 148-157
7. Graham, D.: Requirements and testing: Seven missing-link myths. IEEE Software 19 (2002) 15-17
8. Groves, L., Nickson, R., Reeve, G., Reeves, S., Utting, M.: A survey of software development practices in the New Zealand software industry. In: Proc. Software Engineering Conference (2000) 189-201
9. Harrold, M. J.: Testing: A Roadmap. In: Proc. International Conference on Software Engineering (2000) 61-72

10. Jones, E. L.: Software testing in the computer science curriculum -- a holistic approach. In: Proc. Proceedings of the Australasian conference on Computing education (2000) 153-157
11. Jones, E. L., Chatmon, C. L.: A perspective on teaching software testing. In: Proc. Proceedings of the seventh annual consortium for computing in small colleges central plains conference on The journal of computing in small colleges (2001) 92-100
12. Keil, M., Cule, P. E., Lyytinen, K., Schmidt, R. C.: A Framework for Identifying Software Project Risks. Communications of the ACM 41 (1998)
13. Kit, E.: Software Testing in the Real World: Improving the Process. Addison-Wesley, Reading, MA (1995)
14. Moore, J. W.: Software engineering standards: a user's roadmap. IEEE Computer Society, Los Alamitos, CA (1998)
15. Morris, P., Masera, M., Wilikens, M.: Requirements Engineering and Industrial Uptake. Requirements Engineering 3 (1998) 79-83
16. Myers, G. J.: The Art of Software Testing. John Wiley & Sons, NY (1976)
17. Ng, S. P., Murnane, T., Reed, K., Grant, D., Chen, T. Y.: A preliminary survey on software testing practices in Australia. In: Proc. 2004 Australian Software Engineering Conference. 2004: 116-25 (2004)
18. Osterweil, L., Clarke, L. A., DeMillo, R. A., Feldman, S. I., McKeeman, B., Salasin, E. F. M., Jackson, D., Wallace, D., Harrold, M. J.: Strategic Directions in Software Quality. ACM Computing Surveys 28 (1996)
19. Poston, R. M.: Automating specification-based software testing. IEEE Computer Society Press (1996)
20. Schmidt, R. C.: Managing Delphi surveys using nonparametric statistical techniques. Decision Sciences 28 (1997) 763-774
21. Torkar, R., Mankefors, S.: A survey on testing and reuse. In: Proc. IEEE International Conference on Software - Science, Technology and Engineering (SwSTE'03) (2003)
22. Vassiliou-Gioles, T., Din, G., Schieferdecker, I.: Execution of External Applications Using TTCN-3. In: Proc. 16th IFIP International Conference, TestCom 2004, Testing of Communicating Systems (2004)
23. Whittaker, J. A.: What is software testing? And why is it so hard? IEEE Software 17 (2000) 70-79
24. Voas, J.: Software quality's eight greatest myths. IEEE Software 16 (1999) 118-120

Quality: Attitudes and Experience Within the Irish Software Industry

Brendan Keane and Ita Richardson

Computer Science and Information Systems Department, University of Limerick,
Castletroy, Limerick, Ireland
{Brendan.Keane, Ita.Richardson}@ul.ie
http://www.csis.ul.ie

Abstract. The Irish software industry is facing a new challenge. Prior to this, Ireland had emerged as one of the leading software exporters in the world. Then came the downturn in the global economy, the burst of the 'dot com' bubble and now Ireland faces competition in the form of developing third world economies. The Irish software industry will struggle to compete with the vast, skilled but cheap labour force that these economies can offer in abundance. Is there any other field in which the Irish software industry can compete? Quality in Ireland had traditionally only been applied to the manufacturing industry. However, since the continued development of the Irish software industry, have the Irish software community taken software quality seriously enough? This paper presents the results of research conducted with members of the Irish software community to gauge their attitudes and opinions towards software quality.

1 Introduction

The Irish software industry plays a vital role in the Irish economy. According to reports over the past number of years the Information and Communication Technology (ICT) sector in Ireland employs an estimated 92,000 people within 1,300 companies, with a combined estimated turnover of €52 billion for the year 2003 [1], [2], [3]. Focusing exclusively on the software industry in Ireland, it is estimated that 23,930 people were employed in 2003, a drop of 14% from the previous year. Revenue for the industry in 2003 was estimated around €14.9 billion, a 7% increase on the previous year [4]. The statistics presented here vary to a degree from report to report. However, these statistics highlight the continued importance of the ICT sector to the Irish economy. Despite the downturn in the global economy optimism is still high within the Irish software community that recent success can be continued and improved upon.

1.1 Success Factors for the Irish Software Industry

The Irish software industry has enjoyed the benefits of lucrative outsourcing and foreign direct investment (FDI), particularly from large multi-national corporations.

I. Richardson et al. (Eds.): EuroSPI 2005, LNCS 3792, pp. 49–58, 2005.

Currently, seven of the top ten ICT companies have a base in Ireland: IBM, Intel, HP, Dell, Oracle, Lotus and Microsoft. Worldwide FDI suffered a slump in 2002, though this was not evident in Ireland. FDI to Ireland in 2002 was recorded at €26 billion. This is over two and a half times the amount recorded for 2001 [5]. So what are the reasons behind the Irish software industry's success and growth? There are several factors responsible for the success of the ICT sector in Ireland over the past 20 years. These can be divided into ICT and non-ICT specific factors:

ICT Specific Factors

- Growth in global trade and the expansion of the US economy
- The growth of FDI globally in the 1990s
- Education and technological innovation
- Upgrading of Ireland's telecommunications infrastructure

Non-ICT specific Factors

- Reductions in taxation (corporation tax of 12.5%) and wage moderation
- Labour supply did not limit growth potential
- English speaking workforce
- Deployment of EU structural and cohesion funds to Ireland [6], [7], [8]

1.2 Concerns for the Irish Software Industry

In the last number of years the characteristics that have made Ireland attractive to FDI have been diminishing. With the recent downturn in the global economy, this poses a recognizable problem. Since the 'dot com' bubble burst there has been a reduction in the number of school leavers pursuing college degrees with a technological background, resulting in the possibility of future labor shortages in the ICT sector. There is a distinct worry that there will be a shortfall of supply over demand for ICT graduates to fill jobs currently available to them [9].

The emergence of developing economies such as India and China as major players on the world's technological stage has given the Irish software community cause for concern. These nations and others like them can provide an abundant, well-educated workforce for their ICT sectors. Estimates predict a workforce of almost 17 million available to the ICT sector in India by 2008 [10]. More importantly, this workforce can be delivered at a much lower cost. There also appears to be a higher focus on quality and quality processes within Indian organizations as they seek to surpass their own domestic, continental and western competitors in their bid to secure lucrative foreign investment deals.

1.3 Potential Solutions

In order for the Irish software industry to prosper, the Irish government must continue to lead by example. Ireland's existing financial policies are a big incentive for foreign companies looking to set up a European base. "With one of the lowest corporation tax rates in the European Union, Ireland has seen its economic growth consistently out-pace that of its neighbors" [11]. The Irish government needs to continue its positive economic strategy and further exploit the potential that the ICT sector can bring to the Irish economy.

The potential shortfall of skilled IT graduates in Ireland may eventually be overturned as confidence returns to the ICT sector. Until then, this shortfall could be made up by an influx of skilled foreign workers, particularly from the newly joined member states of the EU.

Possible pay cuts in order to match competitors do not seem plausible in a country where the cost of living is already one of the highest in Europe. Even if it were possible, the cuts would have to be sizable in order to rival Ireland's newly developing competitors. Some hope for the Irish software industry in this regard is the projected rise in wages in India. However, should the balance be met between the Indian and Irish wage costs; other economies such as China still exist to take over the advantage.

One possibility is for the Irish software community to embrace the desire to improve their software processes in the way that Indian companies appear to have. If the Irish software industry could do this and do it right, they would be able to demonstrate mature, repeatable and traceable processes. This could prove the decisive factor for attracting untapped FDI potential, while retaining and developing their existing FDI.

2 Research Overview

The information presented in this paper is the result of research carried out with members of the Irish software community. The aim of this research was to gauge the attitudes and experience of the Irish software community towards quality and quality processes. Given the concerns facing the Irish software industry, the authors wished to explore how or if the Irish software community had catered for quality. A "state of the nation" was proposed whereby the authors would conduct research into these attitudes and opinions and form conclusions and recommendations based on the analyzed data received.

2.1 Research Methods

As this research was intended to discover opinions and experiences, it was decided that interviews would be used as the primary research method. Data from an online questionnaire provided the researcher with a second and separate quantitative bank of data to be analyzed.

2.1.1 Interviews

Interviews bring the researcher closer to the topic, offer flexibility and can be adapted to suit particular situations. They allow the researcher the opportunity to ask complex questions and provide quality data for the researcher to analyze. Interviews were semi-structured in nature allowing the researcher to pursue any emerging trends. A mixture of open-ended and closed questions were used, depending on the type of information the researcher wished to elicit. Voice recording equipment and note taking, were used to record the interviews.

Interview questions were based around the five perceptions of quality as presented by Garvin [12]. Given that there can be a variety of different ways to view quality, by basing the interview questions around Garvin's views on quality, it was intended to discover the different attitudes and opinions of each respondent towards each perspective.

Personal contacts secured many interviews, while other companies upon being informed of the research were also willing to cooperate. In total, 53 interviews were conducted with members of the Irish software community. It was hoped to gain as many perspectives as possible regarding quality in the Irish software industry. As such a variety of personnel were interviewed ranging from CEO's to software engineers. Once transcribed, interview data was coded and hand analyzed for emerging trends.

2.1.2 Online Questionnaire

Data from an online questionnaire was made available to the authors for the purpose of their research. This questionnaire sought to examine quality model adoption rates within the Irish software industry. The questionnaire provided a mix of qualitative and quantitative based questions, allowing respondents to tick a box or in some cases offer a few short words for an answer. Background information about the respondents' organizations was collected. Data relating to organizations focus on quality, as well as data regarding respondent's' experience with a variety of quality models was also gathered.

The raw data from this questionnaire was input into a statistical analysis software tool, which was used to produce tables and graphs to aid the authors in their analysis of the data.

3 Research Findings

3.1 Background of the Irish Software Community

The aim of this research was to gauge the attitudes and experiences of the Irish software community towards quality. The pie chart below (Fig. 1.) presents the information received in a graphical context. Only one interviewee had no formal third level education, but was working in the industry for 20 years. Several interviewees had achieved postgraduate awards in various disciplines.

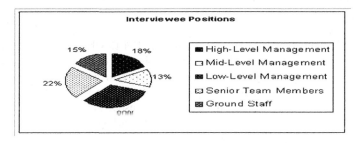

Fig. 1. Employee level of the respondents

3.2 Quality Definitions

Interviewees were asked, "How do you define quality?" When analyzed, these definitions were categorized into 4 areas. In order of importance, these were: customer oriented, meeting requirements, reliability / efficiency and process oriented. Over half gave a definition resembling "A system that reliably satisfies the customers needs". But what does satisfying a customer mean? Further analysis revealed that satisfying a customer can be achieved through one or all of the following; meeting customer needs or requirements, ensuring good product performance and value for money.

3.3 Customers of the Irish Software Industry

Eighty four percent of interviewee's customers are external i.e. outside their organization. The majority of customers fall into the category of IT service users. The main industries catered for are telecommunications, medical, governmental, automotive and construction / engineering.

Customers are shown to have varying attitudes and knowledge regarding the software process within their supplier organizations. Fifty one percent of interviewees said that their customers do not know nor do they wish to know what software processes are in place: *"As long as they get a good product, on time and within budget they are happy"*. Those customers that did care, were either involved in the medical industry and as such were under strict guidelines on quality, or had experience themselves with software quality models.

When asked regarding the main cause of customer complaints, requirement issues were highlighted. Incorrect, changing or misunderstanding requirements were estimated to cause 75% of customer complaints. The remaining 25% of complaints were alleged customer misunderstandings regarding how the product works.

3.4 Software Development Problems

The primary cause of organization's software development problems was issues with requirements. Poor requirements capture or changing requirements caused interviewees the most problems, with one developer saying, *"trying to nail things down and get things done has always been the biggest problem"*. Interviewees were also aware of the difficulty in getting their customers to specify their exact requirements stating, *"It is very hard to pin down specific user requirements"*. Changes can also occur because sometimes the customers themselves do not really know what they want until they see a product in front of them. *"If the customer doesn't know what they want this can be very frustrating"* to developers attempting to anticipate rather than cater for customer needs or wants. The later a requirement change is made, the more expensive and time consuming it can be for an organization to implement.

Incorrect estimates were also considered a major problem. Management figures were seen to play a part in this problem by imposing unrealistic deadlines and/ or budgetary constraints on development teams. According to one interviewee *"They (management) would promise the customer that it would be done in two weeks, when we needed to months to do it"*. Managing management's expectations is a big concern with estimations, but not the only one. In some organizations this can result in *"a trade off between quality and functionality, sometimes shortcuts have to be taken and sometimes functionality has to be curbed"*. Management has a different view on this. One top-level manager in particular bemoans his inability to receive a project plan from his development teams. However this manager believes this is down to the nature of software development itself: *"Every developer will tell you what we're doing is so innovative"*. When developing a new product or using a new method, though they are perhaps not in uncharted territory, they are navigating with new tools. As a result, developers are unwilling to specify how long it will take them to get to their destination, because they are unsure of the answer themselves.

Documentation was the third major software development problem highlighted by interviewees. Having an excessive documentation load can waste time, which developers actually need to spend developing products. According to one developer, an organization's *"heavy handed approach to documentation and procedures"* can waste *"valuable development time and company money, especially if the change involves something small, such as changing a heading"*. However, having too little documentation can lead to variation in practice and having the right amount of documentation will only work if everyone knows how to use it properly and consistently. *"Variations in working practices"* can cause organizations major headaches. Documentation is a very complex issue for organizations and each organization must determine for themselves what is best for them.

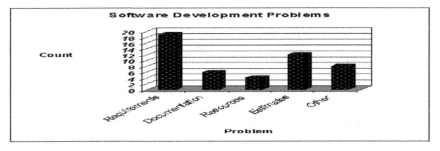

Fig. 2. Main software development problems as reported by the interviewees

3.5   Software Processes: The Good, the Bad and the Confusing

Each interviewee stated that having a good software process positively impacts product quality, *"the more efficiently and effectively a process may be completed, the higher the product quality"*. When asked to give an example of a good software process within their organization 34% of interviewees highlighted their development process as one to be proud of. This was mainly put down to the experience of the individuals running it. One interviewee stated the development process was good because *"it is engrained within the organization, well documented, key deliverables at every stage and risk management is covered"*. Twenty three percent of interviewees highlighted their requirements process as their organization's best example of a good software process. The reason for this was experience, not just of the people involved, but also the experience of the process itself, *"everybody knows why we are doing it, the importance of doing it and we've refined it. It works for us but it took us a while to get there"*.

An issue with requirements again reared its head, this time as organization's primary example of a bad software process. Thirty seven percent of interviewees highlighted their requirements process as a bad software process. The main reasons for requirements causing problems were; having multiple people involved in sign off, reported skills shortages in gathering requirements, not enough accurate documentation for requirements and requirements needing constant revision. Other examples of bad software processes within organizations include; testing, documentation, estimation and the development process.

A confusing development in this research was requirements being highlighted as the second most popular choice for a good software process within organizations. Given the problems associated with requirements i.e. it was, according to interviewees, the main cause of software development problems and the most popular choice for a bad software process. How then could it be held up as the second most example of a good software process? Upon further examination it was revealed that 33% of those that gave requirements as their "good software process" also listed requirements as their main software development problem! A further 33% had estimates as their software development problem; of these, each one stated estimates were a problem, particularly when requirements change. In total this means that either directly or indirectly, 66% of interviewees that highlighted requirements as their "good software process" had issues with requirements during software development.

3.6 Software Quality Models

Fifty two percent of interviewees stated that their organization used a recognized quality model. The most common model used by interviewee's organizations was the ISO series of standards. Tick IT and then CMM follow ISO in popularity here. Thirty seven percent of organizations used none, while 11% of organizations used an internal model. Those not using any model primarily listed cost and overhead as their reasons for not having one. However another reason given was *"at the moment we are not too concerned about having a standard process model. Customers don't ask about it, they don't seem to be aware about it"*. This information is supported by the results from the online questionnaire in which 49% of respondents listed *"too costly or difficult to implement"* as their primary reason for not implementing a quality model. For those with a quality model, it was found that in the majority of cases, market forces were the impetus behind the model's implementation. A customer requirement was also an important factor here. One interviewee from an organization with customers in the United States stated, *"they (our customers) don't have clear visibility at times into our process... so they regard ISO registration as being a key indicator that our quality is up to scratch"*.

Respondents to the online questionnaire were asked how often they get customer enquiries as to their certification if any with quality models. The vast majority (61%) of organizations were asked for certification between 0-20 percent of the time. Not surprising when one considers the lack of customer interest in software processes in the first place, but a worrying trend nonetheless, that suggests that customers do not know enough about software quality models to ask about them or insist on their use.

4 Conclusions and Discussion

This paper has presented the results of research conducted within the Irish software industry. An overview of attitudes, opinions and experience of the Irish software community towards software quality, processes and software models has been presented, but what can be learned from this, not only from an Irish but also from a European perspective?

4.1 Advice for Software Organizations

Software organizations and in particular Small to Medium Enterprises (SME's) generally cannot afford to make mistakes. Without a larger parent to absorb costs and without aid from external organizations, how can small indigenous software companies set about improving their software development process [13]? One customer lost to an SME could potentially put it out of business. So what can SME's do to help themselves? From this research it is evident that requirements are a major issue for software organizations. The requirements process needs to be prioritized, this is particularly pertinent for SME's. There is a clear need for a well defined requirements document, customer and management sign off on such a document and customer involvement in the whole development process right from the beginning. Having customers involved from the start of a project keeps them aware of what is going on but also gives them a better idea of how it will all turn out. This gives customers the opportunity to correct any requirements issues from a very early stage resulting in less trouble had these issues not been spotted until later in the development process.

Incorrect estimates were identified as a serious problem. Estimating how long a project will take or how much it will cost can be a difficult thing. Developers and management must learn from their experiences, retain knowledge from each project completed and carry this forward to the next endeavor. Some estimation problems can be traced back to issues with requirements, so SME's need to ensure that their requirements process is up to scratch or it is bound to have a negative effect on estimates. Communication channels must be kept open between developers and management and each group must be aware of the others situation.

Documentation can help or be a hindrance for any organization. There is no quick fix. Some organizations need heavy documentation, some organizations want heavy documentation. Other organizations want flexibility, through little or no documentation. Whichever the case, all organizations must ensure that all employees using documentation know how to use it right.

4.2 Attitudes Towards Quality

There is a definite disregard within some sections of the Irish software community towards quality. This appears to be down to the ignorance of individuals to the possible benefits of software process improvement techniques. One interviewee of a multi national company with bases in Ireland, India and elsewhere pointed out "the Indian divisions are CMM certified to get more project work"! The Irish division was not CMM certified nor was it pursuing it. Was this because the Irish division does not want more work? Those working in the Irish software industry are not the only ones who show a disregard and lack of knowledge towards software quality. Customers also appear to be in the dark when it comes to processes or process quality. This is reflected in their attitude towards software processes and their lack of desire to know if their supplier organization is at least accredited or certified in a quality model or standard. If the Irish and European software industries are to compete with their Indian and Chinese counterparts, change is required. The industry itself and those that use software products in their day-to-day business must realize the positive benefits that software process improvement can bring to organizations.

Companies appear to be focusing on quick fixes, one problem at a time. These problems include requirements, documentation and estimation. Each of these can be a serious problem for organizations if not managed correctly. However standardizing the organization's processes or even following a quality model or tailored quality model could not only solve these problems, but bring unforeseen return on investment (ROI) benefits to these organizations [14]. Structured process or quality models do not guarantee any ROI, but they can provide an organization with a solid platform to build on.

What can be done to change this? The answer lies in two parts. Firstly management of software organizations need to be made aware of the benefits and pitfalls that structured software process improvement can bring to an organization. They need to know that models can be tailored for use, how to tailor the models and how to get their staff on board as well. Secondly, once in place, management should treat the quality model, or structured processes as a marketing tool, educating customers with regards to their "top quality procedures". Once customers are aware of a process to improve quality, it is likely that they would insist on this as a requirement on all of their suppliers. The more customers ask, the more pressure software organizations will be under to provide.

This could very much be a case of the chicken and the egg. Who goes first, do management start improving their process? Why should they if their customers are not that interested in it? Should customers start asking? Why would they? They do not know about it. Education can play a pivotal role here. Ninety seven percent of those interviewed from the Irish software industry had a third level education. Third level institutions across Ireland have the opportunity and the motive to reach out to future employees of the industry. Were 97% of future employees to be educated in software processes and see their benefits, they would take this with them to the workplace where they would be in a position to positively affect the future of the Irish software industry.

References

1. Central Statistics Office: Information Society Statistics – Ireland 2004. Central Statistics Office, Government of Ireland. Dublin, Ireland. (2004) 7
2. ICT Ireland: ICT sector costs have increased by almost 20% in 2 years. ICT Ireland http://www.ictireland.ie/ibec/press/presspublicationsdoclib3.nsf/wvICTNews/BC8ADB4F FD87A57680256FC4003EB612?OpenDocument 05/04/2005. Dublin, Ireland (2005).
3. ICT Ireland: Key Industry Statistics. ICT Ireland http://www.ictireland.ie/Sectors/ict/ ictDoclib4.nsf/vlookupHTML/key_industry_statistics?OpenDocument 05/04/2005. Dublin, Ireland. (2005)

4. NSD: Software Industry Statistics for 1991-2003. http://www.nsd.ie/htm/ssii/stat.htm 15/05/2005. Dublin, Ireland. (2004)
5. Enterprise Ireland: Economic Profile – Ireland. Enterprise Ireland. Dublin, Ireland. Sept04, (2004) 8-9
6. Enterprise Ireland: Economic Profile – Ireland. Enterprise Ireland. Dublin, Ireland. Sept04, (2004) 3
7. Forfas: Enterprise Strategy Group Report. Dublin, Ireland. (2004) 4
8. Trauth, Eileen M.: The Culture of an Information Economy: Influences and Impacts in the Republic of Ireland. Boston, MA., Kluwer Academic Publishers. (2000)
9. EGFSN: Fourth Report of the Expert Group on Future Skills Needs. Forfas – Expert Group on Future Skills Needs. Dublin, Ireland. (2003) 3
10. Accenture: ICT – the Indispensable Sector in the Knowledge Based Economy. ICT Ireland, Dublin, Ireland. (2004) 5
11. Phillips, Cathy: Worldwide Tax Overview. Tax Notes International. (2005) 37 (7)
12. Garvin, David: What does product quality really mean? Sloan Management Review. (1984) 26(1)
13. Richardson, Ita: Software Process Matrix: A Small Company SPI Model. Sofw. Process Improve. Pract. 2001; 6: 157-165 (DOI: 10.1002/spip.144)
14. Goldenson, D.R. and D.L. Gibson: Demonstrating the Impact and Benefits of CMMI: An Update and Preliminary Results. Software Engineering Institute. (2003)

How Things Should Not Be Done: A Real-World Horror Story of Software Engineering Process Improvement

Jarmo J. Ahonen* and Hanna-Miina Sihvonen

Department of Computer Science, University of Kuopio,
P.O.Box 1627, 70211 Kuopio, Finland
`Jarmo.Ahonen@uku.fi`

Abstract. In this article a real-world story of a 2.5 year period is told. The story is told mostly from the point of view of an individual software engineer with several organizational aspects included. The story illustrates some of the common problems encountered in software process improvement efforts. The story is instructive in the way that many of the strange things and problems encountered in it are something to be avoided. Both engineers and managers should note the problems, their reasons, and make sure that those problems will not be encountered in their own organizations.

1   Introduction

This article illustrates some of the most common pitfalls or hindrances encountered in software process improvement (SPI) efforts with a real-world horror story, which documents a 2.5 year period from the point of view of a software developer. During that time the developer, who will be called Joe in this article, saw a whole spectrum of changes and a remarkable amount SPI lip-service. In this article, we will sum up what various software process improvement efforts Joe perceived and how he observed various improvement efforts from the shop-floor point of view.

The story told in this article is based mainly on the personal experiences of a single software engineer. Those experiences have been documented by the engineer himself and clarified in interviews, but those experiences have been checked by interviewing several other people. Therefore the documented story is not just individual opinions, although the individual point of view has been retained.

The reason why a story like this should be interesting for others is that the mistakes made in SPI efforts during the documented time are quite universal. The interesting issue is that many books tell that those mistakes are serious mistakes, but they are still repeated again and again. Therefore stories like the one told in this article should be interesting to both academia and industry. We hope that the readers of this story will at least try to avoid making similar mistakes and, which is even better, help to find ways to prevent others from making such mistakes.

The engineer, named Joe, worked for a domestically oriented company of about 200 employees and later for a listed company of about 500 employees and branch offices around the world. Both of the companies were old software houses, established in 1960's.

---

* Corresponding author.

I. Richardson et al. (Eds.): EuroSPI 2005, LNCS 3792, pp. 59–70, 2005.

Both of them had strong background in software development, well established customer relations and strong domain expertise. The smaller company will be referred as Company A and larger company as Company B.[1] Joe started working for Company A, but was transferred to Company B in a business unit trade as employees were sold along. The old Company A's business area unit became the new Company B's distant branch office. The main offices of Company B were located in other part of the country. All product development groups, managerial positions, tasks and premises were reorganized. Also interdependencies to the products that remained in Company A's ownership had to be clarified. The observations that we describe here on the behalf of Joe regarding Company B, are concentrated mostly on the purchased business unit.

2   In the Real World

In this section Joe's story will be told. The comments and opinions of the authors will be presented as footnotes[2] in this section.

2.1   The First Assignment in Company A

First Joe was assigned to work in a group that provided web portal services. He was included in a project of five people. He was not given any introduction to his work. One of the project members merely gave him a software functional design document and told him to code needed parts according instructions in that document. Joe had been expecting some kind of small training and orientation period before being put into an actual project. So, he had to ask for more advice and explain that he had no previous experience of being involved in a project like this. Then Joe was given more documents and told to read those for background information. That gave him bit more insight of the project. Finally, as Joe reached the busy project manager, he summarized Joe's job description and introduced him to other project members and told whom to ask advice if Joe needed assistance.[3]

In the beginning, the situation in the group was slightly chaotic, since project groups had been lately formed, people did not know each other, projects had just begun and there was no standard procedure how to handle things. However, there were already minor process improvements to be seen and process thinking was adopted at least at some level. The group leader had acknowledged the need for a more organized way of handling software process and he actually wanted everyone to participate and contribute SPI. The group was working on quite different projects compared to what the other groups in the company were doing, and therefore others were not very familiar with the work processes or goals. The group did not interact with other groups at any level.[4].

---

[1] For obvious reasons we cannot use the real names of the companies.

[2] Like this.

[3] We, the authors, would say including Joe to project work went in a completely wrong order in this case. The introductory part should have been first, after that job description and finally actual involvement in the project. This is the case in the light of the fact that we know that some other employees that were hired about month before Joe had had at least programming training and short introduction to upcoming projects.

[4] This type of isolation is very scary, especially in the light of future events.

The group was working in customer projects that were very carefully planned and strictly scheduled. In these projects they also had to interact with other companies that were providing software products for the same customer. Some of the outside parties were even involved in the same project as Joe's group. In order to work efficiently with other parties involved, Joe's group was required to follow documented instructions and to keep the process as continuous and consistent as possible. All parties had to be aware what stage of the project was currently under development. There were altogether three outside parties involved in the project: the client and two other software houses. The client was a large scale company that required everything to go according to standards. The client's premises were located in another part of the country and these projects required traveling and communicating. Mostly communications were handled via email and telephone and the project managers were in the key positions keeping the communication smooth.

One thing that bothered Joe was the client's project management reachability and the role in the projects.[5] Joe got the impression they were more interested in their own work than what project members were working on. That caused delays in the project, because project manager had not informed properly on the current project status and still expected everything to be ready. Joe did not know how project management level work was followed, but he thinks that they had more flexibility in their work schedules.

Joe's group consisted of many student trainees or recently graduated employees and a few older and more experienced project managers. They all had much enthusiasm to apply knowledge they had acquired in their studies, to real-life software process development. They helped to define the processes. That was very rewarding and made one feel important. They defined several internal processes for their group, for example how projects are accepted, how training is arranged and how invoicing is handled.

They arranged internal training and were planning to get Java certificates. In the internal training they took turns and each one of them arranged a little training session on the topic he/she had knowledge of. Since their group did such a good work and the work was productive for the company, they were given some benefits like money for external training courses or money for experimenting new software products that might be useful to their work. They got external training in tools, but they also had an English course to support their documentation skills. All the training proved to be useful in their work. Contributing to external training was a sign from the management that they supported the group and appreciated the readiness of the members of the group to develop themselves.

To track what employees were doing, the group leader required them to write weekly reports on what they had been doing. Joe assumes that project managers reported on how projects progressed. They also had weekly meetings, where the group leader informed them on the current and upcoming events. They also inserted their work hours into a work hour follow-up system. They never got any feedback or such that would have proved that someone really cared what they had inserted into the follow-up system. Everything seemed to be very trust-based.

---

[5] The unavailability should bother everyone. We have, however, seen similar cases in various types of industry.

2.2 The Second Assignment in Company A

All improvement ideas were forgotten and buried when the group leader resigned because of internal conflicts. At the same time, several other employees decided to resign, because they did not see any future in the company without the strong group leader.

As Joe and others were trying to evolve "what was left of the group", the work environment was not very encouraging or supportive but more hostile and tense.[6] The group was a bit lost and confused how they should rearrange project groups and who would be their group leader. Other groups had envied the development and progress Joe's group had succeeded in. Moreover they had looked down on the projects of Joe's group, even though those had brought lots of money to the company. Now as the group was torn apart, and the projects were appointed to another parts of the company, they were forced back to the company's normal processless way of working. The members of the group were divided into other groups based on their skills and work experience.

Originally Joe was hired for web portal service development, so Joe had not much of an idea about what tools, skills and knowledge other projects required. Also, Joe was not very familiar with company's software product portfolio. They had had only few little training sessions on those products. However, Joe and few other co-workers were appointed to a product development group. The project was an important one and the company had great expectations on the product. Their fresh knowledge and techniques were said to be welcome. The project manager himself did not come to greet them or to introduce the project and project members. One lower lever project member gave brief instructions. They were given the task to produce interface programs. The instructions were more or less vague. They did not get any project schedule or any background information on the project, nor did they have any clue in what context this program was supposed to be included. They found some documentation of the project later on but those documents were not really useful. Based on the little information they got to start with, it was very difficult to create a correctly functioning program. "Use what ever techniques suit you, document it as you wish, create your own plans" were the basic instructions. Sounds like a dream, much freedom and possibilities to use your own creative resources.[7]

2.3 The Transition from Company A to Company B

After the company purchase they were introduced a whole new approach to the software design process. In Company B, all processes were done according standards, and that was very new to most employees. The new rules and working methods seemed very strict and exact compared to the old routines. Implementing new ideas and spreading the new working concept was, as easily figured, an extremely difficult a task for Company B's management and even more difficult since people were rather reluctant to obey the new employer and disliked the company's administrative ways. The reluctance was caused by the fear of losing one's job. All talk about synergy benefits, overlapping in

---

[6] In this sense the isolation backfired, which was something to be expected.

[7] But it really was not an ideal situation. Anyway, this ignorant and careless attitude from project management was to backfire later, since the technical solution the group had chosen to implement was not compatible with the actual product.

operations and how well all the products complement each other just increased the fear. The atmosphere was very tense and therefore timing was not very favorable for new working methods. As expected, a little later the company fired a bunch of people. After that, situation settled down slowly. It was a long process to get things back to normal. Slowly and not so surely, people started to adjust to the new environment and even applied some of the new policies in their work.

A new product management group was founded. The product management group created road-maps for each product to support long term planning. After the road-maps were approved and ready, those were still available for suggestions and improvement ideas. Yet, these ideas were only implemented in next road-map and caused delays in including useful features and properties. The road-maps clarified each products role in company's product portfolio. Managing project resources and schedules was easier as employees had a clear plan how to progress and what to expect. [8]

2.4   The First Assignment in Company B

After a while, as things settled down, the new owner had time to get acquainted with all projects, groups and products. They selected Joe's project, as it was a product development project, to be a pilot project. Joe's group had to start from the beginning, though the project was already halfway completed. They had to rewrite new more exact documentation of each stage of the project and create documentation that was missing. The project plan, schedule, requirements etc. were all rewritten and refined. The most disturbing change was the technology change. It seemed like a waste of time to study new techniques and then implement the already existing program with a new one.

In order to enhance product quality, their project group had to arrange document and code inspections. Joe believes that project managers got some short training, but for others inspections were new and they were not sure how those should be performed in order to be useful. After an inspection they had to sign agreements that they all approved the results. This was a part of Company B's effort to apply the standards and SPI in their new business area unit. One novelty that was also applied in this pilot project was an external evaluation of product's usability.

As the first stage of the project was finished, they had a big meeting, where the project manager presented some results of the project and various metrics that described how well project had been carried out. The metrics were like "how many hours a developer spent in a task". Since that metric was based on the information collected from the work hour follow-up system, Joe thought that the numbers were not realistic. Joe tried to ask what those metrics meant, but did not get a clear answer. Anyway, Joe thinks that the project manager was not aware of what those "carefully selected metrics" presented.

2.5   The Last Assignment in Company B

As the project was in a transitional stage from the phase one to the phase two, there was a quite long waiting period. So, meanwhile Joe was assigned to write a functional specification and plans and schedules for the implementation and documentation of a new

---

[8] Establishing the product management group was definitely a step towards more organized SPI.

integration software that was to connect a legacy system to new systems. Before writing the functional document, Joe had to plan a schedule for documentation and implementation of this project. Joe was given a ready requirements specification document. Joe had no previous knowledge of the legacy system, and he was somewhat confused and lost how could he manage this project. It was a difficult task to schedule a project with Joe's little background expertise. Joe was encouraged to study and explore the legacy system independently.[9]

Joe noticed that it was really hard to find a person who would explain the unclarities. However, the good news was that there was an internal training arranged on the legacy system that Joe could participate in. Based on the information Joe had gathered, Joe succeeded in creating a schedule for the project and to complete the functional specification document. Though, Joe was still convinced this project would have gone much more smoothly if someone with more expertise would have commented it. In addition, Joe was told to create a test case document for the project. At this point, it felt that the amount of self-educating Joe had to do was overwhelming. He never actually got to complete that phase of the project, since Joe and several other people lost their jobs.[10]

In this integration project a quite strict quality and process policy was adopted and there were several document inspections. The inspections were done in a little group, where Joe, who had actually written the document to be inspected, was left outside the conversation. The inspections were done so hastily and negligently that it was hard to separate the changes Joe had to make to the document.[11]

3   Why Things Went Wrong — The Soft Issues

In this section we will consider the educational, cultural, social and psychological aspects of the SPI problems encountered.

3.1   Educational Aspects

In all the groups that were transferred from Company A to Company B, educational backgrounds varied a lot, which of course reflected in each employee's skills, working methods and in the enthusiasm or lack of it to develop oneself.

One of the main problems in both companies was the lack of knowledge of languages, communication skills and general writing skills. In this case, English proved to

---

[9] That was not a productive idea and Joe had major difficulties to get any kind of understanding of the system, since it was very large and complex. In cases like this, the employer should provide necessary education in a planned way.

[10] Joe would have appreciated constructive critique on the schedule Joe had come up with for the project. Joe know that the project manager could have given some realistic perspective, but he had no interest to "interfere". It was not easy to estimate how much time each project phase would take, especially because Joe was not familiar with legacy system's technical solutions nor did have any idea who would be appointed to implement that part of the project. Joe heard later that the schedule and project hour estimations had been underestimated.

[11] This type of "lip-service" inspections are very counterproductive. as we have seen in many cases. Proper procedures are outlined in many sources, e.g. [1].

be one of the most needed in addition to the software engineering skills. In Company B the existing documentation and the documentation to be written were in English. There were many people who managed English at some level or even very well, but the skills could have been much better. We assume that the employees' age structure had some effects on language skills, since the employees' average age was close to 45 and earlier it has not been that easy to obtain fluent skills in foreign languages.

The heterogeneous educational background within the company is a richness and also a useful resource, it may aid in providing inventive solutions and new knowledge. The educational differences may, however, cause some minor understanding and co-operation problems. There may be conceptual differences and misunderstanding and also difficulties in interpreting instructions. There may be major variety in how different areas of software development are seen and valued, for example quality issues, requirement definition, coding standards, implementation issues etc. Such concepts should be defined by the company in order to avoid different interpretations. Neither Company A or Company B had done that in a sufficient detail.

Both Company A and Company B arranged internal training for using different software development tools, especially company's self-developed tools that are not taught anywhere else. Training for the companies' own software products was arranged too, but only in small scale. For the employees, training for the software house's own tools and products increases competence mostly within that company and learned skills may not be useful later. But it is essential to train employees to keep them competent for the company. In both companies the training sessions were arranged secretively and employees were not aware of those. Furthermore, the employees did not feel they are obligated to attend training, because training was not mandatory. Company B arranged training for not only their own tools but on how to use their document templates and document naming conventions, unfortunately this training was mostly arranged to group managers. In addition to internal training, some external training was arranged, but mostly for higher level management and project managers. Those who attended training were supposed to spread the learned information afterwards. In practice that spreading of knowledge never happened. Education should have been provided to everyone.

One field that is part of the educational aspect is the employees' domain expertise and capability to understand customers' concepts and work processes. Although the customer training was open for the employees, the domain education was forgotten in both companies. Each employee's and each group's need of domain expertise varies according to given work assignments. Nevertheless, all of the employees should have at least some idea of the customer's work processes and business domain, even if they do not have to interact with the customer.

It is often pointed out that the domain expertise is not necessary for a software developer in order to produce correctly functioning applications. Certainly all the products can be implemented according to given instructions, but if domain expertise is lacking and the developer has no idea what the concepts mean, there is a risk that the efforts produce an incorrectly functioning program. If the developer has no idea in what context application is to function, a more strict follow-up methods from the project management are required and a much more effective approach to testing in order to assure product quality.

3.2 Psychological Aspects

One of the most visible issues concerning the software improvement efforts in both companies seem to be the lack motivation along with the attitude problem. However, that was not really a surprise considering all the major changes employees had to go through. All this caused insecurity, reluctance and reduced motivation to work. All this reflected directly into the product quality and even more into the customer relationships. An especially demanding phase for the employees was the transitional stage from the old employer to the new one. Soon after the company purchase, the new employer arranged psychological assistance for employees to recover from the shock and turmoil caused by this dramatic change. After the employer employee negotiations dismissed employees got training and psychological help. That was well arranged and helpful but the employees who remained in the company would have needed assistance too. It is an exhausting experience for the remaining employees to see co-workers dismissed and that affects work motivation.

One thing that has a direct effect on psychological motivation is feedback. Of course the way how negative feedback is presented has a great importance. Feedback helps to notice weaknesses and strengths and it is essential for an individual in order to develop oneself. Pointing out positive sides increases motivation and self-esteem and pointing out negative sides in a positive way increases interest to evolve better in the area of perceived weaknesses. During the documented period Joe got hardly any feedback, it seemed that nobody was really interested in his work quality. We have observed similar lack of feedback in other companies also.

There was a strong resistance to change all the time, which is expected. In the early stages while Joe still working for Company A, employees seemed to resist changes because they did not want to change their working methods. They were happy with the way things were. Unfortunately their working methods were not even close to efficient and well organized. Rapid changes would have probably backfired, as often is the case [2]. In Company A all work reporting and interaction was very trust-based, it might have been seen as a sign of mistrust from the organization's management if they had interfered very radically with the working methods.

3.3 Cultural and Social Aspects

Cultural and social aspects are somewhat closely related to psychological motivation. The cultural and social settings affect how individuals act in their daily activities, what set of values an individual has and how the individual interacts with other people. These considerations are based on the considerations presented in [3].

The surrounding environment layers of the organization affect organization's need for change. They affect organization's values, missions and strategies and what skills and qualities of the personnel are valued and when. The organization's values on the other hand reflect to the employees and how they work for the benefit of the organization. In individual level how people see their work and what they consider important in their work is a result of individual's own set of values and what aspects the organization has offered to them.

The most important part of the company culture in both companies was strong traditions in customer relations and customer service. The prevailing business culture in both companies was a result of long and hard work. In Company A, the organization was a distant concept. The surrounding culture was quiet, and the values and strategies were not clear to employees. In Company B, the organization levels were more reachable and socialization was important. The company's values and mission were introduced in every informative meeting. Company A seemed to be a more secure work place, since it was not so profit driven as Company B. Company B was constantly exploring new possibilities, new market areas and efficient ways to increase profit. Therefore it should not have been a surprise that Company B had a real challenge introducing its existing organizational culture to the unit bought from Company A.

Within the cultural and social settings the knowledge sharing has a major role. Often only few individuals possess vast knowledge of a certain software area expertise within the company. That knowledge is tacit knowledge, residing in their mind, not written anywhere. In this context we refer to [4] and [5]. That was the case in both Company A and B. The ideal situation would be to share knowledge with other employees contributing to organizational learning process, since all are involved in a common enterprise using the same tools and techniques. In Company B higher management supported knowledge sharing so that it would not be focused in one irreplaceable individual. In Company A, sharing was not acknowledged to be of importance and therefore was not encouraged. This is somewhat amazing because there already had been loss of tacit knowledge as people had left the company or retired. This should have increased the awareness and need to convert tacit knowledge to explicit. In Company B the insecure and unstable atmosphere reduced the willingness to share knowledge and give up the irreplaceable role. Individual people wanted to secure their position and enjoy the important role. This had negative consequences to SPI and the company in general.

4   Why Things Went Wrong — The Hard Issues

In this section the infrastructure, organization, management and measuring issues are considered.

4.1   Infrastructure

There was a very bad example of how to handle things in the actions of Company B. Company B carried out an ergonomics mapping in order to provide a more employee friendly working environment. The purpose of the mapping was to provide various ergonomic aids to people who need those. The mapping was planned to be implemented carefully. A physiotherapist and the personnel manager visited each work post and evaluated each individual's ergonomic needs. After the mapping the news was that the company can not afford to provide the aids just yet. So the whole mapping process had been only a waste of time and money. Eventually, no improvements were done and that just added the employees' dislike and mistrust towards the employer.

4.2   Organization and Management

In Company A the organization was quite well structured. All of the groups were working on products assigned to them and each group had a leader, who acted as an interface between other groups and the management. The management was distant and old-fashioned. A certain level of respect and distance was expected from the employees. Informing was very casual, small informative meetings were arranged during morning coffee breaks.

Some processes did exist in Company A, the process thinking clearly was gaining ground and there were some people defining processes. The processes were defined at the managerial levels of the organization and applied to the most important activities. The processes for lower level groups were defined by people who did not have actual knowledge of how things should be done. Although these processes were defined at some level, they were not introduced properly to employees to adopt and thereby not implemented effectively, which is something that has been described as a mistake in [2]. In Company A, there was some process documentation available in the intranet, but not many people were even aware of or interested in it. Such use of documentation is not fruitful without training on how to apply the instructions in daily activities.

Company B was a more modern and profit driven organization than Company A. The organization was "alive" and changing. The managerial level was more reachable. Informing was organized and arranged regularly. Informative meetings were kept "even if there was nothing new to inform". Those meetings gave a chance to make suggestions and present questions.

Company B was involved in defining ISO 9000 standard. Several processes were defined, but at the time when Joe worked for the company they were used only in the company's main offices. The process documentation was available in the intranet as electronic process guides. Those were easily reachable but not eagerly used, due to a very natural reason. Those guides were exact and helpful in principle, but they were very large and a way too exhausting to read alone and to comprehend.

4.3 Monitoring, Measuring and Tools for Follow-Ups

In order to keep track what employees are working on, how they advance, and what is their current attitude, it is important to have some kind of follow-up methods and metrics. Such metrics are very important in order to know how things really are proceeding [2] and such metrics have been considered for fairly small organization also [6].

One important follow-up method was weekly group meetings, a habit that was exercised in both companies. In every meeting each group member listed what tasks they had completed during the week and what they were currently working on. The group leader wrote a weekly report. Joe told us that although some members of higher level management might have read through those reports he did not believe that to be true because nobody realized clear errors in those reports.

Questionnaires were send to employees via e-mail to inquire about "opinions of our employer" and "how do you view our company". Hard to say how many employees cared to fill in those questionnaires. The results of those inquiries remained a secret to employees.

Both Company A and Company B arranged development discussions once a year. The goal of the development discussions was to find out employees current work situation and skills and to clarify employees chances for new more demanding tasks. The managerial person who arranges discussions should have enough skills to carry out the discussion in a productive manner. In the discussions Joe wanted to take advantage of the opportunity to share his thoughts, visions and readiness to evolve himself. Joe's boss added several improvement ideas to the discussion report. To Joe's great disappointment none of these ideas ever actually took place. The lack of concrete results of the development discussions was a very bad disappointment for Joe. In our opinion the development discussions should not be held if no real action will be taken.

The work hour follow-up system was one option to survey the progress. In early stages in Company A the work hour reporting did not have such importance and people did not pay attention if you even forgot or did not care to report. In Company B work hours were followed more strictly and project managers required project members to fill in hours in weekly meetings if someone had not done it yet. Particularly in projects that were valuable for invoicing, the work hour reporting was to be done on daily basis. Two different follow-up systems were used, one for product development and another for customer projects. The two systems were different in perspective. In the customer projects follow-up system all employee skills and knowledge and CV-kind of data was collected and that was not implemented in the product development follow-up system. That caused problems for company-wide tracking and result evaluation.

5 Discussion

During the outlined period there were, however, some visible improvements to be seen from Joe's point of view. For example, in early stages, working hours were reported on paper, but later on a work hour follow-up system was used for that purpose. However, such programs seem to be a bit defective, since in the end nobody really follows what has been registered. That type of neglect in really using the metric data is not uncommon, but it is a very serious one. Proper use of such data is outlined in several books, for example in [7] and [8].

Furthermore, a more advanced follow-up system that collected employees' skill data was introduced. That made it easer to find people whom to ask advice for specific problems when needed. The possibility to find assistance was even used. Also one improvement was to arrange work places for all groups according to their work description. Informing became more efficient, the intranet was used more effectively for informing, informative meetings were arranged more often, the management level became more reachable. The document standards were absorbed into daily use and all documents were created in ready templates, although the use was forced on the employees without proper training. Even a document naming policy was slowly adopted. Also each group's tasks were defined better and product road-mapping gave guidelines that did not exist before.

In both Company A and Company B process thinking was not, however, exactly visible for lower level employees and thereby it was hard for them to adopt. Those few processes that were used did not seem efficient. In fact, those out-of-reality processes even slowed down project work by causing too much time to be wasted in idling instead of effective work. There were several examples of how things were delayed because of the ineffective process definition and implementation. The document inspections easily caused delay, because the person who was supposed to approve the document was busy and the inspection meetings had to be arranged according to that person's timetable. This might cause even a week or longer delay, and while waiting, money was lost. Another example found in many companies is the distribution of work and knowledge. One person is totally overworked while others lose time looking for some pieces of knowledge possessed by that person. This happens partly because of bad management but also because of employees "not sharing the tacit knowledge" issue.

If the circumstances would have been stabler and the atmosphere more secure, the management could have been more successful in carrying out SPI efforts. Those efforts were, however, somewhat half-hearted due to the fact that training and personal involvement of employees were neglected. The unavoidable impression is that the management had got the idea that SPI is important but had not bothered to gain real understanding of SPI and the effort it would require. In both companies SPI was still a managerial game, a type of lip-service.

The lip-service attitude to SPI is not uncommon. We have seen it in many companies and the main difficulties seem to be the same in many cases: the employees are not involved, the management is not properly committed to providing the necessary resources, the organization of SPI is too complex, the management fears to let software engineers to handle as many things as possible. Those difficulties are somewhat disappointing because nowadays there exists a whole bunch of good books, like e.g. [2], and articles, like e.g. [9][10], on how to make SPI a success. In the light of Joe's story we can just hope that both managers and employees who are faced with SPI challenges would read at least some of the books and articles before proceeding.

References

1. Gilb, T., Graham, D.: Software Inspection. Addison-Wesley, London (1993)
2. Zahran, S.: Software Process Improvement. Addison-Wesley, London (1998)
3. Sharp, H., Woodman, M., Hoveden, F., Robinson, H.: The role of 'culture' in successful software process improvement. In: Proceedings of 25th Euromicro Conference. (1999)
4. Nonaka, I., Takeuchi, H.: The Knowledge Creating Company. How Japanese Companies Create the Dynamics of Innovation. Oxford University Press (1995)
5. Pourkomeylian, P.: Knowledge creation in improving a software organization. In: Proceedings of Scandinavian Conference in Information Systems, IRIS23. (2001)
6. Kautz, K.: Making sense of measurements for small organizations. IEEE Software (1999)
7. Fenton, N.E., Pfleeger, S.L.: Software Metrics: A Rigorous and Practical Approach. 2nd edn. PWS Publishing Company, Boston (1997)
8. Florac, W.A., Carleton, A.D.: Measuring the Software Process. Addison-Wesley, New York (1999)
9. Arent, J., Nordbjerg, J.: Software process improvement as organizational knowledge creation: A multiple case analysis. (In: Proc. of 33rd Hawaii Int. Conf. on Syst. Sci.)
10. Stelzer, D., Mellis, W.: Success factors of organization change in software process improvement. Sotware Process Improvement and Practice 4 (1998) 227–250

AIM – Ability Improvement Model

Jan Pries-Heje[1] and Jørn Johansen[2]

[1] IT University Copenhagen, Department of Design and Use of IT,
Rued Langgaards Vej 7, DK-2300 Copenhagen S, Denmark
jph@itu.dk
www.itu.dk
[2] DELTA, Focusgroup IT-Processes,
Venlighedsvej 4, DK-2970 Hørsholm, Denmark
joj@delta.dk
www.delta.dk

Abstract. Too many improvement and innovation projects fail. We have studied characteristics of successful and failed projects. From this study we derived 19 parameters that influence success and failure. We used the parameters to build an Ability Improvement Model (AIM), which is a model that can be used to measure an organizations or a projects ability to succeed with improvement. After having build AIM we tested it in real life in a large organization, learned from the experience and improved the model. Then we tested it again in two organizations with promising results. In the paper we report on the considerations and research behind AIM. Finally we describe the method, and how the model can be used in practice.

1 Introduction

The Software Process Improvement (SPI) is about systematically evaluating your current status in relation to software processes, doing something to improve, and measuring whether the things done improved the situation? Many IT organizations have used considerable resources for SPI. However, investments in SPI often have not led to the changes and improvements expected. For example Goldenson and Herbsleb [1] found in a study of a larger number of organizations that had invested in SPI that 26% agreed that "nothing much has changed" and 49% declared themselves to be disillusioned due to lack of improvements. And this study is not alone. Several others have found that SPI initiatives can fail (cf. [2], [3], [4]).

Thus unsuccessful SPI initiatives led to an interest in what is needed to achieve successful implementation of SPI (cf. [5], [6], [7], [8]).. Grady [5] directs attention to the fact that an organization must be ready for SPI. If that is not the case the SPI initiative can be very costly and may fail. Zahran [6] for example points out the importance of understanding the business and organizational context before carrying out an assessment of an organization with the purpose of initiating SPI. Zahran calls this activity a pre-assessment phase and he recommends that this phase should be carried out before a decision is taken on whether to initiate SPI.

This leads to the research question that we address in this paper: How can you improve an organizations ability to improve?

I. Richardson et al. (Eds.): EuroSPI 2005, LNCS 3792, pp. 71–82, 2005.
© Springer-Verlag Berlin Heidelberg 2005

Or said in another way: Can you, by examining some parameters, get a picture of whether you will succeed or fail with an Improvement initiative – being at the organizational or the project level - prior to launching it?

So to sum up we believe that it is important to focus on an organizations *ability to improve*. In this paper we will report on our findings from an in-depth study of success and failure when improving and a model - called Ability Improvement Model (AIM) - build from the results. First we describe our research methodology, a qualitative interview study with more than 50 interviewees from four 4 organizations followed by an action research undertaking to build a model of ability improvement. Second we report the findings from the interview study and how our findings were grouped into 19 influential parameters. We then give an account of the model we developed based on the parameters and how that model can be used to assess an organization. This leads to a discussion of what factors contribute to readiness for SPI. And we end the paper by outlining a way to gauge the readiness for SPI in an organization.

2   Interview Study Research Method

We selected successful and failed projects as an arena of particular interest from the viewpoint of improving the ability to improve. We can highlight two key reasons for this interest. First, we appreciate the learning that can be harvested by looking at projects in retrospective. Second, in opposition to many other studies we decided to look at both SPI projects where other software developers are the users and at traditional IT projects in IT organizations.

We used an existing research collaboration called Talent@IT to select companies. There are four companies that participate in the research collaboration. Each of the companies was asked to appoint two successful and two failed projects. We asked that the companies appointed two SPI projects and two normal innovation projects, preferably a successful and a failed one of each type. Furthermore we asked to have SPI projects that had delivered results that were used in the innovation projects.

We then conducted interviews in the projects. We interviewed the project manager and 1-2 project members. We interviewed the sponsor or owner of the project, typically a manager in the organization. We interviewed the users; for an SPI-project that meant other developers, and for innovation projects that typically meant end users. In 16 projects we conducted more than 50 interviews in the period from summer 2003 to summer 2004.

Typically every interview was conducted by two people. One interviewing and one taking notes. Subsequently all interviews was transcribed and analyzed using Grounded Theory techniques.

Grounded Theory (GT) is a qualitative research methodology that has its name from the practice of discovering theory that is grounded in data. GT is best used in research where one has relatively "uncharted land", as for example the notion and meaning of Internet Speed. Grounded theories are inductively discovered by careful collection and analysis of qualitative empirical data. That is, this method does not begin with a theory, and then seek proof. Instead, it begins with an area of study and allows the relevant theory to emerge from that area [9].

After having collected our interview data we applied the three coding procedures of GT. According to [10], analysis in a grounded theory approach is composed of three groups of coding procedures called open, axial and selective coding. These procedures do not entirely occur as a sequence, but each overlaps the others and iterates throughout the research project.

The goal of open coding is to reveal the essential ideas found in the data. Open coding involves two essential tasks. The first task is labelling phenomena. This task involves decomposing an observation into discrete incidents or ideas. Each discrete incident or idea receives a name or label that represents the phenomenon. These names represent a concept inherent in the observation.

The second essential open-coding task is discovering categories. Categorizing is the process of finding related phenomena or common concepts and themes in the accumulated data and to group them under joint headings and thus identifying categories and sub-categories of data.

In our analysis, we found 54 categories that all contributed to either success or failure of a project. Three examples of categories are: (1) User involvement, (2) Defect in product, and (3) Stakeholder involvement.

Developing a better and deeper understanding of how the identified categories are related is the purpose of axial coding. Axial coding involves two tasks further developing the categories and properties. The first task connects categories in terms of a sequence of relationships. For example, a causal condition or a consequence can connect two categories, or a category and a sub-category. The second task turns back to the data for validation of the relationships. This return gives rise to the discovery and specification of the differences and similarities among and within the categories. This discovery adds variation and depth of understanding.

The first part of the axial coding was done together by four people. Similarities and differences were noted and discussed. Categories and relationships were identified, discussed, corrected, and changed, until a common understanding of the categories, sub-categories and their relationships was reached. In the concrete we ended up with 19 categories. To distinguish the 19 categories from the 54 coming out of the open coding we called it the 19 *parameters*.

Selective Coding involves the integration of the categories that have been developed to form the initial theoretical framework. Firstly, in Selective Coding, a story line is either generated or made explicit. A story is simply a descriptive narrative about the central phenomenon of study and the story line is the conceptualization of this story (abstracting). When analyzed, the story line becomes the core category that is related to all the categories found in axial coding, validating these relationships, and elaborating the categories that need further refinement and development.

The story line we ended up with was in fact a story that says that the ability of an organization to produce success and avoid failure – the ability to improve - depends on the organizations ability in coping with four groups of parameters:

- Parameters related to initiation of projects typically ideas for new SPI or Innovation projects
- Parameters related to *projects*, from the very first hour and until a result is taken into use

- Parameters related to results *in use*, from the first user uses the new process or product for the first time and until full deployment
- Parameters related to the enterprise *foundation*

After having identified the story line and the parameters we decided to build a model out of it. One could say that we at this point turned away from grounded theory and started applying design science research [11].

3   Ability Improvement Model

The resulting model with 19 parameters in four groups looks like depicted in figure 1. The core assumption behind this model is that the parameters identified from success and failure projects can be used to identify an organizations ability to improve by encouraging activity that has shown to be related to success and avoiding activities that has shown to lead to failure.

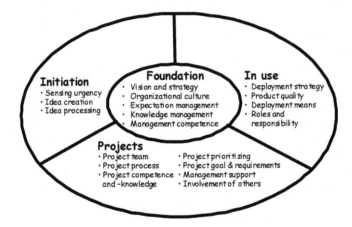

Fig. 1. AIM – Ability Improvement Model – with 19 parameters in 4 groups

Each of the 19 parameters in the model is shortly described in Table 1 – 4 below.

Table 1. Foundation Parameters

Vision And strategy	To what extent has the organisation a business strategy and/or a vision that is decided and communicated?
Organisational culture	To what extent has the organisation a culture that encourages improvement and innovation?
Expectation management	To what extent has the organisation systematic management of expectations in relation to both organisational changes and daily work?
Knowledge management	To what extent is knowledge systematically gathered, stored and used?
Management competence	To what extent has the organisation the necessary competence at the management level?

Table 2. Initiation Parameters

Sensing urgency	To what extent is the organisation able to sense the urgency for change? For example because existing ways of working have become obsolete or because existing products are too old or maybe the organisation has simply arrived in an untenable position.
Idea creation	To what extent is the organisation able to identify, foster and create many ideas for new SPI and IT processes or products? Preferably form many different sources such as user needs, new technology or new strategies.
Idea processing	To what extent are new ideas captured and decided on?

Table 3. Project Parameters

Project team	To what extent are the people allocated to projects highly motivated and are they having the right attitude and profile for the projects? Competent project management? Team sitting physically together and close to users? Does the team work as a team?
Project process	To what extend do the projects have good estimates, plans, follow-up, risk management, testing and quality reviews?
Project competence and knowledge	To what extent do the projects have the necessary technical knowledge? Domain knowledge? Development model and method(s)?
Project prioritizing	To what extent are projects prioritized in relation to each other? And in relation to schedule, cost, scope and quality? Are priorities communicated and understood? Are priorities stable?
Project goal and requirements	To what extend are project goals, expected benefits and formulated requirements precise, unambiguous and stable? Do the projects – developers as well as users - perceive their goals and the rationale behind as reasonable?
Management support	To what extend is management in the organisation supporting the projects? That could be allocating the right resources at the right time. It could also be about participation in a steering committee. Or it could involve demanding results.
Involvement of others	To what extent are other stakeholders (than the team and management) involved? This could for example include early user involvement. External resources? Consultants? At the right time and in the right way?

Table 4. In Use Parameters

Deployment strategy	To what extent is a deployment strategy for new processes or products decided on and followed?
Product quality	To what extend are new processes and products that are deployed of high quality? Few defects? User friendly? Low complexity? Compatible? Efficient? Have relative advantages for the user?
Deployment means	To what extend is the optimal mix of information, communication, education and training, plus marketing of new processes and products applied?
Roles and responsibility	To what extend are roles and responsibilities in relation to deployment and use well defined and enacted?

For each of 19 parameters in the four groups we have formulated a number of questions. The questions are based on our observations (the transcribed interviews) and the grounded theory coding.

3.1   An Example of Questions for a Parameter

Let us as an example take the parameter deployment strategy. This parameter was identified in our coding based on the grouping and sequencing of a number of categories. One of the categories was called implementation strategies. In table 5 we have shown an excerpt from this category. Behind each of the coded observations to the right in the table there is a citation in one of our interviews that the coding represents. Two of the coded observation in the table (followed by a parenthesis saying "caused failure") is codes from failure projects. They represent things that the interviewees have told us was the cause of failure.

Table 5. Example of 1 of 54 categories from open coding

	Coded observation
Implementation strategy	Put it to the test
	Took small steps
	Forced Use – Demand that things are 100% ok
	Hard follow-up – scare lists
	Used ambassadors
	Had the right tool at right moment
	Review ensured use
	When the users needed it
	Project by project implementation
	Nothing mandatory (*caused failure*)
	Parallel running experienced as wasted effort
	Punished non-users
	"The door to change has to be opened from inside"
	Slow learning curve (*caused failure*)
	… and 15 more

Deployment strategy		N	P	L	F	N A
1.	To what extent is a deployment strategy for new processes or products decided on and followed?	Score:50				
1.a	To what extent is there a procedure for selecting a deployment strategy?			X		
1.b	To what extend are risks in relation to deployment uncovered?		X			
1.c	To what extend is there a plan for deployment (time, milestones, responsible)?				X	
1.d	To what extend are deployment strategies and plans followed?	X				

Fig. 2. Excerpt form spreadsheet with questions used to measure the ability for the parameter deployment strategy. The scale used is "N" for not (counting as zero), "P" for partly (counting as 1/3), "L" for largely (counting as 2/3), and "F" for fully (counting as 3/3). The score is then calculated as a percentage of fully answers on. Here it is (2/3+1/3+3/3+0/3)/4*100 = 50.

Several categories were grouped into a parameter. The category in table 5 became part of the parameter "deployment strategy". In figure 2 we have shown the questions we derived for this specific parameter. The figure shows part of a spreadsheet that can be used to measure the *ability to improve* by an organisation.

4   Process to Measure Ability with AIM

To bring AIM into use a method and some techniques are necessary. We have designed such a process to be used in an organization by assessors from outside. The process includes a number of meetings and activities as shown in figure 3. In the process we use different materials such as presentations, questionnaires, descriptions of the model and a spreadsheet (from which figure 2 was taken).

Before an assessment of an organizations ability to improve can take place, several practical works has to be done. Selection of employees for interview, calendar synchronization, reservation of meeting rooms, order food and so on. This has to be done at least a month before the assessment.

The method for gathering information during an assessment is inspired primarily by the Bootstrap method [12]. An assessment starts with a preparatory meeting, where respectively the assessors and key persons in the organization prepare for the assessment, gather facts on the organization, and clarify who is to say what at the opening meeting. This meeting is scheduled to one hour.

At the opening meeting all persons involved should be present. At this meeting the concept of the model and method, the purpose of the assessment, the plan and activities, the type of results and the use and the results are explained in detail.

Then follows a group interview with management typically with 5 to 7 persons from the organization participating. At this 4-hour group interview the parameters of AIM are discussed. Such an interview provides the managers with an organizational view of the situation in relation to AIM, across the many projects in the organization; process improvement projects as well ad product innovation projects.

After this follows a similar group interviews with a number of projects; process improvement projects as well ad product development projects. In these interviews 5 to 7 key persons in relation to the four groups in AIM are invited. For example we interview a group of users to make sure to cover the parameters from the "In Use" group. And we also interview a group of project participants including the project manager.

The interviews are carried out by two trained assessors, who during the assessment take interview and notes by turns. The interviews are performed as open dialogues where the assessors ensure that the discussions cover the subjects and all 19 parameters. After a group interview the assessors answer the questionnaire in form of a spreadsheet (as shown in figure 2). The spreadsheet generates a picture of strong and weak parameters on a scale from 0 to 100. To consolidate the result the assessors then combine the parameter scores with the notes from the interview. This is done for each interview.

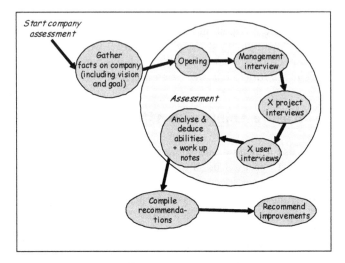

Fig. 3. How an assessment with AIM is conducted

To be able to select parameters for improvement it is necessary to prioritize the parameters. This is done during a prioritizing practice with management. In an open discussion the managers are asked to prioritize the 19 parameters in four groups: (1) very low importance, (2) normal, (3) high importance, and (4) essential. Before they prioritize they are given two rules. First, at most three parameters must be essential. Second, at least three parameters should be low. Our experience shows that these two simple rules create and stimulates a good discussion. This meeting takes 45 minutes.

The 19 parameters are then positioned in a 4-by-4 matrix. The x-axis represents the relative parameter score and the y-axis represents the priority given at the management meeting. In the upper right corner of the matrix we now have the essential parameters with a low score; parameters which are candidates for improvement. And in the lower left corner of the matrix we have the parameters of low importance with a high score; probably parameters where too much effort has been invested and therefore with a potential for saving money in the future?

From the 4-by-4 matrix three to five parameters are then selected. It is here that we recommend that the organization focus their attention so they can improve their ability to improve.

To derive the concrete recommendation we use a catalogue of improvement methods and techniques. In fact as part of AIM we have a catalogue where we for each parameter can find inspiration on how to improve the concrete parameter. The catalogue is also a product of our coding of interview data for successful techniques and methods plus a literature study.

During the assessment factual data about the organization and its current strategic improvement initiatives are deducted. This is used to describe and illustrate the scope for the planned or already initiated changes. This information is gathered with a questionnaire used in connection with the group interviews.

Finally the assessors use all the collected data, parameter scores, the completed 4-by-4 matrix, the overall improvement practice, and the scope of strategic improvement initiatives to generate recommendations produce a presentation for the closing meeting. The notes written by one assessor in all the group interviews are used for consolidation of the result. The presentation is shown to management and afterwards shown to all involved in the assessment at the closing meeting. Depending on what the organization wants, a more or less detailed report can be prepared to document the assessment result.

5   Testing AIM

For testing AIM we decided to apply an action research approach. Galliers [13] describes action research as an approach that allows us to create new theoretical knowledge in addition to something that has practical value for the organization under research. The approach that we adopted in our action research is based on the five phases recommended by Susman & Evered [14]: (1) Specification of infrastructure in project. (2) Diagnosis of problem. (3) Planning of actions. (4) Implementing actions. (5) Evaluation of results. Repeat phase (2) to (5), if necessary.

Our first action research cycle (referring to the five phases above) took place in the first part of 2004. We had built a first version of AIM that we tested it in real life in Danske Bank.

Our second action research cycle took place in the second half of 2004. Here we had a significantly updated version of AIM – actually the version presented here in this paper. We tested it in PBS – Payment Business Services – with quite good results.

Finally our third action research cycle took place in April 2005 in SimCorp. Here we focused on whether AIM could be used to generate improvement recommendations at the project level.

5.1   Learning from the First Action Research Cycle

The Danske Bank group is a financial institution that provides all types of financial services such as banking, mortgaging and insurance in northern Europe. Danske Bank employs 17.000 employees and has more than 3 million private customers in Scandinavia. As part of the Danske Bank Group there is an IT department with 1700 employees located at four development centres; three in Denmark and one in Ireland.

We had designed a first version of AIM and Danske Bank volunteered to test it. We had group interviews with the management from the software producing part of the organisation and with four projects. The overall conclusions from the test were that:

- The overall model was useful. The grouping in four (corresponding to our grounded theory story line) was easy to explain and understand.
- To get a complete picture of especially the parameters in the "In Use" group we needed to include interviews with users.
- It was not enough to provide the organisation with the scoring of the 19 parameters. They wanted more. They wanted some concrete recommendation.

We addressed these comments by adding user group interviews and generate a list of possible recommendations – methods and techniques – for each parameter as explained in section 4 of this paper.

5.2 Learning from the Second Action Research Cycle

PBS specializes in electronic payment services. They employ 750 people of which half is working within the IT Division. They develop and operate solutions for payment systems and are a leading supplier of payment solutions and related services to banks, private associations and public institutions. Last year 1.3 billion transactions were processed via PBS.

We had re-designed AIM after the first test. It now looked as described in section 3 and 4 of this paper. PBS volunteered to test the updated model. And so in October we used two weeks in the organization to test the model. One of the major differences between the first and the second test were that we included two user group interviews. The overall conclusions from this second test were that:

- The overall model was now very useful. Both the four groups and the 19 parameters were easy to explain and understand.
- The manager of the IT Division was most enthusiastic about the overall improvement strategy that we suggested. Based on our interviews we suggested that they used learning and socialisation as their main strategies for changing the organisation. The manager called this the major "Aha!" experience for him.
- At the closing meeting management from PBS committed to following the recommendations – not in detail but in principle. This, we believe, is the best possible recommendation of the model.

5.3 Learning from the Third Action Research Cycle

SimCorp is a leading supplier of highly specialised software and expertise for financial institutions and corporations. They aim at establishing their reputation as "the house of financial know-how". SimCorp has one main product – the system called SimCorp Dimension - that they sell world wide.

For this test we did not redesign the model. But we tested whether it could be used at another level and at another time. Namely for projects that were starting as opposed to the other two tests where we had asked for project that were either closed or very near to ending.

Two projects were chosen for the test. In each of them we conducted two group interviews one with project participants and one with management and other key stakeholders for the specific project. The overall conclusions from this second test were that:

- AIM is also quite useful at the project level. The recommendations that we generated were well received.
- One of the two projects committed to doing most of things we recommended. We were even asked to present our findings and recommendations to the steering board that included two people from SimCorp top management. Our interpretation of this is that the outcome of using AIM must be valuable

– In the second project we came to disagree on how to prioritise the importance of the parameters for a project. We realised that we need a better procedure for that
– When interviewing projects early in their life-cycle we ask the interviewees to imagine how they will work – as opposed to asking them how they have worked. That worked ok. But some of our recommendation on "In Use" parameters were seen as too far away (in the project) to be of immediate value. We need to address this.

6 Conclusion

We are often asked how AIM compares with traditional maturity models like CMMI [15]. Our answer is that we have tried to group all the categories of our findings that were related to CMMI into the group called "Projects" and more specifically into the parameters called "Project team", "Project process" and "Project goal and requirements". Thus we believe that AIM has much more to offer – from an organisational point of view aiming at becoming better at improving - than CMMI.

An advantage of our model is that it is so solidly grounded in empirical observations. The model consists of four groups. The groups consist of parameters. Each parameter consists of categories. Each category is based on a large number of observations from 16 different projects and from many interviews in each project.

Finally, even though we have now reached a stage where we find it fruitful to report our findings in this paper we have already planned the fourth action research testing. So the story will be continued ...

References

1. Goldenson, Dennis R. & Hersleb, James D. (1995). After the Appraisal: A systematic Survey of Process Improvement, its Benefits, and Factors that Influence Success. Technical Report CMU/SEI-95-TR-009. Software Engineering Institute, Carnegie Mellon University, Pittsburgh
2. El-Emam, Khaled et al. (2001). Modelling the Likelihood of Software Process Improvement: An Exploratory Study. Empirical Software Engineering. 6. P. 207-229. Kluwer Academic Publishers. The Netherlands.
3. Blanco et al. (2001). SPI Patterns: Learning from Experience. IEEE Software, May/June 2001, pp. 28-35..
4. Rainer, Austen & Hall, Tracy. (2002). Key success factors for implementing software process improvement: a maturity-based analysis. The Journal of Systems and Software 62 (2002). pp. 71-84.
5. Grady, Robert. (1997). Successful Software process improvement, Pentice Hall PTR, ISBN: 0-13-626623-1
6. Zahran, Sami (1998). Software Process Improvement – Practical Guidelines for Business Success. Addison-Wesley, ISBN 0-201-17782-X
7. Stelzer, Dirk & Mellis, Werner (1999) Success Factors of Organizational Change in Software Process Improvement. Software Process Improvement and Practice, Volume 4, Issue 4

8. Dybå, Tore. (2000). An Instrument for Measuring the Key Factors of Success in Software Process Improvement. Empirical Software Engineering. 5. P. 357-390. Kluwer Academic Publishers. The Netherlands.
9. Strauss, A. and J. Corbin (1990). Basics of Qualitative Research: Techniques and Procedures for Developing Grounded Theory, Sage Publications, Beverly Hills, CA, USA.
10. Strauss, A. and J. Corbin (1998). Basics of Qualitative Research: Techniques and Procedures for Developing Grounded Theory, Sage Publications, Beverly Hills, CA, USA.
11. Hevner, A., S. March, J. Park, and S. Ram (2004), "Design Science in Information Systems Research", MIS Quarterly, 28, 1, pp. 75-106.
12. Kuvaja, Pasi, Jouni Similä, Lech Krzanik, Adriana Bicego, Samuli Saukkonen, Günter Koch (1994). "Software Process Assessment & Improvement. The BOOTSTRAP Approach." Blackwell Publishers.
13. Galliers, R. (1992). Choosing Information Systems Research Approaches. In: Galliers, R. (Ed.). Information Systems research. Blackwell scientific Publications. Oxford, England.
14. Susman, G. and Evered, R. (1978). An assessment of the scientific merits of action research. Administrative Science Quarterly 23 (4): 582-603.
15. Chrissis, Mary Beth, Mike Konrad & Sandy Shrum (2003). CMMI – Guidelines for Process Integration and Product Improvement. Addison-Wesley. ISBN 0-321-15496-7.

Customer-Oriented Specification and Evaluation of IT Service Level Agreements

Wolfram Pietsch

Aachen University of Applied Sciences,
QFD-Institut Deutschland e.V.
Eupener Str. 70, 52066 Aachen, Germany
pietsch@fh-aachen.de
http://www.fh-aachen.de/pietsch.html

Abstract. Service Level Agreements (SLA) are used to determine required and actual performance of IT departments. According to current research and practice, SLA definitions are based on technical performance criteria that may be captured easily such as 'system availability'; the specific needs of the IT system are not considered explicitly. Hence, high system performance does not lead to high customer satisfaction in practice. A methodology based on Quality Function Deployment (QFD) for the customer-oriented specification of SLAs for IT Services is presented and validated in a case study. At first, elementary service requirements of the customers must be separated from service functions and technical performance criteria. Then performance requirements are correlated with performance criteria and evaluated with regard to effectiveness. A case study employing the method is presented and finally, strategic options for the improvement and positioning of IT Services in an organisation are discussed.

1 IT Service Level Management

Process improvement has traditionally a strong focus on the development stages within the software life cycle. The operational stage is gaining more attention lately, i.e. for such companies with primary Information Technology (IT) processes in the value chain such as telecommunication and financial services. Process improvement for IT operations is a lever for business success but may be a threat if quality is not sufficient. In order to improve the quality of IT, IT operations must be conceived as a process. This process delivers an IT-based service such as the Internet Service, which is available only if several components and activities are orchestrated properly. The term 'IT Services' is used for such processes commonly with a broad spectrum of meanings from simple help desk dispatching to comprehensive outsourcing.

So-called Service Level Agreements (SLAs) emerged as common practice in business in order to track and improve performance of such IT Services and as a basis for the calculation of charges [1]. For example, a provider of corporate network services offers its services with a promise of availability for 99% of regular office hours time at a specific price. Both parties agree that there will be a price cut of 10% for each hour of unavailability, if this promise is not kept.

SLAs might be used also for internal charging or accounting of IT Services. A well-defined specification and quantification of SLAs is inevitable in order to track

I. Richardson et al. (Eds.): EuroSPI 2005, LNCS 3792, pp. 83–94, 2005.
© Springer-Verlag Berlin Heidelberg 2005

SLAs for accounting or charging. However, the most precise specification is not always the one that meets customer expectations best. SLA-reports delivered by the providers of IT Services are not easy to comprehend and often meaningless to end-users [2]. They are structured by IT components and not by business processes. Perception of availability by users depends on many contextual and subjective factors. Availability is crucial when processing a customer order but plays a minor role for system administration. Systems are more likely to break down during peak time e.g. short before the noon break, where availability is critical for the user but a promise is very difficult to keep for the provider.

IT management that focuses on technical aspects, tends to employ SLAs for justification of IT performance ('We can prove, we did our best!'). But when SLAs improve, the performance as perceived by customers of IT Services does often not change or becomes even worse ('IT does only stick to the rules, but does not care for our needs!'). If IT is reduced to a fundamental technical commodity like a power supply, its business value will degrade – then "IT doesn't matter" [3]. In order to survive the outsourcing battle, the full potential of IT Services must be focused to business requirements in principal and to customer needs specifically.

For ease of tracking and control SLAs are specified independent of application and context. Hence, more differentiated SLAs will be more complex and require extra effort for control. Who decides at what time and for which system availability will be critical? Which level is required for each time and system? Which measures must be taken to control the different service levels? There are many solutions with respect to the type of fault, context and infrastructure components: fault tolerant systems, data replication, audit trails, monitors, additional service personnel or even preventive measures within system development and testing. IT service performance is a compound result of many factors. If measurement will be narrowed to a single dimension, its potential will be strangled. In order to activate IT Services, more complex measurement with regard to customer requirements is necessary. SLAs should relate to the needs regarding the employment of IT Services for business processes. There are different needs for IT Services within Customer Care compared to Supply Chain Management (SCM) or Accounting.

2   QFD for SLA Definition

2.1   Customer Oriented Service Management

The trade-off between measurability and relevance does exist not only for SLAs. The problem of customer-oriented definition of quality criteria has been a Japanese domain within the sixties, moved to America in the seventies and has arrived into Europe in the nineties with the method Quality Function Deployment (QFD). The de-facto standard method for customer-oriented quality management finally was recognised in the revised ISO 9000 for quality management [4]. QFD has been employed for multiple application fields and branches for the definition of products and services. Software development is a prominent application area with a strong focus on Requirements Engineering and the improvement of software development processes [5]. There are few studies on the late stages of the software life cycle [6], but there is no study on the employment for the definition of SLAs yet. Since QFD has been devised to structure complex quality criteria with regard to customer needs. Since this issue has been identified as the crucial issue for customer-oriented SLAs above, QFD should be a suitable tool. However, QFD is not a formal construction method that may be evaluated by theoretical reasoning but a communication process that must be evaluated in a practical setting [7]. Therefore, a QFD-based approach for the specification of SLAs has been developed and validated in a practical business environment.

QFD clarifies and integrates two perspectives: the perspective of customers and engineers. Who is the customer and who is the engineer of IT Services? Customers are the destinators and consumers of the service that is defined by SLAs, i.e. the end user of the IT system. Engineers are the originators and designers of the services, i.e. the IT department or an external provider as suppliers of IT Services. The customers may be also the authorities that are responsible for the business processes that require a specific IT service, i.e. departmental management. Engineers may be also representatives of a subcontractor, i.e. key account manager of an IT service provider. The requirements of the customer and the services provided by the supplier must be clarified: Which services are to be negotiated and what are the quality criteria to measure performance; which hard- and software will be provided and maintained; which additional services like training or a hot-line will be offered?

In order to identify the different types of requirements on IT Services, stereotype roles for customer and engineer may be derived 'top-down' from a value chain analysis of IT Services and employed for the deduction of principal requirements. However, value chains are rather hypotheses and the context of analysis is quite fuzzy and dynamic in practice. Therefore it is straightforward, to employ the 'bottom-up' approach of QFD and to ask a selected group of stakeholders: Which requirements do you have regarding IT Services? The QFD process will lead into customer requirements that are independent of current technology and implementation approaches, opposite to technical SLA. Then it may be questioned, whether specific groups of people view and prioritise these requirements are significantly different.

2.2   IT Service Requirements Analysis

QFD searches for long-term customer requirements without any preconceived solutions [5; 7]. For tangible products like a car "Comfortable transportation" could be a principal requirement that truly has changed over time (Ford 'Model T' vs. Ford 'Mondeo') and depends heavily on the geographic location (downtown London vs. desert Gobi). Is "Fast response time" a principal requirement in the case of IT Services? The key to the identification of principal requirements it the question 'Why?'. If there is more than one answer with different goals, the chances are good, that the statement under consideration contains different aspects, that must be differentiated in order to arrive at principal requirements. The need for fast response time could have different reasons: "Avoid idle time when processing customer orders" or „React faster to customer requests". Both needs may but must not be fulfilled by means of an improvement of the response time. There are many other solutions such as change of the design of the input forms, improved user friendliness, or even organisational changes or training. The absolute level of required response time may vary by system function: it could be high for order input and low for system maintenance. Moreover, a

faulty or impractical system with an immediate response may not fulfil the requirements of the customer whereas the customer may be highly satisfied if response time
is moderate but the system is reliable, well designed etc. There may be a different
scenario, where reaction time is a final objective. In some real-time systems, response
time is a major aspect of the system, therefore a principal requirement. In this case
there is no satisfying answer to the question 'why' (e.g. "It's a MUST") – the customer should decide!

Response time, availability or user friendliness are not final goals but intermediate
measures that may be employed to evaluate the system independently of its functions.
QFD defines such non-functional measures as 'Quality Criteria'. This term does
sometimes lead to confusion due to different definitions of quality. Therefore we will
call such measures for IT Services 'IT Service Performance Criteria', since they
should describe the way a service is performed independently of its functions and
components. The principal requirements will be called 'IT Service Requirements' and
the specific solutions that resemble the functionality of tangible products will be
called 'IT Service Function'. The QFD process that addresses the elicitation of the
principal requirements is called Voice of the Customer Analysis (VoC). It provides a
standard tool with six questions, the 5W1H-questionary (five questions with the initial
'W' and one with the initial 'H') [5]. The following table 1 shows a 5W1H-scheme,
which has been adapted for the requirement analysis for IT Services.

Table 1. 5W1H-scheme for IT-Service Requirements Analysis: Any <*Statement*> of a
customer will be clarified employing the following questions resulting in three types of
concepts, principal Service Requirements and two types of solutions, Performance Criteria and
Service Functions

Why?	What is the final purpose of the requested <*Statement*>?
What?	Which specific service is wanted with regard to <*Statement*> ?
Who?	Which person or system does need <*Statement*> ?
Where?	At which location / system is <*Statement*> needed?
When?	At which time will <*Statement*> be needed?
How much?	To what degree is <*Statement*> needed?
IT Service Requirement	A primary customer requirement, independent of solutions.
IT Performance Criteria	A non-functional measure for the performance of IT Services.
IT Service Function	A specific task or system function that is part of the IT Services provided.

The resulting IT Service Requirements may be more or less detailed, do refer to
different levels of abstraction, and must be clustered into a hierarchical structure for
prioritisation. Standard facilitation techniques may be employed for this step, e.g.
affinity diagrams [5]. The following table 2 provides a simple sketch of a two-level
hierarchy including the weight of each requirement from the perspective of the

customer. The prioritisation may be performed with standard techniques such as the Analytical Hierarchical Process (AHP) and/or pair wise comparisons [5]. The way clustering and prioritisation is performed does influence the quality of the result significantly. It is not constituent for the specific methodology as presented, but a general issue in any Requirements Analysis.

Table 2. Sample Sketch of an IT Service Requirements Table

Category	*IT Service Requirement*	*Weight*
A) Improved Work Productivity		
	A1) Minimise idle time when entering customer documents	10%
	A2) Find customer documents quickly	15%
	…	…
B) Improved Effectiveness of Work		
	B1) Availability of services independent of place	10%
	B2) Support for advanced system customisation	05%
	…	…
C) Competent Support Services		
	C1) Understanding of work environment	25%
	C2) Social competence	15%
	…	…

2.3 IT Service Solution Analysis

After the VoC, the next logical step within QFD is the Voice of the Engineer Analysis (VoE). For IT Services the VoC results in IT Service Requirements according to the scheme presented in Table 1. The following VoE produces Service Performance Criteria and IT Service Functions and will be called IT Service Solution Analysis. The procedure is similar to the VoC. However, not the customers but the engineers of IT Services will be asked about properties and function of IT Services, i.e. Service desk managers and staff or other IT personnel. It is common that the VoC produces already some Performance Criteria's and Functions, since customer statements often include solutions. Nevertheless, there should be specific solutions without any limitations from the current service context as the customer experiences it. Service engineers must be free for innovation. Table 3 gives a sample sketch of an IT Performance Criteria Table.

Whereas the structuring of customer requirements should be adapted to the specific perspective of the customers, the structuring of Performance Criteria and Functions should follow industry standards for many reasons, among others certification and tool support. The three categories A) to C) in the example in table 3 reflect key service processes from the IT Infrastructure Library (ITIL) [8], the de-facto industry standard for Service Management. If ITIL has not been introduced in an IT service organisation yet, it may be not practical to use ITIL-terminology since it is very

Table 3. Sample Sketch of an IT Performance Criteria Table

Category	Performance Criteria
A) Service Desk	
	A1) Response time to requests
	A2) Level of communication skills
	…
B) Incident Management	
	B1) Average time for resolution of critical incidents
	B2) Percentage of incidents solved by First Level Services (1LS)
	…
C) Problem Management	
	C1) Number of anticipated problems per month
	C2) Percentage of critical anticipated problems per month
	…

powerful but not commonsense and thus may lead to misinterpretations. Anyhow, ITIL should be employed whenever it is feasible since it provides a proven structure and supports competitive benchmarking as pointed out below.

2.4 Evaluation of Effectiveness

If VoC and VoE have been completed, the effectiveness of solutions (Product Functions and Quality Criteria) can be analysed with regard to customer requirements employing a correlation matrix, which is often called the House of Quality [5]. For IT Services the Service Performance Criteria (*criteria*) and Functions must be correlated with IT Service Requirements (*rqt*). QFD provides a fixed set of values for correlation measures (*c*) restricted to four different levels that are quantified exponentially with increasing effect as specified below.

$$c_{rqt,criteria} = \begin{cases} 0 \rightarrow \text{no/indirect effect of } criteria \text{ on } rqt \\ 3^0 \rightarrow \text{low effect of } criteria \text{ on } rqt \\ 3^1 \rightarrow \text{medium effect of } criteria \text{ on } rqt \\ 3^2 \rightarrow \text{strong effect of } criteria \text{ on } rqt \end{cases} \tag{1}$$

The correlation measure *c* may neither be deduced from a general framework like ITIL nor captured from empirical analysis. It is a result of a negotiation process between customers and engineers reflecting the current knowledge and attitudes of the participants. Hence, facilitation is the common technique for correlation analysis. Questionnaires may be used supplementary but do not replace personal negotiation and discussion about the impact of criteria's and solutions on customer needs. From a methodological standpoint of view it is rather knowledge engineering than systems analysis resulting in a 'reconstructed model' regarding the effectiveness of service functions and its performance. Figure 1 gives a sample sketch of a correlation matrix for IT Services.

	w	Performance Criteria				Satisfaction	
		Ii)	IIi)	IIIi)	...	S^{actual}	$S^{planned}$
Requirement A1	10	9	0	0	...	1	1
Requirement B1	20	0	3	0	...	2	4
Requirement C1	30	0	0	1	...	3	9
...	...	...	...	...	...	...	...
Target Level		99%	10	1,500	...		
Importance (I)		90	60	30	...		
Difficulty		0.90	1.2	1.8	...		

Fig. 1. Sample Sketch of a Correlation Matrix for IT Services

The Service Requirements from the VoC (Table 2) form the rows and Performance Criteria from the VoE (Table 3) form the columns. The results of the prioritization are included in the column with the customer preference weights w as well. The cells of the matrix contain the correlation measure c for the respective Service Requirements and Performance Criteria assuming a specific target level of performance: How strong would be the positive effect of an improvement of Performance Criteria <Column> up to Target Level <Column> on the fulfillment of Service Requirement <Row>? For the explanation of Importance, Difficulty and Satisfaction see below.

The lever of a specific performance criterion with regard to the fulfilment of Service Requirements may be calculated as a weighted sum of the correlation measures c and customer preference weights w:

$$I_{criteria} = \sum_{Rqts} w_{rqt} \, c_{rqt,criteria} \tag{2}$$

The resulting metric I provides a measure for the importance (I) of a specific Performance Criteria with regard to the needs of the customer. A Performance Criterion with a certain Target Level may serve as a SLA specification; the corresponding importance I may be employed to evaluate its degree of customer orientation. If a SLA should be ruled by customer needs only, performance criteria with a high value of metric I should be chosen. A given set of SLA may be evaluated with metric I with regard to its customer focus.

Nevertheless, products that are geared to current needs only, may be successful in the short run, but do not address competition and innovation properly. Within QFD, a modified measure has been developed that considers the subtle relationship between the fulfilment of requirements and the satisfaction of customers discovered by Kano [9]. The metric I developed above assumes, that an improvement of the fulfilment of requirements in terms of Service Performance leads to a higher satisfaction proportionally. According to Kano, not all requirements behave like such 'normal requirements'. There are other requirements that are perceived as elementary by the customer and taken for granted ('expected requirements'). Current satisfaction level is high and an improvement does not lead to a much higher satisfaction. There is a third kind of requirement, which does not have an effect on customer satisfaction at a low level of fulfilment but an extraordinary high effect or excitement if fulfilment improves ('exciting requirements'). This applies i.e. for innovative solutions, which the customer does not expect if not present, but may excite even on a low level of implementation.

The metric I addresses normal requirements only. For expected and exciting requirements the satisfaction level of customer requirements must be considered also as shown in Table 3. Expected requirements must not be improved, if the satisfaction level is high or if there is no alternative known to the customer, i.e. another supplier offering services at a much higher level. In both cases the difference between the actual and the desired or planned satisfaction level is low. The satisfaction level for exciting requirements is usually low, whereas the planned level is higher and thus there is a significant difference. The difference between actual and desired or planned satisfaction may also be of importance for normal requirements in order to consider competitors. Table 3 may be augmented by the current satisfaction of customers with regard to an alternative product or service offered by a competitor. Differences in satisfaction may reflect unique selling positions or weaknesses of a product or services. Once again, the difference counts: the higher the difference the more important is a solution.

$$I'_{criteria} = \sum_{Rqts} \left\{ w_{rqt} \cdot c_{rqt,criteria} \cdot \left| S_{rqt}^{planned} - S_{rqt}^{actual} \right| \right\} \tag{3}$$

Metric I has been modified to I' by multiplying the weighted contribution of a solution to the customer needs with the absolute difference of satisfaction levels. If the current satisfaction level is higher than necessary, e.g. for an expected requirement, the difference may be negative in order to save resources and avoid 'over-engineering', which is an important objective indeed.

Customer satisfaction surveys are a common practice in IT Service Management. But they are often reduced to overall satisfaction. Furthermore, evaluation criteria for satisfaction are either technical and thus mostly indirect or unspecific and not well defined, i.e. if performed by external marketing-oriented consultancies. IT Service Requirements Analysis does not only provide a framework for Service Level Definition but also provides a structured set of criteria for customer satisfaction surveys that is specific and possesses a high degree of validity.

3 Case Study

A leading telecommunication service provider in Germany has decided to define SLAs for its internal IT Services, i.e. for the IT office automation services. Office automation services such as text processing are demanded from customers of all departments and operated decentrally; the provision and support of the services is centralised. A new central Service Level Management Unit has been founded that is responsible for the definition of SLAs. QFD has been employed in order to find a well-founded SLA specification.

Three workshops have been performed, one VoC-, one VoE- and one Correlation-workshop. In the first workshop, selected members of business units, support and IT have been invited for the discussion of Service Level Agreements. Already this first workshop did lead to a hot discussion between the customers from the business units and the suppliers of IT Services. The customers did complain about technical-focused, sometimes arrogant support, which was not accepted by the support staff. There was a heavy fight about the justification of the customer statement 'IT staff should be more friendly', which was not accepted by the IT staff as a measure for service performance. The methodology did help, since 'Friendly treatment of support requests' was identified as a customer requirement but not defined as a Service Level Requirement at first. After prioritisation of customer requirements it came out, that the absolute intensity of discussion did not reflect the relative importance of this requirement to the customer. The topic has been loaded with personal attitudes and subjective measures leading to a biased discussion. The method did help to master this and other similar problems successfully.

The structure of the correlation matrix from the case is depicted as an example. Due to disclosure rules, a sample is extracted only. The QFD-chart has been produced with the software tool QualicaQFD.

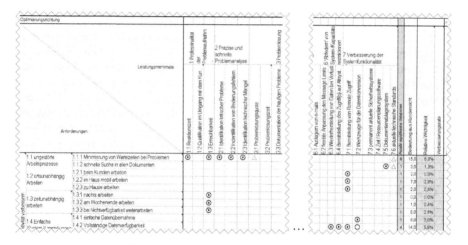

Fig. 2. Sample Correlation Matrix (Extract)

In the second workshop the hot issues cooled down and the bias faded away. A common framework for understanding Service Requirements beyond SLAs has been established. Now an evaluation of the SLAs was feasible, but not simple, indeed. Correlation analysis resulted in a low value of metric I for classical SLAs like 'Response time to support requests', the value for 'Time for resolution of critical incidents' was just moderate. Other performance criteria such as 'Quick identification of incidents caused by inappropriate system usage' had a very high I, but were not considered as an SLA and even rejected by support staff at first.

Innovative measures such as proactive training performed by support staff earned a very high I within the analysis of service functions, but this solution seemed to attack the self-understanding of IT Services as a corrective rather a constructive force. Data security was another top requirement but only partly under control of the IT service unit and user satisfaction was on a high level already. Some of the issues raised by users with regard to IT Services were beyond the influence of the IT service unit, e.g. data migration problems have been caused during the execution of a project but must be mitigated within IT Services.

It was obvious, that classical SLAs reduce the potential of IT Services and are not adequate to address customer needs properly. Moreover, the current role, responsibility and authority of IT Services were not defined in a way, that a service level measure could established as a proper contractual agreement. Strategic questions must be addressed first. This is not a new insight for business process design in general and for IT process improvement in specific: the structure must follow the strategy! But few methods are sensitive with regard to strategic alignment, i.e. classical SLAs. Even if the design process starts from strategic goals like ITIL does [10], specifications do often not match reality like in the case above. The QFD-based method unveils strategic incongruencies in a way that a discussion is triggered and structured constructively.

4 Strategic Options for Service Management

The case study addresses the problem of self-understanding of IT Services within a large enterprise in specific and expands in general on Carr's question mentioned above as follows: What is the purpose of IT Services and IT in general?" An answer could be that IT is a standardised commodity that is exchangeable and that could be provided by an external supplier as well. The opposite answer could be that IT should create value or support the creation of value effectively and more efficient than any external supplier. The answers comprise Porter's generic strategies [11] of cost leadership, focus and differentiation that will be discussed below with regard to the customer oriented specification of SLAs.

4.1 Cost-Oriented SLA Definition

If IT Services are to be standardised in order to provide a large number of customers with a minimum of resources, cost minimisation is the natural strategy. This strategy is likely to be found in large, international providers of software and services. Market power is more important than the satisfaction of customers. IT is considered as a commodity and SLAs are employed for controlling purposes. The method described above may be used as a target-costing tool in order to devise a cost-minimal set of SLAs. In such cases, communication between customers and supplier is very likely to be distorted by politics – a showstopper for successful customer-oriented process improvement. There have been several requests to the author, to introduce the method in organisations of such kind, in order "to discipline IT Services" or "to tame IT users". After explaining the procedure and rules, the interest faded away quickly.

4.2 Focused SLA Definition

If an enterprise or an IT service provider plans to concentrate on specific IT Services in order to improve customer satisfaction, the chances are better for the method. However, if the analysis does lead to a questioning of roles and responsibilities, commitment of management is critical like in the case study presented above and may require a strategic dialogue that is time-consuming with an open end.

Customer-oriented specification of SLAs is powerful for medium or small suppliers of software and services with a particular customer segment or a niche market. The limited resources within IT Services can be focused on customer avoiding ad-hoc assignment of support staff and enforcing professional but lean service processes.

4.3 Differentiated SLA Definition

The third strategy besides cost and focus is differentiation, which is the most challenging in this case. SLAs will be defined in a way, that it differentiates IT service provider from another (internal or external) competitor. Based on a detailed analysis of customer satisfaction the 'Unique Service Position' of an IT service provider may be identified and its services may be modified with regard to exciting requirements. For instance, a small software house could position its products and services comparing to the market leader; an internal consulting team may position its services compared to central IT Services. The method described above does support the identification of strength and weaknesses and the precise positioning of services as a marketing tool. The effectiveness of the SLAs depends on the existence of a sound and feasible product strategy. Product design is the main scope of QFD. The method described above may help to identify strategic flaws but does not support strategy definition. Nevertheless, it could be extended for strategic planning, for instance by employing Shillito's Advanced QFD [12].

5 Conclusion

QFD is a proper tool for the customer-oriented specification of SLAs, but must be modified for this purpose significantly. The method proposed does not only support the specification of new SLAs. It may be employed for the evaluation of the customer focus of existing SLA and may serve as a tool for the design of IT Services and its strategic alignment in principal.

References

1. R. Sturm, W. Morris, M. Jander: Foundations of Service Level Management, Indianapolis IN 2000.
2. M.G. Bernhard, W. Lewandowski, H. Mann: Service Level Management in der IT, Symposion Publishing, Düsseldorf 2001.
3. N.G. Carr: IT Doesn't Matter, in: Harvard Business Review, May 2003.
4. ISO Standards Compendium: ISO 9000 – Quality Management, ISO bookstore, Ed. 10 2003.
5. G. Herzwurm, W. Mellis, S. Schockert: Joint Requirements Engineering. Using QFD for Rapid Customer-Focused Software and Internet Development. Braunschweig - Wiesbaden 2000.

6. G. Herzwurm, W. Pietsch: Risk-based Deployment of Standard Software Rollout Processes - a pragmatic approach, Transactions of the 11th Symposium on Quality Function Deployment, QFD-Institute 1999.
7. W. Pietsch: QFD Dissemination - Principles and Practice. Proceedings of the First National QFD-Conference, Izmir 2002.
8. Office of Government Commerce (OGC): ITIL - Planning to Implement Service Management. The Stationary Office (TSO), Norwich 2002.
9. N. Kano et al., Attractive quality and must-be quality", The Journal of the Japanese Society for Quality Control, 1984.
10. Office of Government Commerce (OGC): ITIL - The Business Perspective. The Stationary Office (TSO), Norwich 2002.
11. M.E: Porter: "Competitive Advantage", New York 1985.
12. L.M. Shillito: Advanced QFD. Linking Technology to Market and Company Needs. New York u. a. 1994.

Safety Methods in Software Process Improvement

Torgrim Lauritsen and Tor Stålhane

NTNU, Norwegian University of Science and Technology
torgriml@idi.ntnu.no

Abstract. Even if the application developers produce software in accordance with the customer requirements, they cannot guarantee that the software will behave in a safe way during the lifetime of the software. We define a system as safe if the risks related to its use are judged to be acceptable [1]. Safety must not be confused with security which broadly is defined as keeping the system unavailable for people who should not be able to access it. In this paper we introduce the Failure Mode and Effect Analysis (FMEA) technique into the software development process to improve the safety of business-critical software. In a business environment this means that the system does not behave in such a way that it causes the customer or his users to lose money or important information. We will use the term "business-safe" for this characteristic.

1 Introduction

The Failure Mode and Effect Analysis (FMEA) [2] technique has been used with success in safety critical systems for cars, aircrafts and trains. Several companies, among them ESA, have worked on applying FMEA to software [3]. In this case we will use it when we focus on the business critical safety of using software. We use cars, trains and aircrafts every day, without being terrified of the possibility that we will crash our car, the train will derail, or the aircraft will loose the power of one of its engines, or two or more aircrafts will collide. We know that if something unexpected happens, we or the transport controllers will be able to manage the transportation equipment in such a way that we will be able to control or avoid catastrophic events. This is because there has been built in hazard reduction and control solutions into safety critical equipment.

But there are seldom built in hazard reduction solutions into business critical software, mainly due to the fact that the application developers mostly are focused on methodologies, classes, and use cases, while clients and business owners worry about the requirements, and seldom think of the possibility that this new software will affect their marketable features, cash flow, or return on investment. Therefore, the stakeholders often neglect the safety aspect of the software. Introducing FMEA into the software development process will help the application developers to be able to increase the quality of the software in a systematic way by making them able to implement barriers. These barriers will reduce the possibilities that the software will fail or cause the users to loose information or money.

The rest of this paper is organized as follows: First we look at why we should do hazard analysis in software development, and introduce the FMEA technique. There-

I. Richardson et al. (Eds.): EuroSPI 2005, LNCS 3792, pp. 95–105, 2005.

after we describe how the hazard analysis affect the software process. Then we describe how FMEA fits into software process improvement (SPI). We then describe how we recommend using FMEA in two steps during the development process, before showing two examples of how FMEA can be used. Finally we conclude the paper and discuss further work on this topic.

2 Why Hazard Analysis

In the Business Critical Software (BUCS) project we focus on hazard prevention rather than hazard detection and hazard reduction. It is easier and cheaper to identify hazards early during development, than doing it for instance during integration and testing. The result will be that the developers produce safer software, which in future will give the application developers more satisfied customers. Ignoring hazard prevention will get the customers into problems when using the software. Then it will be harder to fix, and more expensive to repair.

A system should be analyzed for business safety in the context of its environment and modes of operation to identify possible hazardous events [2]. A hazard is a state or set of conditions of a system or an object that, together with other conditions in the environment of the system or object, will lead to an accident. Using Failure and Effect Analysis (FMEA) will help us to reduce the product risk stemming from these accidents. While many software methodologies pay lip service to the need to monitor risk, there is little help offered in methodologies such as Rational Unified Process (RUP) and eXtreme Programming (XP) on how to reduce the product risk. In these frameworks, risk is only treated as a project risk.

Risk is defined as the product of an event's consequence and its probability of occurrence or as its hazard level (severity and likelihood of an occurrence) combined with 1) the likelihood of the hazard leading to an accident and 2) hazard exposure or duration. When a company is looking for a new software product, they deal with three factors; "What suppliers should we use?", "Which psychosocial influence will this new software product have in our organization?" and "Will the software product function in accordance to our requirements?" The supplier factor deals with uncertainty concerning the relationships of the potential supplier, like "Can we trust this supplier, do they produce the "best" product for us?", "Does this supplier stay "alive" both during the development time and during the maintenance time limit of our product?", "How financial strong is the supplier?", etc. Psychosocial factors deals with how this new product will affect our organization, like "Will this product improve our productivity and profitability?", "Will we be able to reduce / increase our staff?", etc. Product factors deals with "Does this product meet our requirements?", "How is the quality of this new software product as opposed to our existing product?", "What will happen if the product fails?" FMEA is a tool that can be used to consider the product factors.

Using FMEA will not make it cheaper to develop software, at least not in a short term perspective. Applying FMEA to increase the products' business-safety must be viewed as an investment. The return of investment will be software products with higher quality, which will lead to more business from existing customers and new business from new customers. In addition, we will have less need for fire-fighting.

The workload will be larger in the beginning of the project. This bigger workload will reduce the rework later in the project, because now latent hazards are identified and the developers can use their new knowledge to limit, reduce or eliminate these hazards.

The results of the FMEA should be used as input to the further development and as input to tests that verify that the software is safe to use. Tests unambiguously communicate how things are supposed to work and provide feedback on whether the system actually works the way it is supposed to work. Tests also provide the scaffolding that allows developers to make changes throughout the development process. The FMEA results may be re-used in later projects, so the developers do not repeat implementing possible latent hazards in future products. In this way we accomplish a software process improvement.

3   Software Process Improvements (SPI)

The goal of software process improvement (SPI) is to increase the quality of the software by improving the development process. Quality can be defined as properties of products or services that satisfy the customers and users of the product. Software developers should build in integrity that balances functionality, usability, reliability and economical aspects in a way that satisfies the customer [4]. Using FMEA early in the software development will help the developers to prevent damage and accidents, so that they don't have to resist to a reactive response when damage or accident already has happened. The developers will thus avoid implementing latent hazards that might lead to catastrophic events, and thus, will increase the quality of the software. Introducing FMEA in software development process will lead to a more safe software product.

Figure 1 shows both the RUP and the XP development process augmented with two FMEA activities. In principle, the software development process runs as usual, with the additional FMEA activities taking input from and affecting the architecture and coding activities, as well as giving output for tests on identified failure modes and their barriers. The same figure will, with possible minor modifications, apply to any other development processes.

As we see in the Figure 1, FMEA should be used as a guiding and documenting tool when the developers has received the requirements from the customers and started to describe the requirements into use cases in RUP or user stories in XP. Some people [5] have extended the use cases with negative use cases, which they called misuse cases.

Already in this early stage of development the developers will be able to identify and document possible hazards and find solutions that will avoid or reduce the consequences of such hazards. The developers should use the FMEA analysis in cooperation with the customers, so that they together can find solutions that will avoid a possible damage.

The results from this functional FMEA will be new requirements that should be added to the original customer requirements. The developers should bring these new requirements into the design phase, where they describe abstract models based on the requirements. These models can be class diagrams, sequence diagrams, and other models which developers has sketched before they came up with the UML diagrams. These pre-UML diagrams models are used in agile modeling, where the developers start almost immediate to code, following the test-driven development approach.

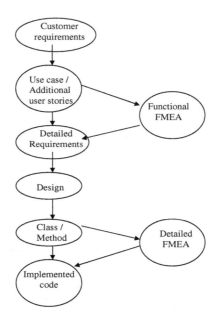

Fig. 1. FMEA in the development phase

In the detailed FMEA the developers analyze all the requirements, i.e. both the original requirements and the requirements from the functional FMEA, since the additional requirements could add new hazards into the software solution.

Introducing FMEA in today's software processes will result in more focus on "hazard scenarios", i.e. the developers will be more focused on "what can go wrong", and "what consequences will that have for ….", in contrast to today's focus on "happy scenarios", where the developers only focus on implementing the functional requirements from the customers. The results from the FMEA should be used as basis for tests, both developer and customer tests [4].

4   The Many Faces of FMEA

4.1   Failure Method and Effect Analysis

During every development project some kind of safety evaluations is performed, but the results from these evaluations are seldom documented. Our solution at the early stages, when we have no design description, to analyze, is to use a simple Preliminary Hazard Analysis (PHA), Functional Failure Analysis (FHA) or Functional Failure Analysis (FHA) [6]. Later in the development process, when developers have made a design, for instance, described in UML, they can use FMEA to identify hazards that can arise, and what effects these hazards will have. FMEA gives guidelines on how to execute a systematic analysis of all components in a system – for object oriented development this can be all classes and their methods. The systematic approach makes the FMEA more effective than just a simple, unstructured analysis. The quality of the result of the FMEA process is, however, strongly dependent on the experience and knowledge of the participants. For this reason both developers and customer must participate in the analysis.

The procedure for the FMEA is as follows: Each method in a class is analyzed for possible failure modes. This is done by asking "how can this method fail and what happens if it does?" The developers write their answers to this question in the FMEA table - see table 1.

Table 1. A general FMEA table

Method	Failure Description	Effect(s) of failure	Actions / barriers	Severity
Account.find Accountnumber ()	No connection to the database	No account number found	Ensure that the DB connection is establisehed before asking Account.find Account Number	High

The weakness of the FMEA method is that each method is assessed one failure at a time. The developers thus miss the opportunity to identify and test sequences of several failures in a row. All failures and associated effects are described and collected in FMEA tables. The developers should sort the failure modes according to the severity classification and methods with major failures are considered for redesign or for insertion of a barrier to avert the danger [7].

The FMEA table contains fields where the developers fill in the description of the effect of the failure, both locally - for the unit - and for the system. The developers shall, together with the customers, assess and insert the severity of each fault. We propose to use a simple ranking for severity – for instance high, medium or low. An alternative could be to use a combination of occurrence frequency, severity and detection [8]. From the FMEA table the developers will be able to start working with identifying actions and barriers that can be used to avoid or reduce the possibility of the hazards. These actions and barriers must not be in conflict with the originally requirements.

Simple arithmetic methods that only could give erroneous output because of overflow or underflow should not be analyzed, nor should the developers analyze methods concerning exception handling. Including these in the analysis will be time consuming and clutter the analysis, without adding any significant information. The developers should, however, be aware that using exceptions will introduce more code and increase risk. This again, can lead to new faults.

For each method relevant to the analysis, the developers have to identify the failure modes of the methods and possible failure causes. If the failure cause cannot be removed, it has to be dealt in another way, for instance by implementing a barrier. The barrier has to detect the failure and perform an action that will rectify or notify a controller function about this failure.

The most effective barriers are those inserted immediately after an error-prone step, such as data input, non-trivial mathematical or logical operations, and before data output. In many cases the detection is in the form of an assertion which, if not true, causes the program to enter an exception handling routine. Other detection provisions, typically found in system software (schedulers, operating systems, middleware) protect against incorrect message passing, exceeding time limits, and anomalous event sequences [9].

The closer to the source of failure the barrier is inserted, the better is the chance of picking it up before it contaminates the rest of the system. This can, however, lead to a high number of barriers, and therefore a more complex system. Another possibility is to organize all classes into packages and implement barriers in supervising façade-class.

Effect propagation can be assessed by also analyzing classes that depend on methods from the class whose methods are being analyzed. This can be done by using information from the relevant sequence diagrams. The development team can go on to analyze the effects on the related classes, or they can decide to take action to prevent the failure modes from occurring in the local class, thereby removing any negative effects on related classes and their methods. When every method has been analyzed, or deemed exempt from analysis, the FMEA of the class methods is complete.

The identification of possible failure modes in a class will help the developers to choose among alternative solutions during implementation. By changing the system design by inserting a barrier, or by just rewriting some of the code, the developers may be able to eliminate the problem instead of inserting extra code for checking or control.

4.2 Functional FMEA

A functional FMEA is performed based on the requirements the developers receive from the customers and can be started when the developers have described the requirements as use cases in RUP or as user stories in XP, and they have chosen different architecture and design solutions. Later, when the developers have implemented and tested their code, they can perform a more detailed FMEA. The developers will then be able to identify possible failure modes both in the inception and elaboration phases of RUP and in the construction phase on the code that is used to implement the system. Some issues the FMEA should handle are shown in table 2:

Table 2. Examples of failure modes that can be found using FMEA

Initial FMEA		Detailed FMEA	
Design defects	Critical implementation areas	Logical code defects	Code detail defects
Design pattern not followed Incorrect class relationships Class inheritance faults Object instantiation faults Over-complex class structure Omissions Incorrect facts Inconsistencies Ambiguities Extraneous information [10]	Critical methods that require additional attention in testing	Logical defects in method design Lack of error handling for a method Methods never called Methods called in wrong order Methods called with wrong parameters Methods called at the wrong time Missing methods Algorithms are not robust	Initialization of class instances Code typing errors that are compliable Data retrieval Data storage Wrong variable types Incomplete code - methods returning mock / test / no data

4.3 Detailed FMEA

During the functional FMEA, the information available was quite limited. The developers now have more available knowledge about the system to be built. This knowledge stems both from the previous functional FMEA and from all the other tasks done during the development process. The classes will have attributes, methods and relations to other classes and requirements for barriers are available from the functional FMEA. The detailed FMEA will further help the developers to describe how to make tests concerning the identified hazards and their barriers. This will give the developers knowledge about the classes' responsibilities and relationships to each other and they can thus produce:

- Barriers that can be used to reduce or eliminate hazards.
- Detailed tests that can be implemented and run as unit tests.

From a detailed FMEA the developers get information that will influence tests and already implemented code. There should preferably not be any changes to the architecture at this stage. The developers will have a better understanding and more information about the failure and the effects they will have.

The results of the detailed FMEA will be recommendations for concrete actions used to evade the identified failure modes. This will be in the form of suggestions for code alteration and barrier implementation, as well as tests concerning the suggested alterations and implementations.

5   Two Small Examples

5.1   Class Fragment

A company needs a software system for handling customer orders. They contact a software company and from the requirements the developers come up with the class diagram shown in figure 2. The developers decide that they need a database that contains information about the customers and the products of the company. The orders the company receive from their customers, will contain the number of items ordered for each product. The company has an order limit of each product.

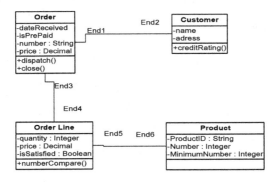

Fig. 2. Example of a high level class diagram [11]

5.2   Example of a Functional FMEA

The following FMEA fragment analyzes the customer's credit rating. If the credit rating is too high, the customer can order for more than he should be allowed to. This

Table 3. A FMEA table for credit rating

Class / Method	Failure mode	Effects of failure	Action or barriers	Severity
Customer. creditRating	creditRating is too high	Customer orders for more than his credit rating	1) Manual check when setting or changing credit rating	High
	creditRating is too low	Customer is not allowed to use his full credit rating	2) Implement function to obtain credit rating from external sources	Medium
	no creditRating	The company might loose money by selling too much products to customers that will not be able to pay		High

might cause a loss for the company since they run the risk that the customer will not be able to pay. If the credit rating is set too low, the customer will not be allowed to order as much as he wants to and he will thus be less than satisfied. He might then start to buy the products from another company, and the company will loose a customer. If there is no credit rating at all, the company will not have any idea of whether they will get the money for their products. The FMEA table, partly filled out for our example, is shown below in Table 3.

Note that we can implement the barriers to this failure mode either as a manual control procedure or as a barrier in the code. If the barrier is implemented as code, this will be a critical implementation area and it should thus be analyzed further in a detailed FMEA.

5.3   Example of a Detailed FMEA

After further development of the system, the developers can perform a detailed FMEA. They will now have more knowledge about the inner workings of the class, as well as how the class under consideration relates to other classes. The example in table 4 shows an FMEA concerning the potential event that the customer orders more than the company have in the stock. By using FMEA, the developers can identify the possible occurrences of this failure mode and identify possible barriers and barriers that will assure the business safety of the software product.

Table 4. Detailed FMEA

Method	Failure mode	Effects of failure	Cause(s) of Failure	Action, barriers	Severity
Order-Line.numb erCompare()	Order-Line.isSatis fied = true, when it should be false	Order will be processed even if the available stock should not allow this	Wrong information about stock available	Product (class) must update stock information before every order by calling the method Product.numberUpdate()	High
			Faulty check of stock versus order	OrderLine (class) must ensure that the comparison of order and stock is correct by checking that the inputs to Order-Line.numberCompare() are correct	High

If the order is larger than the available stock, this should be discovered in the application, and a message should be sent to the user that the number of products ordered is too large. On the other hand, if the system's knowledge about current stock numbers is not updated, it can not send this information.

Relevant items:
Classes: Order, Product, OrderLine
Variables: Order.number, Product.number, OrderLine.isSatisfied
Methods: OrderLine.numberCompare()

The identified failure mode is that the system does not recognize that the ordered number of items is larger than the number of items in stock. The FMEA identifies some possible causes of this failure mode and what could be done to prevent it.

6 Conclusions and Further Work

By using the FMEA, the developers can identify possible failure modes in the system and include code that will prevent the problem or at least reduce its impact on system behavior. In this way, they can increase the probability that the system will behave in such a way that it will not cause losses to the user.

FMEA is a proactive tool that helps developers to become aware of possible failures, their affects on the sub-system and on the complete system. The strength of the FMEA is that it focuses on only one failure mode at time, and offers a documentation tool for developing more business safe software. The results from one FMEA could also be used in later projects, so the developers reduce later workload. In this way the developers will gain more knowledge, and make safer software products.

The next step in the BUCS project is to run an industrial experiment to see if they find FMEA suitable for use in a real project and whether there are situations where the FMEA technique will break down. One of the interesting topics is to see how the results from an FMEA could be used in later projects. One other interesting topic is how easy it is for the developers to convert the results from the FMEA to tests, which will be used to identify the software system quality.

References

1. Lowrance, William W: "Of acceptable risk: Science and the determination of safety", William Kaufman, Inc., Los Altos, Calif., 1976
2. Leveson, Nancy G. "Safeware – System safety and computers", Addison-Wesley Publishing Company, Inc. ISBN: 0-201-11972-2, 1995
3. Guidelines for Considering a Software Intensive System within FMECA Studies, ESTEC, January, 1992
4. Poppendieck, Mary, Poppendieck, Tom: "Lean Software Development – An agile toolkit", Addison-Wesley, ISBN: 0-321-15078-3, 2003
5. Guttorm Sindre, Andreas L. Opdahl, "Eliciting Security Requirements with Misuse Cases", Requirements Engineering Journal, 10(1):34-44, January 2005.
6. Johannessen, Per, Christian Grante, Anders Alminger, Ulrik Eklund, Jan Torin: "Hazard Analysis in Object Oriented Design of Dependable Systems", IEEE, 2001
7. Craig, J.H.: "A software reliability methodology using software sneak analysis, SW FMEA and the integrated system analysis approach", in Reliability and Maintainability Symposium, 2003. Annual, 27-30 Jan. 2003

8. Samatis, D.H.: "Failure Mode and Affect Analysis. FMEA from theory to Execution", ASQ Quality Press, Milwaukee, Wisconsin, 1995, ISBN: 087389300X
9. Hecht, H. Xuegao A. and Hecht, M. "Computer-Aided Software FMEA", SoHaR Incorporated, Culver City CA Los Angeles, May, 2003,
10. Travassos, Guilherme H., Shull, Forrest, Carver, Jeffrey R., Basili, V.R.: "Reading Techniques for OO Design Inspections", Proceedings of the Twenty-fourth Annual Software Engineering Workshop, 1999.
11. Fowler, M. and Scott, K.: "UML distilled : second edition", Addison-Wesley, ISBN: 0-201-65783-X

RAMALA: A Knowledge Base for Software Process Improvement

Javier Garcia, Yaser Rimawi, Maria Isabel Sánchez, and Antonio Amescua

Computer Science Department, Carlos III University of Madrid, Avda. de la Universidad 30,
28911 Leganes, Madrid, Spain
jgarciag@inf.uc3m.es, yrimawi@gmail.com, misanche@inf.uc3m.es,
amescua@inf.uc3m.es

Abstract. The actual situation of small software organizations in software process definition and improvement is chaotic. Actually, deploying a software process improvement program within such organizations is very difficult, due to its high cost and small ROI percentage that could be obtained. RAMALA is a knowledge base, supported by a software tool called also RAMALA, that contains a software process framework, which is mainly based on the PMBOK process framework [9], detailed by software engineering experts using the best practices of the main software reference models like CMMI [11] and ISO 15504 [3], and enriched with process assets of the most outstanding software development methodologies. RAMALA is a platform where best practices of any software engineering process are recollected in a process definition form. Small software organizations can define, assess and improve their software processes economically using RAMALA.

1 Introduction

Software production in most small software organizations is characterized by poor management and individual skills, which are typical features of the "Software Crisis". These features cause serious problems, such as, project delay, high costs, and poor quality products.

Software community is trying to deal with this problem since almost four decades. In 1968, Nato held a conference in which the term "Software Engineering" was born [7]. Since then, Software Engineering is a growing discipline. Two basic movements have enriched this discipline: technological and process. Programming languages, software tools and techniques characterize the technological movement while the process movement is focused on software process improvement elements and their support activities.

Within the last decade, the process movement has expanded widely in numerous software organizations where it has been proved that the major software problems are due to the inefficient management of the software process. One of the reports of the Department of Defense of the United States of America [1] states: "After two decades of largely unfulfilled promises about productivity and quality gains from applying new software methodologies and technologies, industry and government organizations are realizing that their fundamental problem is the inability to manage the software process".

I. Richardson et al. (Eds.): EuroSPI 2005, LNCS 3792, pp. 106–117, 2005.

Several organizations contribute to the process movement developing reference models and standards like CMM [5] [6], CMMI [11], ISO 15504 [3], and PMBOK [9]. Although there are several software reference models and standards that software organization can implement in order to improve their software processes, few organizations apply them. For example, in the world, just 567 organizations have conducted SCAMPI v1.1 class A appraisals from April 2002 through December 2004 [12]. This small number of organizations is due, among other reasons, to the high cost associated to deploy a software process improvement program.

SEI carried out a study in response to a demand for information on the results of software process improvement efforts [4]. This study covered 13 organizations that represent a variety of maturity levels. The results showed that the average yearly cost of software process improvement was $245,000 and the average number of years engaged in software process improvement was 3.5. This means that implementing a software process improvement program is very expensive, especially for small and medium-sized companies.

The results of another study carried out to calculate the cost of CMM deployment by activities in a conventional IT organization [8] is shown in Table 1.

Table 1. Cost of CMM deployment activities

Activity Category	Percent of Improvement Project Effort
CMM Process Flow Specification	19.90%
CMM Control Flow Specification	13.92%
CMM Data Flow Specification	11.53%
Decision Maker Management	26.70%
Product Related Process Assurance Activity	22.29%
Initial Training	3.48%
On going training	2.18%

As we can see from the table, the first three activities (underlined) are related to process definition and their costs are more than 45% of the total, the cost of the process assurance activity (also underlined) is more than 22%. The cost of these four activities makes up 67.64% of the total cost.

This means that the major part of the cost of deploying the software reference model is the cost of software engineering experts. We believe that this percentage can be reduced, using a knowledge base supported by a software tool where the expert's knowledge can be gathered and managed.

RAMALA knowledge base, supported by a software tool called also RAMALA, gathers the software engineering knowledge needed to deploy a software process improvement program within a software organization. RAMALA knowledge base contains a software process framework, which is mainly based on the PMBOK [9] process framework, detailed by software engineering experts using the best practices of the main software reference models like CMMI [11] and ISO 15504 [3], and enriched with process assets of the most outstanding software development methodologies.

RAMALA knowledge base fulfills three main functionalities in a software process improvement deployment program: process assessment, process definition, and process improvement tracking.

2 RAMALA Knowledge Base

RAMALA knowledge base is the result of a research work developed in the Computer Science Department at Carlos III University of Madrid [13]. Its main scope and goal was to model and develop a software engineering knowledge base for software process improvement supported by a software tool that enable the definition, assessment, and improvement tracking of organization's software processes.

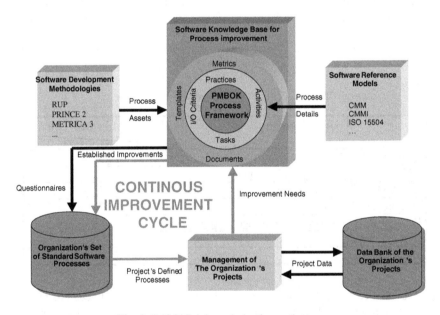

Fig. 1. RAMALA knowledge base structure

RAMALA knowledge base structure is shown in Figure1. As we can see, the process definition functionality is covered by the software knowledge base for process improvement component, where the PMBOK Guide Process Framework [9] is its core. Software engineering experts using the best practices of the software reference models and process assets of the most outstanding software development methodologies detail the process framework.

Implementing a formal assessment method valid for any software reference model covers the process assessment functionality. During the assessment, RAMALA gathers and classifies all process assets in the organization and links them to the related software process elements. Along with the assessment result, which is a color snapshot of the knowledge base, RAMALA provides the organization's set of standard software processes.

The improvement tracking functionality is covered by providing a mechanism to establish the project's defined processes, managing the project's process assets instances, and gathering measure data to verify the fulfillment of the improvements.

RAMALA knowledge base is described in more details in the following sections.

2.1 Software Engineering Knowledge Base for Software Process Improvement

In order to build a standard and robust software engineering knowledge base for software process improvement, we think that it had to satisfy the following requirements:

1. Standard structure for software reference models
2. Standard process framework
3. Formal process definition

2.1.1 Standard Structure for Software Reference Models
RAMALA uses a generic data model where it is able to save in one repository all the elements of each software reference model; in this way organizations could have in one tool several reference models like CMM [5] [6], CMMI [11], and ISO 15504 [3].

2.1.2 Standard Process Framework
Software reference models help organizations to define their software processes, but organizations need a standard framework to define these processes in an integrated way.

The Project Management Institute (PMI) has developed an international project management standard: the Project Management Body of Knowledge (PMBOK) Guide [9]. This standard offers a process framework where all the necessary processes to manage any project are identified with all their dependencies. RAMALA uses the PMBOK Guide as its standard process framework

The PMBOK Guide just cover the project management process area, it does not cover in detail the rest of engineering process areas involved in the software development process. We believe that the main process area within the software development process is the project management process area, and that engineering process areas are support processes that the project management process area uses in different moments.

What we do is extend the PMBOK process framework integrating process frameworks for each engineering process area involved in the software development process.

With the new extended PMBOK process framework and the practices of a selected software reference model, software engineering experts detail all processes within the process framework creating a meta software process definition.

RAMALA has several meta software process definitions according to the number of software reference models stored in it.

2.1.3 Formal Process Definition
RAMALA uses the Entry Task Verification eXit (ETVX) definition process technique [10], which has the advantage that it can be extended by adding more

process definition elements that help us to obtain a meta process definition. The process definition elements that RAMALA uses are:

- Purpose
- Preceding Processes/Activities
- Subsequent Processes /Activities
- Entry Criteria
- Inputs
- Activities / Tasks
- Outputs
- Exit Criteria

- Practices
- Tools and techniques
- Metrics/Measurements
- Interfaces with other processes
- Roles
- Notes

In order to enrich process definitions, RAMALA permits linking process assets of any software development methodology to some process elements (those underlined), i.e. RAMALA as a software engineering knowledge base gathers, and classifies process assets like templates, documents, or metrics of different software development methodologies such as Prince 2, METRICA 3, RUP, etc., and links them to the corresponding process elements. RAMALA provides these process assets to organizations to adapt them or improve their own process assets.

2.2 Definition and Assessment of Organization's Software Process

In order to enable organizations obtain an assessment and a definition of their actual software process, we think that RAMALA had to fulfill the following requirements:

1. Formal software assessment method
2. Process asset manager

2.2.1 Formal Software Assessment Method

In order to determine the actual capacity of the organization's software process according to a certain software reference model, we have to use a formal assessment method that covers the selected software reference model. RAMALA has stored in its knowledge base several software reference models that organizations can select to determine the capacity of their software processes. This means that there must be at least a formal assessment method for each software reference model stored in RAMALA, which makes RAMALA a complex tool. To solve this problem, RAMALA implements the Formal Approximation for Software Process Improvement method [2]. This is a generic assessment method that covers any software reference model stored in RAMALA.

The assessment result will be a color snapshot of the meta process definition of the selected software reference model where colors reflect the fulfillment degree of each process generic or specific practice.

Along with the assessment result, the organization will also obtain the definition of their standard software processes that will be a subset of the RAMALA meta process definition of the selected software reference model.

2.2.2 Process Asset Manager

RAMALA, during the assessment, gathers and classifies all direct evidences that indicate the implementation of the selected software reference model practices creating the organization's process assets repository, i.e. all documents and templates are gathered during the assessment and associated with the corresponding process elements within the organization's set of standard software processes. Also, organizations will have available process assets of different software development methodologies that can use to adapt or improve their own process assets.

The assessment result will be a color snapshot of the meta process definition of the selected software reference model where colors reflect the fulfillment degree of each process element.

2.3 Tracking of Implemented Software Process Improvements

In order to assure that new implemented software processes are institutionalized within the organization, we think that RAMALA had to satisfy the following requirements:

1. Project's defined processes mechanism
2. Process improvement tracking mechanism

2.3.1 Project's Defined Processes Mechanism

Once the organization's set of standard software processes is established, it has to be improved continuously according to the results of its own projects, where project results determine the processes' strengths and weaknesses.

For each project, RAMALA allows the organization establish the project's defined processes that will be a subset of the organization's set of standard software processes. Project results and documents will be stored in RAMALA as instances of the corresponding organization's process assets. In this case, RAMALA will also act as an historical database that helps project managers manage current and future projects.

Analyzing projects results stored in RAMALA, software process improvement plans can be developed and later implemented.

2.3.2 Process Improvement Tracking Mechanism

Once software improvement plans are implemented, it is necessary to have evidence that improvements have really been implemented and followed. RAMALA helps organizations in this aspect by making queries and comparisons on instances of the project's process assets, gathering and analyzing measure data in order to track the improvement fulfillment.

3   How to Use RAMALA Knowledge Base

The most important features in using RAMALA will be described in this section. RAMALA software applies the Application Service Provider (ASP) concept, where what software organizations only need is an Internet browser and an Internet connection. Software organizations, before signing on RAMALA, can make a tour within the knowledge base. Once, they sign on, the first thing that a software organization had to do is selecting a software reference model that wants to follow. Actually, RAMALA knowledge base has stored CMMI and ISO 15504 models. Figure 2 shows elements of the CMMI as a selected software reference model.

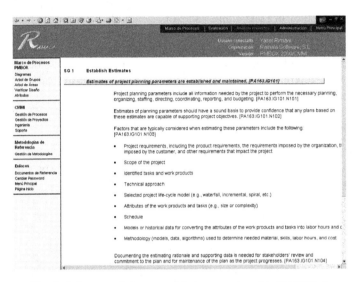

Fig. 2. Software reference model elements stored in RAMALA

RAMALA, as described before, has stored for each software reference model a meta software process definition based on the PMBOK process framework. The relevant next step that the software organization should do is selecting a set of processes that whish to assess. Figure 3 shows how processes are selected for assessment in RAMALA.

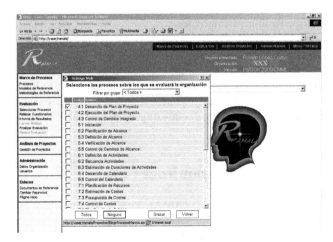

Fig. 3. Selecting processes from the PMBOK process framework for assessment

In order to carry out the assessment, special members of the organization had to fulfill a detailed questionnaire for each process selected and its elements. During the assessment, direct evidences (organization's process assets), which indicate that the organization is satisfying the software reference model practices are collected, classified, associated to the corresponding software process elements, and stored within the organization's particular knowledge base in RAMALA. Once the organization finish filling questionnaires, an automatic algorithm is executed, which calculates the capacity of each process and its elements. Figure 4 shows a report with the process capacity.

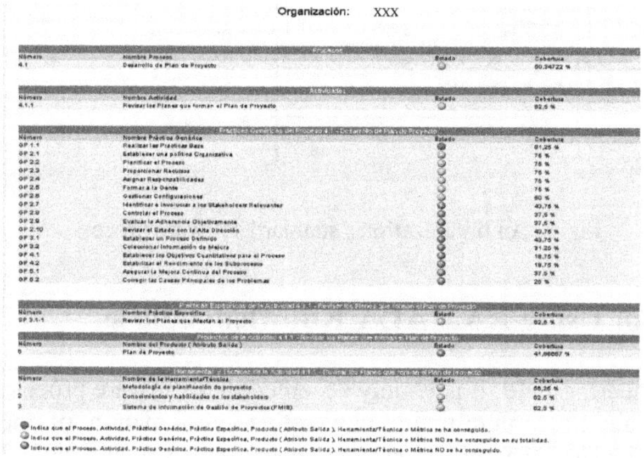

Fig. 4. Organization software process capacity

Along with the assessment results, the organization will obtain its own software engineering knowledge base where the definition of its set of standard software processes is stored as a color snapshot of the meta software process.

Later, the organization can manage its own knowledge base adapting its process assets. RAMALA offers process assets of the most outstanding software development methodologies that the organization can use to adapt their own process assets. Figure 5 shows an organization's process description stored within its knowledge base.

Once the organization implements a software process improvement plan based on the assessment results, RAMALA helps organizations assure the institutionalizing of the new processes acting as an historical database of organization projects' software process assets instances. An organization that uses RAMALA can:

1. Create projects
2. Establish the project's defined processes for each project
3. Gather project's results (process assets instances) and associate them to the corresponding project's defined process elements.
4. Analyzing project's results
5. Determine the fulfillment degree of new implemented processes.

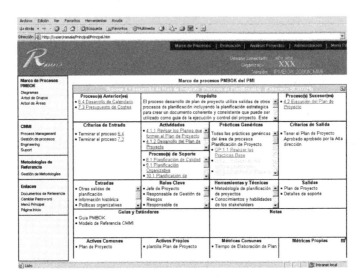

Fig. 5. An organization's standard software process

4 Benefits of Using RAMALA Knowledge Base

In software engineering field, it is widely accepted that software process improvement should contemplate the commitment and active participation of the organization personnel at all levels. Therefore, as a process improvement tool of the software organization, RAMALA has to be productive at all levels of the organization: strategic, tactical and operative.

- At the strategic level, because management, as the driving force of software process improvement, has to decide on the strategic objectives of the organization's software project improvement. At this level RAMALA provides the mechanisms to define the improvement objectives and track the evolution of the improvement.

  Consequently, at this level, the model sought to obtain evidence to ensure that RAMALA:

  - Identifies the weaknesses of the current software project management processes.
  - Helps to continuously track the improvement actions.
  - Provides adequate mechanisms for the original knowledge management of the organization's software project management.

  The decision makers of 8 software organizations in which the RAMALA model was used were surveyed to compile evidence. At this level, those surveyed should be the decision makers who determine the strategy of the organization and are committed to carrying out an improvement programme. As there are few of this type of public objective, the sample (8 people) collected is representative, because the access to this kind of people (Software Company High Level Manager, CEO or someone with similar responsibilities) is difficult and its number is low.

Generally speaking, it is important to indicate that everyone surveyed knew the improvement models and they all appreciated that the approach and focus of the RAMALA model offered significant improvement over the rest of the models they know.

In every case, they also considered that the process defined in RAMALA for process definition is useful and easy for top management and strategic consultants who are responsible for defining the organization's strategies.

With regards to the use of the knowledge base as a support for the RAMALA model, top management and the strategic consultants evaluated positively (85%) the possibility of defining quantifiable objectives for process improvement and providing metrical objectives for the organization's software process improvement in real time.

To confirm the validity of the results, the disparity between the answers was studied. As the disparity in the answers obtained is 0.33 out of 1.2 (less than 30%), so we can state that the level of dispersion is low, and, consequently, we can consider the results to be representative.

- At the tactical level because middle management plan, control and track the organization's different software projects undertaken. At this level RAMALA provides efficient mechanisms for software project management process definition and assessment of the efficiency and quality of the work procedures to carry out the projects mentioned.

  Therefore, at this level, the aim of the model was to gather evidence to ensure:
  – the process representation capacity with RAMALA.
  – the evaluation capacity of the organization's current practice with RAMALA.

  The team leaders responsible for improvement or the experts in software improvement processes who had used the RAMALA tool filled in questionnaires in order to gather evidence. Eleven questionnaires were registered.

  To assess the results of the capacity verification of the RAMALA tool, the data gathered from the evaluation questionnaires filled in by the 11 improvement team managers or the software improvement experts were analyzed.

  All of them were familiar with software improvement methods and all rated the RAMALA model positively. The representation capacity and software project management process assessment which the RAMALA model offers were analyzed separately.

  At a general level, the representation capacity of the RAMALA software was considered to be high and capable of meeting the organization's objectives. In this respect, therefore, all the replies were rated HIGH or VERY HIGH. Only 10% of the replies were partially unfavourable.

  The analysis of the RAMALA's capacity to assess the quality and efficiency of an organization's software project management processes were rated very high. At the same time, 37.5% of those surveyed thought that the results with RAMALA reflected reality and were very easy to understand, while 62.5% considered them useful, in general terms.

- At the operational level, in the field of research, the activities consisted of designing and implementing project management work procedures and instructions. Thus, at this level, the aim of the model was to gather data to verify effort reduction RAMALA provides in the definition and implementation of project management processes.

During this validation phase, the researchers controlled the effort spent by seven groups in charge of defining and implementing a software project management process using RAMALA was analyzed. This data was obtained from seven teams, totalizing 32 people. This information, obtained from set of workgroups, was checked against the information gathered from other workgroups that, in the previous months, had to define and implement a software project management process without using RAMALA. This control data was obtained from six teams, grouping 33 people.

The effort data used for this validation was accounted using an effort registry form (specially designed for this purpose) that had to be filled in each week by each member of the working groups. Table 2 shows the effort the software project management processes definition and implementation work teams accumulated.

Table 2. Effort of Software Process Improvement activities

	Number of Groups	Time (minutes)	Average (minutes)
Without Ramala	6	62099	10349,8
With Ramala	7	44706	6386,5

Analyzing table 2, we can say that RAMALA reduces costs in assessing and defining the organization's set of standard software processes. RAMALA offers a simple formal software process assessment method, where as a result, the organization can obtain its software process definition that can be maintained and updated easily.

5   Conclusion

In this work, we have presented RAMALA knowledge base, which contains all the necessary knowledge to carry out all the software process improvement activities. RAMALA permits:

– Assess and define the organization's set of standard software processes with respect to the most outstanding software reference models like CMMI [11], ISO 15505 [3], and the most important project management standard: the PMBOK Guide [9].
– Gather all the software development knowledge of the organization (process assets) and associate them with the corresponding process elements.
– Provide software organizations with a software development thesaurus to re-use methodologies, standards, and products.
– Identify for each project the processes and activities needed to be carried out.
– Store all the project's results in an historical database in order to be used in future projects.
– Assure software process institutionalizing.

References

[1] Dept. of Defense United States, *"Report of the Defense Science Board Task Force on Military Software"*, Office Secretary of Defense for Acquisition, Sept.1987.

[2] Javier Garcia, *"Formal Approximation for Software Process Improvement"* Ph.D. Thesis, Carlos III University of Madrid, November 2001.

[3] International Organisation for Standardization. *"ISO/IEC 15504 Software Process Improvement and Capability dEtermination Model (SPICE)"*, 1997.

[4] J. Herbsleb, A. Carleton, J. Rozum, J. Siegel, and D. Zubrow, *"Benefits of CMM-Based Software Process Improvement: Initial Results (CMU/SEI-94-TR-013)"*. Software Engineering Institute. 1994.

[5] M. C. Paulk, B. Curtis, M. B. Chrissis, and C. V. Weber, *"Capability Maturity Model for Software, Version 1.1 (CMU/SEI-93-TR-024)"*, Software Engineering Institute, 1993.

[6] M. C. Paulk, B. Curtis, M. B. Chrissis, and C. V. Weber, *"Capability Maturity Model for Software, Version 1.1 (CMU/SEI-93-TR-025)*, Software Engineering Institute, 1993.

[7] P. Naur, and B. Randell, *"Software Engineering: Report of a conference sponsored by the NATO Science Committee"*, NATO Scientific Affairs Division, Belgium, October 1968.

[8] P. Roshan, *"The Cost of CMM in a Conventional IT Organisation: A Field Study"*, Ph.D. Thesis, University of Detroit Mercy, 2002.

[9] Project Management Institute. *"A guide to the project management body of knowledge (PMBOK)"*, ISBN: 1-880410-22-2, 2000.

[10] R. Radice, N. Roth, Jr. O'Hara, and W. Ciarfella, *"A Programming Process Architecture"*. IBM Systems Journal, 24(2), pp 79-90, 1985.

[11] Software Engineering Institute. *"CMMI for Systems Engineering, Software Engineering, Integrated Product and Process Development, and Supplier Sourcing"*, March 2002.

[12] Software Engineering Institute. *"Process Maturity Profile CMMI V1.1 SCAMPI V1.1 Appraisal Results 2004 Year End Update"*, Carnegie Mellon University, March 2005.

[13] Yaser Rimawi, *"RAMALA: A Model for Software Project Management Process Improvement"* Ph.D. Thesis, Carlos III University of Madrid, September 2004.

A Process Based Model for Measuring
Process Quality Attributes

A. Selcuk Guceglioglu and Onur Demirors

Informatics Institute, Middle East Technical University, Inonu Bulvari,
06531, Ankara, Turkey, +90 312 210 3741
aselcuk@ieee.org, demirors@metu.edu.tr

Abstract. Organizations frequently use product based organizational performance models to measure the effects of information system (IS) on their organizations. This paper introduces a complementary process based approach that is founded on measuring business process quality attributes. These quality attributes are defined on the basis of ISO/IEC 9126 Software Product Quality Model. The new process quality attributes are applied in an experiment and results are discussed in the paper.

1 Introduction

IS capabilities have been advancing at a rapid rate and motivating organizations to investment in IS. In 2002, $780 billion was spent for IS in the United States alone [1]. Although IS expenditures seem quite high, there are few systematic guidelines to measure the organizational impact of IS investments [2], [3]. Available studies on organizational impact of IS focus on the product based organizational performance models to manage IS investment. These studies provide organizations with guidelines for measuring cost and time related issues, but they have some constraints in identifying IS effects, isolating the contributions of IS effects from other contributors and using the performance measures in specific categories of organizations such as in public organizations. DeLone & McLean IS Success Model, one of the most well known models for measuring the IS effects, states these difficulties and emphasizes that the studies for measuring IS effects on the organizations are at the initial stage and much work is needed [2], [4].

In this paper, a complementary process-based approach, developed to measure the effects of IS on business process, is discussed. This new approach focuses on the quality aspects of the processes. As business processes are one of the most fundamental assets of organizations, modifications performed on them whether in the way of improvements or innovations cause immediate effects on the success of the organizations. This approach therefore enables organizations to get early feedback for the potential IS investment.

Our studies in the literature demonstrated the lack of business process attribute based frameworks for measuring process quality. As there are close relationships between software and business processes [5], we also investigated software quality frameworks as a potential to measure process quality. ISO/IEC 9126 Software

I. Richardson et al. (Eds.): EuroSPI 2005, LNCS 3792, pp. 118–129, 2005.

Product Quality Model [6] is one of them. This model presents a comprehensive specification and evaluation framework for ensuring software product quality. The structure of the model that we have developed is based on the ISO/IEC 9126. After the evaluation of the ISO/IEC 9126, some software quality metrics that can be used for measuring process quality are chosen. The business process quality attributes are defined according to these selected metrics and then, guidelines of how they can be measured are detailed. In order to observe the applicability of the model and to measure the attributes, the model is applied to a sample business process.

In the remaining chapters of the paper first, related search is summarized as a background to depict the relation of our model within the IS literature. The business process concept is summarized and IS effects on business process are defined. Secondly, the new model is introduced and its measurement categories are given. Thirdly, implementation of the model and its results are summarized. Finally, conclusions and future works are stated.

2 Background

2.1 Measuring the Effects of IS

There are some models for measuring the effects of IS in the literature. One of the most widely known of them is DeLone and McLean IS Success Model [2], [4]. With this model, they introduce a comprehensive taxonomy to organize different research studies as well as to present a more integrated view of the IS success concept. This taxonomy has six major dimensions of IS success as System Quality, Information Quality, Information Use, User Satisfaction, Individual Impact and Organizational Impact. Available studies in Organizational Impact dimension include organizational performance based models and measures. These studies concentrate on the effects of IS for creating organizational changes and relations of these changes with the firm level output measures such as productivity growth and market value [3]. There are some limitations in these present studies for measuring IS effects. The first one is limited understanding of the IS effects. The focus on the firm level output variables, while important, does not clearly identify IS effects on organizations and its working. The second one is difficulty of isolating contributions of the IS effects from other contributors on the organizational performance. The third one is difficulties of using the organizational performance measures in public organizations. As the economic criteria are not so meaningful for these nonprofit organizations, especially government agencies, only productivity gains can be used to measure the effects of IS on the such organizations [7]. In this circumstance, DeLone & McLean IS Success Model states that the studies in Organizational Impact dimension are at beginning stage and much work is required to be done in categorizing and measuring the changes in the organizations and work practices, and to establish their relations with IS.

Another well-known model is Seddon's IS Effectiveness Matrix [8]. He proposes a two-dimensional matrix for classifying IS effectiveness measures. The first dimension is the type of system studied and the second dimension is the stakeholder whose interest the system is being evaluated. This matrix emphasizes that different stakeholders in an organization may validly come to different conclusions about the success of the same IS and, therefore, he suggests measuring IS effectiveness of the systems according to the stakeholders' criteria. In similar to the DeLone & McLean model, this model focuses on the organizational performance based measures such as firm growth, return on assets, percent change in labor, and market share.

In addition to the product based models mentioned in IS Success Models, there are also process oriented studies for assessing IS effects on the organizations. Mooney's study is of them [9]. Although IS effects on business processes are dealt with in this study, it is not precisely defined to measure these effects on the process. The changes occurred in organizations due to IS effects are given in conceptual level. The other process based approaches [10], [11], [12] assess the IS effects on the organizations, but they do not focus on the process attributes in detail for measuring the IS effects.

2.2 Business Process and IS Effects

Davenport [13] defines process as "a structured, measured set of activities designed to produce a specified output for a particular customer or market," and business process as "a set of logically related tasks performed to achieve a defined business outcome." These definitions imply a strong emphasis on how work is done within an organization. Another implication is about measurement of the activities. On the other hand, Hammer [14] concentrates on the importance of the business process oriented thinking and emphasizes that organizations must arrange and manage themselves around the axis of the business process, in order to achieve the performance levels that customers now demand.

There are some factors which affect business processes, and IS is one of the most considerable of them [9]. When available studies are investigated, it is noticed that few of them have focused on interactions between the IS effects and business processes. However, IS affects both operational and managerial processes. IS influences operational processes by automating them with providing technologies of work flow systems, flexible manufacturing, data capture devices, imaging and computer aided design tools (CAD). IS can improve the efficiency of the operational processes through automation or enhance their effectiveness and reliability by establishing linkage among them. Similarly, IS influences managerial processes by providing electronic mail, database and decision support tools. These tools improve the efficiency and effectiveness of communications and decisions. These examples clarify the effects of IS on business processes, especially in process improvement studies, but the effects of IS are not limited to only automational supports in process improvement. IS is also recognized as having a critical role in business process reengineering efforts, primarily as an enabler of new operational and managerial processes [13].

The effects of IS on the business processes can be categorized. For instance, Davenport [13] concentrates on the effects of IS in business process reengineering perspective and identifies nine opportunities for business process innovation through IS effects as automational, informational, sequential, tracking, analytical, geographical, integrative, intellectual, and disintermediating. In another categorization [9], IS can have three separate but complementary effects on business processes. First, automational effects refer to the efficiency perspective in the business process changes with the role of IS effects. The automational effects are derived primarily from impacts such as productivity improvements, labor savings, and cost reductions. Second, informational effects emerge primarily from IS's capacity to collect, store, process, and disseminate information. Following these operations, effects are accrued from improved decision quality, employee empowerment, decreased use of resources, enhanced organizational effectiveness, and better quality. Third, transformational effects refer to the business process changes with IS's ability to facilitate and support process innovation and transformation. The business process changes associated with these effects will be manifested as reduced cycle times, improved responsiveness, downsizing, and service and product enhancement.

3 A Process Based Model for Measuring IS Effects on Business Process Quality

The definitions of business process quality attributes constitute main point of our model. At the beginning, Goal Question Metric (GQM) method [15] was used to find out these attributes. Some of the attributes were defined such as complexity, dependency, and accuracy, but, in order to present a more complete and widely acceptable attribute set, we extended our model by utilizing ISO/IEC 9126 Software Product Quality Model [6]. The close relationships between software product and business process [5] helped us. For instance, both of them have logical structures with inputs, operations and outputs whether in the form of functions or activities. The "software product" logically matches with "business process", and "function" of software product with "activity" of business process. A similar relation between software product and function exists in the business process and activity as "activity is one of the subunits or functions of the business process and represents a logical completeness in its context." They constitute a part of the whole and have interactions with other parts. In addition, high quality is of prime importance for both of them.

3.1 Measurement Structure of the Model

The model is designed in four-leveled structure that is similar to the ISO/IEC 9126. The first level is called as category. There is one category as "quality". The second level is called as characteristic. The quality category includes Functionality, Reliability, Usability and Maintainability characteristics. The third level is for subcharacteristics and finally, fourth level is for metrics to measure the business process quality attributes. The quality category is given with its levels in Figure 1.

Functionality characteristic is defined for evaluating the capability of the process to provide functionality properties in the subcharacteristics of Suitability, Information Technology (IT) based Functionality, Accuracy, Interoperability and Security. Suitability metrics are used for ensuring that business process activities are complete and adequate for performing the tasks. IT-based Functionality metrics examine the IT usages in the process activities. Accuracy metrics investigate the capability of the process to achieve correct or agreeable results. Interoperability metrics investigate the capability of the process interactions with other processes and problems experienced during the interactions. The interoperability can be seen as dependency of a process

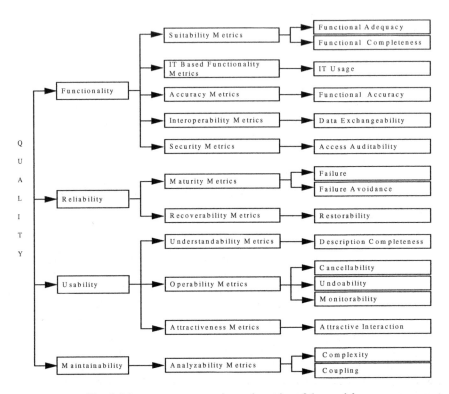

Fig. 1. Measurement categories and metrics of the model

to other processes. Security metrics investigate protecting information and data so that unauthorized persons or systems cannot read or modify them and authorized persons or systems are not denied access to them.

Reliability characteristic is used for evaluating the capability of the process to provide reliability properties in the subcharacteristics of Maturity and Recoverability. Maturity metrics investigate the failures that may happen in the process activities and failure avoidance mechanisms employed for preventing from the failures. Recoverability metrics investigate the capability of the process to continue with minimum data lost when abnormal events occur. The restorability mechanisms provide re-establishing an adequate level of performance and recovering the data in case of a failure.

Usability characteristic is used for evaluating the capability of the process to provide usability properties in the subcharacteristics of Understandability, Operability and Attractiveness. Understandability metrics investigate the understandability of the process activities. This subcharacteristic assesses that new users can understand whether the process is suitable, and how it can be used for particular tasks. Operability metrics investigate the capability of the process to be operated and controlled. The possibility of the process activities cancellability prior to completion of the activity, the possibility of the process activities undoability after completion of the activity and the monitoring the status of the process activities are investigated in the scope of this subcharacteristic.

Attractiveness metrics investigate the capability of the process to attract the users with its documents' structures and/or user interfaces' designs.

Maintainability characteristic is used for evaluating the capability of the process to provide maintainability properties in the subcharacteristic of Analyzability. Analyzability metrics investigate the maintainer's or user's spent effort and resources in trying to diagnose for deficiencies or causes of failure, or for identification of parts to be modified in the process. The measurement of this subcharacteristic gives insights about the comprehensibility of process activities and interconnections between other processes.

In the model, all attributes are defined and tabulated with the information of metric name, purpose, application, measurement and interpretation. In order to present a short summary, only four sample metrics, one example metric for each characteristic, are given in Table 1. The full detailed descriptions about categories, characteristics, subcharacteristics and metrics are given in the Technical Report [16].

Table 1. Additional information about four sample metrics

Metric Name	Purpose	Application	Measurement	Interpretation
Functional Adequacy	Investigating the business process for determining functional adequacy	Count the number of activities that are not functionally adequate, and compare with the number of activities	$X=1-A/B$ A= Number of activities in which problems about functional adequacy are detected in evaluation, B= Number of activities	$0 <= X <= 1$ The closer to 1, the more functional adequacy of the business process
Failure Avoidance	Investigating the business process for determining failure avoidance mechanisms	Count the number of mechanisms that will provide failure avoidance	$X=$Number of failure avoidance mechanisms	The higher value of X, the more failure avoidance of the business process
Monitorability	Investigating the business process for determining monitorability status	Count the number of activities whose status can not be monitored and compare with the number of activities	$X=1- A/B$ A=Number of activities whose status can not be monitored, B=Number of activities	$0 <= X <= 1$ The closer to 1, the better monitoring capability of the business process
Complexity	Calculating the complexity of the business process	Find complexity of the business process by means of cyclomatic complexity technique [17]	$X=$Cyclomatic complexity of the business process (number of decision points)	The lower value of complexity, the better

4   The Implementation of the Model for Measuring IS Effects on a Sample Business Process

4.1   Information About the Implementation

The implementation of the model is accomplished on a sample business process in an organization [16]. In the implementation, a business process, named as "Meeting Material Request", is selected from Warehouse Department of the organization. In addition to Warehouse Department, this organization has 5 more departments. Each department has its own head manager, secretary and other staff in sections according to their duties. While the departments are performing their tasks, they meet material needs from the Warehouse Department. For this purpose, department secretaries communicate with Warehouse department secretary to inform the material requests. Warehouse Department is organized to meet these material requests and also purchase new material, repair and maintain existing material and produce special purpose material. It has approximately 40 staff and 7 basic business processes about material operations including Material Purchasing, Material Counting, Material Registration, Material Record Deletion, Material Return, Material Repair and Maintenance.

In the implementation of the model, static business process definitions were used. The implementation was performed in the two stages. In the first stage, the current state (AS-IS) of the process, Meeting Material Request, was taken into consideration. This process has 29 activities. Each activity was clearly identified by explaining with actors who took part in, forms, tools and applications that were used in. Unified Modeling Language (UML) Activity Diagram was used for modeling the process. When the modeling of the process was examined, it was recognized that the process had document based manual works and nonintegrated software tools. The same data is kept in more than one place such as in private inventory records. All departments keep their material movements in department stock cards in addition to Warehouse Department. These problems increase the number of activities and cycle time. The new model was applied to the AS-IS modeling of process and quality attributes were measured by evaluating its activities and the attributes definitions in the model. The quantified attributes' values address the hidden problems and duplications in the process.

In the second stage, a new form (TO-BE) of process was modeled according to specifications of an IS project. In the IS project, an integrated workflow was defined and endorsed by a software application and a central database. The numbers of document-based works are decreased and data is kept only in one place that can be accessed by users in accord with their privileges. There is also decline in the number of activities (from 29 to 24). Similar to the first stage, the process modeling of the new process was drawn and quality attributes were calculated. The new values of the attributes depict the effects of IS on the process.

4.2   Results of the Implementation

The results of the first characteristic, functionality, are given in Table 2. The common desirable features of the functionality metrics are their closeness to the 1.

Table 2. Results of the functionality characteristic

Subcharacteristic	Attribute	AS-IS	TO-BE
Suitability	Functional Adequacy	0.793	0.916
	Functional Completeness	0.759	0.875
IT Based Functionality	IT Usage	0.241	0.667
Accuracy	Functional Accuracy	0.518	0.792
Interoperability	Data Exchangeability	0.857	1
Security	Access Auditability	0.931	1

AS-IS results of the functional characteristics can reveal some beneficial insights about the present state of the process. Access Auditability of the activities is near to 1. It can be considered as satisfactory. The accesses of the users to the resources such as reading or updating inventory records and document record books are under the control. Unlike the Access Auditability, IT Usage is the most far away from 1. This low value shows improvement opportunities. On the other hand, another low value is about Functional Accuracy. It shows that process has critical functional accuracy problems and needs to be improved. The results of Functional Adequacy and Functional Completeness are close to each other and also to 1. It can be said that process activities are almost adequate and complete. The last result is for Data Exchangeability. Its value emphasizes that the business process can be interoperable with other processes in the Warehouse Department.

When TO-BE results of the functional characteristics are compared with the AS-IS counterparts, some improvements take attention. The most improved results are about IT Usage and Functional Accuracy. The use of workflow in software system with a central database provides controlled and consistent environment to the users. This reduces the user based errors and misconceptions. The use of material code, automatic inventory record update and sharing resources instantaneously guide users. The effects of IS can also be observed in Access Auditability and Data Exchangeability values. As users are defined in the system with proper roles and responsibilities and their accesses to the resources are performed with the username and password, Access Auditability attribute equals to 1. Data Exchangeability also equals to 1 as it has no problems during the interactions between Material Purchase and Material Registration processes. The inputs and outputs between the processes are automated and also can be monitored by users. Other improvements occurred in Functional Adequacy and Functional Completeness attributes. The process activities are redefined and their incompleteness are reduced and more compact activities are formed.

AS-IS results of the reliability characteristics are given in Table 3. Failure attribute shows the number of user based errors. These errors hinder the process from reaching the expected results. According to the measurement, 23 failures may be happened in the process (one activity may have more than one failure). When the failures are investigated, it is recognized that most of the failures are originated from users such as writing incorrect material name, updating incorrect material number and delivering wrong material. The second attribute is Failure Avoidance. 6 Failure Avoidance mechanisms are detected in the current state of the process such as using the previous document template. The last attribute is about Restorability. There is 1 Restorability mechanisms as daily backups of inventory records to floppy disks.

In the TO-BE column of the reliability, failure attribute value decreases to 11. The IS project on the process limits the number of user based errors. For instance, user cannot deliver a material that is not selected in Material Request Form, and software itself accomplishes automatic inventory records updating. Another improvement occurs in the second attribute. New Failure Avoidance mechanisms can be defined in the workflow of the software such as selecting material code from Material Catalogue rather than writing material name and its characteristics. The value of third attribute, Restorability, seems not changed after the implementation of IS project. Although it has the same value, the process has more sophisticated daily database backup utility and also instantaneous transaction logs.

AS-IS results of the third characteristic, usability, are given in Table 4. According to the results, Description Completeness attribute is near to 1. It can be said that process can be understandable with its current definitions. This thought may be supported by Attractiveness Interaction attribute with its high value. The other attributes that are close to 1 are Cancellability and Undoability. These attributes show that the process activities can be undone or canceled before they are completed. On the other hand, Monitorability attribute has the lowest value. This indicates that status of the process activities cannot be monitored satisfactorily.

Table 3. Results of the reliability characteristic

Subcharacteristic	Attribute	AS-IS	TO-BE
Maturity	Failure	23	11
	Failure Avoidance	6	9
Recoverability	Restorability	1	1

In the TO-BE column, the most increase happens in the value of Monitorability attribute. The users can now follow the status of their request easily in the software such as following Material Request Form's status (as "initial", "met", "rejected", "to be delivered" and "to be bought"). There are other increases in the values of Description Completeness and Attractive Interaction. The users have more complete activity descriptions and user-friendly interfaces. Some of the fields in the forms are filled by the software automatically such as form number, date and department name. The other fields are whether selected from combo boxes such as material code or entered by users. This new environment presents users more understandable process activities. Although there are increases in most of the attributes' values, the values of Cancellability and Undoability attributes slightly decrease. The new form of the process presents users more controlled activities with cancellability and undoability facilities.

Table 4. Results of the usability characteristic

Subcharacteristic	Attribute	AS-IS	TO-BE
Understandability	Description Completeness	0.828	0.875
Operability	Cancellability	0.793	0.792
	Undoability	0.793	0.792
	Monitorability	0.138	0.584
Attractiveness	Attractive Interaction	4 good, 4 very good	8 very good

AS-IS results of the fourth characteristic, maintainability, are given in Table 5. Complexity attribute indicates the number of decision points as 3. The other attribute, Coupling, implies the number of business processes that are communicated as 2. As the number of decision points and number of communicated processes do not change in the new form of the process, TO-BE values of the attributes are same with the AS-IS values.

Table 5. Results of the maintainability characteristic

Subcharacteristic	Attribute	AS-IS	TO-BE
Analyzability	Complexity	3	3
	Coupling	2	2

In order to give additional information about the process, cycle time and cost values are measured. Cycle time is calculated by adding the elapsed time in each activity. According to the results, there is a considerable decrease, from 260 minutes in AS-IS to 144 minutes in TO-BE. The reasons of this improvement are decrease in the number of activities (from 29 to 24), increase in the operations that are performed by the software automatically such as updating inventory records, filling some of the fields in the forms (e.g. formal number, date, department name, material name) and monitorability of the activities status (users can learn the status of their requests by following the status field in the software rather than making telephone conversation). The other information is about cost. Although cost includes wide range coverage, we only calculate actors' salary-based cost. The actors' (e.g. department secretary, department manager, store section manager) salary (converting one month salary to minute salary) and elapsed time in each activity are multiplied to find the cost. As there is decrease in cycle time, cost also reduces from \$25.340 in AS-IS to \$16.075 in TO-BE for one cycle.

5   Conclusions

In this paper, a new process based model is developed as a complementary to the available product based models to measure the quality of processes. The model is implemented in an organization to calculate the quality attributes on the sample process. When the effects of IS on processes are considered in process improvement scope, the implementation of the model shows that the new model can be useful in process improvement studies. The changes in the process quality attributes after implementation of a process improvement study demonstrate the impacts of the study. The results of a process improvement study can be used for directing the designs of evolving process improvement studies for decreasing the value of specific attributes (e.g. complexity, and coupling) or increasing the other ones (e.g. IT usage, restorability). In this way, organizations can control process quality attributes and have gradual improvements.

The model can also be used with product based models to evaluate different IS investment alternatives. For this purpose, organizations can apply the model in the evaluations of IS investment alternatives. The product based measurements and results of the model can help the organizations for selecting the most suitable alternatives to their processes.

As a prerequisite, organizations must model their business processes to apply the new model. It may be thought as a possible restriction, but, today, organizations should already have modeling of their processes to follow and improve them. Another possible restriction may be high number of process. This makes difficult the implementation of the model. In this case, a sample business process set can be formed according to the criticality of the processes before applying the model.

In the future, further experiments will be performed to improve the model. These studies provide significant feedbacks to the model. The definitions of the attributes will be more clear and concrete. New measurement categories or attributes can be added to extent the scope of the model. The correlations between the attributes can also be examined and defined. Therefore, the benefits of the model to organizations will increase and organizations will benchmark their quality attributes with other organizations' processes.

References

1. Jeffery, M., Leliveld, I., Best Practices in IT Portfolio Management, MIT Sloan Management Review (2004)
2. DeLone, W.H., McLean, E.R., Information System Success: The Quest for the Dependent Variable, Information Systems Research, 3, 1 (1992) 60-95
3. Brynjolfsson, E., Hitt L., The Three Faces of IT Value: Theory and Evidence, Proceedings of the Fifteenth International Conference on Information Systems, Vancouver, BC (1994) 263-276
4. DeLone, W.H., McLean, E.R., The DeLone and McLean Model of Information Systems Success: A Ten-Year Update, Journal of Management Information Systems, Vol. 19, No. 4 (2003) 9-30
5. Osterweil, L., Software Processes are Software Too, Proceedings of the Ninth International Conference on Software Engineering, Monterey, CA (1987) 2-13
6. ISO/IEC FCD 9126-1.2: Information Technology - Software product quality -Part 1: Quality model

7. Danziger, J. N., Politics, Productivity and Computers: A Contingency Analysis in Local Governments, Proceeding of the Ninth Annual Society for Management Information Systems Conference (1987) 213-221
8. Seddon P.B., Staples S., Patnayakuni R., Bowtell M., Dimensions of Information Systems Success, Communications of the Association for Information Systems, Vol.2 Article 20 (1999)
9. Mooney J.G., Gurbaxani V., Kraemer K.L., A Process Oriented Framework for Assessing the Business Value of Information Technology, The Data Base for Advances in Information Systems, Vol. 27, No. 2 (1996)
10. Beath, C. M., Goodhue, D. L. Ross, J. R., Partnering for business value: The shared management of IS infrastructure. In J. I. DeGross, S. L. Huff and M. C. Munro (Eds.), Proceedings of the Fifteenth International Conference on Information Systems, Vancouver, British Columbia, (1994) 459-460
11. Sambamurthy, V. and Zmud, R. W., IT management competency assessment: A tool for creating business value through IT. Working Paper, Financial Executives Research Foundations (1994)
12. Soh, C. and Markus, M. L., How IT creates business value: A process theory synthesis. Proceedings of the Sixteenth International Conference on Information Systems, Amsterdam, The Netherlands, (1995) 29-42
13. Davenport, T.H., Process innovation: reengineering work through information technology, Boston, Mass: Harvard Business School Press, 062117110523 (1993)
14. Hammer, M., Steven S., The reengineering revolution, New York: Harper Business, 062117110523 (1994)
15. Basili, V.R., Software modeling and measurement: The Goal/Question/Metric paradigm, Technical Report, CS-TR-2956, Department of Computer Science, University of Maryland, College Park, MD 20742 (1992)
16. Demirors, O., Guceglioglu, A.S., A Model for Using Software Quality Characteristic to Measure Business Process Quality, Technical Report, METU/II-TR-2005-08, Department of Information System, University of METU (2005)
17. McCabe, T. J., A Complexity Measure, Software Engineering SE-2, 4 (1976) 308-320

Reference Model for Software Process Improvement: A Brazilian Experience

Ana Regina Rocha, Mariano Montoni, Gleison Santos, Sômulo Mafra,
Sávio Figueiredo, Adriano Albuquerque, and Paula Mian

COPPE/Federal University of Rio de Janeiro,
Caixa Postal 68511 CEP 21945 –970 Rio de Janeiro - RJ, Brazil
{darocha, mmontoni, gleison, somulo, savio, bessa, pgmian}
@cos.ufrj.br

Abstract. Recent research efforts about quality in the software area demonstrate that a concentrated effort is necessary to improve software process. Mainly in Brazil, there is an urge to enhance software processes performance aiming to improve the quality of software products and to increase Brazilian organizations competitive advantages both in the national and international markets. This work describes an approach developed to establish the base for Brazilian organizations to improve software processes. The focus of this work is to increase the software development capability of small and medium size companies in a fast pace. The presented approach consists of the development of a Reference Model for software process improvement and an appraisal method for the Brazilian software industry. This model has been deployed in several Brazilian companies thorough the support of Software Development Environments. The pilot experience and empirical validation results of application of the presented approach are also described in this paper.

1 Introduction

Recent research efforts about quality in the software area demonstrate that a concentrated effort is imperative to improve software process in software development companies [1]. Mainly in Brazil, there is an urge to enhance software processes performance aiming to improve the quality of software products and to increase Brazilian companies' competitive advantages both in the national and international markets. Since 1993, with the foundation of PBQP Software (Subcommittee of Software of the Brazilian Program for Software Quality and Productivity), Brazil invests on Software Quality improvement [2, 3].

Nevertheless, a comparative study of the MIT (Massachusetts Institute of Technology) [4] concluded that Brazilian companies have more interest on ISO 9000 [5] than other models and standards specifically oriented to software. This information is corroborated by the results of a research of the MCT (Ministry of Science and Technology of Brazil). According to this research, the number of software development companies in Brazil in 2003 with ISO 9000 certificate was 214, and the number of companies with SW-CMM (Capability Maturity Model for Software) official evaluations was 30 and none with CMMI (Capability Maturity Model Integration) official evaluation.

I. Richardson et al. (Eds.): EuroSPI 2005, LNCS 3792, pp. 130 – 141, 2005.

Considering the 30 companies with SW-CMM official evaluations, we can verify that at the base of the pyramid there are 24 companies in the Maturity Level 2, and 5 companies in the Maturity Level 3. At the top of the pyramid, there is a single company in the Maturity Level 4 and none at the Maturity Level 5. Beginning in 2006, organizations must start working on implementing CMMI, since the SW-CMM will no longer be supported by the SEI-CMU (Software Engineering Institute – Carnegie Mellon University).

These data evidence that in order to improve software processes in Brazil, there are two major problems to solve: (i) concerning the top of the pyramid, the question to be solved is: *How to significantly increase the number of Brazilian companies with CMMI official appraisals in Maturity Levels 4 and 5 focusing the companies that export software and other large companies?*; (ii) concerning the base of the pyramid, there is another question that needs to be answered: *How to radically improve software processes in Brazil focusing on a significant number of small and medium size companies so that these companies can achieve CMMI Maturity Levels 2 or 3 within feasible costs?*

This work describes an approach to solve the second problem in the context of the Brazilian Software Process Improvement (mps Br) Project. The approach consists of the development of a Reference Model for software process improvement (MR mps Br) and an appraisal method. The MR mps Br has been deployed in several Brazilian companies located in the state of Rio de Janeiro. Moreover, a Software Development Environment (SDE), named **Taba Workstation**, were configured and installed in each of these companies aiming to facilitate and accelerate the software processes definition, deployment, and improvement. In order to evaluate the adequacy of the deployed processes and supporting SDE, a survey was planned and implemented.

The next section presents the mps Br Project main objectives and characteristics. Section 3 presents the Reference Model for Software Process Improvement and the appraisal method developed. The pilot experience concerning the deployment of the presented approach in Brazilian software companies, and the main functionalities of the supporting SDE are presented in section 4. Practical results from MR mps Br deployment in small and medium size Brazilian companies, and the empirical evaluation execution results are presented in section 5. Finally, sections 6 and 7 present some lessons learned, and point out future directions and conclusions, respectively.

2   The mps Br Project

Since 2003, 7 Brazilian institutions, with complementary competencies in software process improvement, have participated in the Brazilian Software Process Improvement (mps Br) Project coordinated by SOFTEX (Association for Promoting the Brazilian Software Excellence), a national entity responsible for the SOFTEX program that coordinates the actions of 31 SOFTEX Agents located in 23 cities of the country and with more than 1,300 associated companies. Among these institutions, there are COPPE/UFRJ and RioSoft.

The mps Br Project aims to improve software processes in small and medium size Brazilian companies within feasible costs. It is not an objective of this project to define something completely new concerning standards and maturity models.

In Brazil, some institutions and a reasonable number of SOFTEX Agents have experience in forming and managing groups of companies aiming to improve software processes through the implementation and certification of ISO 9000 standard [6], and to implement and perform SW-CMM evaluations and CMMI appraisals. From this experiences the mps Br Project was conceived aiming to address two situations: (i) to tailor and deploy a Reference Model for software process improvement (MR mps Br) to companies individually; and (ii) to tailor and deploy the MR mps Br cooperatively in small and medium size companies organized in groups to diminish the deployment costs through the division of the overall costs and facilitation of search for financial support sources.

The mps Br Project consists of 6 phases. The objective of the first phase, concluded in March 2004, was to organize the project, to establish its objectives and to define the first version of the Reference Model. The second phase, concluded in June 2004, had the objective to improve the Reference Model, to start the training activities on the model, and to execute the initial experiments deploying the MR mps Br in software development companies. One of these experiments was executed in Rio de Janeiro and is described in this paper. The other phases consist of parallel deployment of the Reference Model in different parts of the country.

3   The Reference Model for Software Process Improvement

The main objective of the mps Br Project is to create and to disseminate the Reference Model for software process improvement (MR mps Br). It is not an objective of the project, as stated before, to define something new concerning standards and maturity models. The novelty of the project is the strategy adopted for its deployment, which considered the characteristics of Brazilian companies. Besides that, the Model has great potential to be replicated in different regions of Brazil and in other countries with similar characteristics, for instance Latin-American countries.

Therefore, the starting point for the definition of the MR mps Br was the analysis of the characteristics of Brazilian companies, the ISO/IEC 12207 and ISO/IEC 15504 standards, and the CMMI model [7, 8, 9].

The reference standard for the software processes of MR mps Br is the ISO/IEC 12207, i.e., this standard is the framework for the definition of the processes that constitute the MR mps Br. Similarly to the ISO/IEC 12207 standard, the MR mps Br defines fundamental processes, supporting processes and an adaptation process. Each company interested in deploying the MR mps Br should select the pertinent processes from that set according to the adaptation process. The expected results for the deployment of the MR mps Br processes are an adaptation of the expected results of the ISO/IEC 12207 processes and activities.

Seven maturity levels were established in the MR mps Br: Level A (Optimization), Level B (Quantitatively Managed), Level C (Defined), Level D (Largely Defined), Level E (Partially Defined), Level F (Managed), and Level G (Partially Managed). Table 1 illustrates how the five maturity levels of the seven CMMI maturity levels are mapped to MR mps Br maturity levels.

Table 1. Mapping of the MR mps Br maturity levels to CMMI maturity levels

MR mps Br Maturity Levels	CMMI Maturity Levels	Processes Names
A (highest)	5	Organizational Innovation and Deployment, Causal Analysis and Resolution
B	4	Organizational Process Performance, Quantitative Project Management
C	3	Decision Analysis and Resolution, Risk Management
D	3	Requirements Development, Technical Solution, Software Integration, Software Installation, Product Release, Verification, Validation
E	3	Training, Process Assessment and Improvement, Process Establishment, Tailoring Process for Project Management
F	2	Measurement, Configuration Management Acquisition, Quality Assurance
G (lowest)	2	Requirements Management, Project Management

For each of these maturity levels, processes were assigned based on the ISO/IEC 12207 standard and on the process areas of levels 2, 3, 4 and 5 of CMMI staged representation. This division has a different graduation of the CMMI staged representation aiming to enable a more gradual and adequate deployment in small and medium size Brazilian companies. The possibility of rating companies maturity considering more levels, not only diminishes the cost and effort of achieving a certain maturity level, but also allows the visibility of the results of the software process improvement within the company and across the country in a shorter time when compared to other models, such as CMMI. The criteria used to divide the processes across the maturity levels G-C were the importance of the process to the company, the facility to implement it and the dependency of the process to the others.

The MR mps Br Appraisal Method for Process Improvement was defined based on the ISO/IEC 15504 standard. The level of deployment of the expected results related to a specific process is evaluated based on indicators that evidence such deployment. These indicators are defined for each company, related to the expected results of a process, and can be one of the following types: (i) Direct, (ii) Indirect, or (iii) Affirmations. Direct indicators are intermediate work products that result from an activity. Indirect indicators are generally documents that indicate that an activity was executed. Affirmations are results of interviews with the project teams of the evaluated projects.

The implementation of an expected result is evaluated according to four levels: (i) TI – Totally Implemented; (ii) LI – Largely Implemented; (iii) PI – Partially Implemented, and (iv) NI – Not Implemented. The appraisal method adheres completely the ISO/IEC 15504 standard appraisal method [8] defined to the staged representation.

A company is considered mps Br level A, B, C, D, E, F or G if and only if all of its units, divisions or sectors had been rated as such level. Since one or more appraisals can be executed in a company, it is possible that parts of a company are rated with different levels. No matter the appraisal context, the evidential document of the appraisal must explicitly state the objective of the appraisal (appraisal scope), and the maturity level ratings.

In order to execute an appraisal, all completed and on going projects started after the deployment of the MR mps Br in the company or the organization unit to be evaluated must be submitted for the appraisal. During the appraisal planning, the appraiser institution must select a sufficient subset of projects that guarantee the representatively of the company or organization unit to be evaluated. Nevertheless, this number should not be less than two completed projects and two on going projects. The result of an appraisal is valid for two years. After this period, the organization must be evaluated either to maintain the same level, or to try to achieve a higher maturity level.

4 Pilot Experience and Supporting Environment

The MR mps Br was deployed by COPPE/UFRJ in 18 small and medium size companies located in Rio de Janeiro forming two groups organized by RioSoft. These companies shared the same training activities, that constituted 44 hours of classes on Software Engineering topics and 20 hours on the MR mps Br and on the organizational processes to be deployed.

Three strategies for deployment of the processes were defined. Some companies opted for starting their improvement process following rigorously the MR mps Br maturity levels, and, consequently, concentrating their initial efforts on the maturity level G process areas. Another set of companies decided to start the work focusing the maturity levels F and G, i.e., these companies decided to address all process areas equivalent to CMMI maturity level 2. One single company decided to start from the maturity level E, because its processes were already defined and institutionalized. These three strategies are perfectly compatible with the MR mps Br and aligned to mps Br Project objectives.

In order to support the deployment of the model, those companies counted on the software process consultants of COPPE/UFRJ, and the CASE tools integrated into a Software Development Environment, named Taba Workstation [10, 11, 12, 13, 14].

4.1 The Taba Workstation: A Software Development Environment to Support Processes Definition, Deployment, and Improvement

Software Development Environments (SDE) have been playing an important role to support software engineers in the execution of software processes through the application of specific procedures that combine integrated tools and techniques in accordance to particular software paradigms. Moreover, SDE are evolving to integrate knowledge management activities within software processes aiming to support developers to produce better software products based on organizational knowledge and previous experiences more effectively [10].

The Taba Workstation is a SDE created to support individual and group activities, project management activities, enhancement of software products quality, and increase of the productivity, providing the means for the software engineers to control the project and measure the activities evolution based on information gathered across the development. The Taba Workstation also provides the infrastructure to the development and integration of tools to support the execution of software processes. Moreover, this infrastructure maintains a useful repository containing software project information gathered across its life cycle.

In order to support the definition, deployment, and improvement of processes defined according to the Reference Model presented in the last section, the Taba Workstation supports the definition of organizational standard processes and tailoring of these processes to specific projects aiming to increase the control and improve the quality of software products. Therefore, the Taba Workstation not only supports software engineers in the execution of software development processes activities, but also provides the means to execute these processes according to organizational software development processes.

The Taba Workstation evolved during the last years to support knowledge management activities integrated to the software processes aiming to preserve organizational knowledge and foster the institutionalization of a learning software organization. Therefore, the main objectives of Taba Workstation are: (i) to support the configuration of process-centered software development environments for different organizations (Configured SDE); (ii) to support the automatic generation (i.e., instantiation) of software development environments for specific projects (Enterprise-Oriented SDE); (iii) to support software development using the instantiated environment; and (iv) to support the management of organizational knowledge related to software processes.

The Taba Workstation tools offer automated support to: (i) adaptation of the organization standard processes for a specific project; (ii) definition of the organizational structure [10]; (iii) acquisition, filtering, packaging and dissemination of organizational knowledge [10]; (iv) planning the organization of specific projects; (v) time, costs, risks [10], human resources planning, monitoring and control [10]; (vi) planning and execution of Configuration Management activities; (vii) identification of software product quality requirements; (viii) documentation planning; (ix) supporting the planning and monitoring of corrective actions; (x) supporting measurement and analysis activities based on the GQM (Goal-Question-Metric) method; (xi) project monitoring through the generation of periodic reports and measures; (xii) controlling of the activities executed during a specific project; (xiii) requirements management; and (xiv) post mortem analysis.

The figure 1, for instance, presents a screenshot of a tool named AdaptPro aiming to support the institutionalization of the standard processes since it facilitates the adoption of these processes in all the projects of the organization. By using the AdaptPro tool, the software engineering can execute the following activities: (i) characterize the project; (ii) plan the process that will guide the project through the adaptation of the organizational standard process considering the project characteristics; and (iii) instantiate a SDE to support the execution of the planned process. On the left side of figure 1, the system presents the activities that guide the execution of the tool.

On the right side of the figure, the system presents another screen to support the execution of the selected activity; in this case, it is presented the screen that supports the definition of a life cycle model to a specific project as part of the process planning activity. A list of life cycle models and the respective level of adequacy to the project considering its characteristics are presented on the right side of the screen. Besides that, the user can consult the justification of the automatic identification of the adequacy level and can consult the software processes defined for similar projects that used the same specialized process and life cycle model facilitating the selection of an adequate project life cycle model by the user. Moreover, the user can consult knowledge related to life cycle models directly from this screen and register knowledge related to the planning process activity, such as lessons learned.

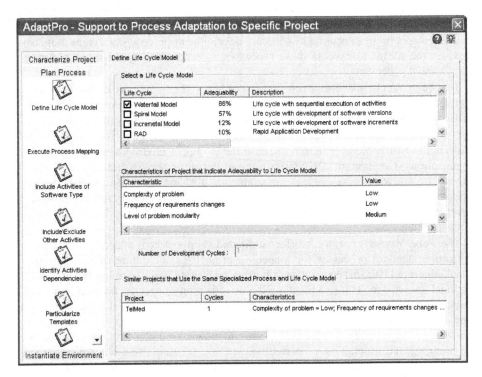

Fig. 1. AdaptPro – a tool to support process adaptation to specific projects

After planning the process, the project manager uses the AdaptPro tool to instantiate the specific process to the project based on its particularities. The product of this tool is the process plan (including adaptations to support the life cycle model chosen) and a SDE to support the execution of the planned process.

The AdaptPro tool, just like the other tools of the **Taba Workstation**, is integrated into the **Taba Workstation** Knowledge Management tools. The practical results obtained from the MR mps Br deployment with the support of the **Taba Workstation** tools are presented in the next section.

5 Practical Results from MR mps Br Deployment in Small and Medium Size Brazilian Companies

The processes deployment in small and medium size companies demonstrated several benefits, such an increase of product and process quality, and preservation of organizational knowledge related to software processes. A direct benefit obtained from the processes deployment can be exemplified by three companies that obtained ISO 9000:2000 certification based on the software process deployed.

The first company to obtain the ISO certification is a software development company that during the previous two years was involved in software processes definition, preparation and deployment without success. One year after the beginning of the mps Br Project, the company obtained the ISO 9000:2000 certification [15].

The second company to obtain the ISO certification is a software development company that already had the ISO 9000:1994 certification and had to be compliant with the ISO 9000:2000 standards in order to renew their certificate. According to the software engineers of the company, the deployed processes and the Taba Workstation support were decisive to obtain the certification renewal, because it has speeded the deployment of software processes, and had facilitated the dissemination of organizational best practices.

The third company to obtain the ISO certification achieved this goal on February of this year. Moreover, a successful SCAMPI official appraisal was conducted on March of this year aiming to evaluate the same company on the CMMI Level 2 process areas [16]. These two evaluations were conducted after only 8 months since the beginning of the processes deployment initial activities.

These results not only demonstrate the feasibility of the deployment of MR mps Br, but also reinforce its compatibility to CMMI process areas and ISO standards. Moreover, the quality of the software processes enhanced because the companies implemented their processes based on standards and maturity models.

Official MR mps Br appraisals are going to be executed aiming to evaluate five companies until the end of this year.

5.1 Empirical Evaluation Results

A survey was planned and executed with the objective to analyze the processes deployed and the Taba Workstation supporting tools, with the purpose of evaluation with respect of the adequacy under the point of view of project managers, system analysts and developers in the context of software engineers executing the deployed processes with the support of the Taba Workstation tools.

The survey was executed through the application of questionnaires to 16 key members of the companies that took part of the initial phase of the mps Br Project. These members had to fill out a form containing sets of questions addressing different concerns. The questions were divided into four sections. The first section contained specific questions concerning the experience of the participant. The second section contained questions related to the deployed process. The third section addressed questions about the Taba Workstation supporting tools. Finally, section four contained questions related to the activities and procedures specific of the process areas. Figure 2 presents the results of the execution of this empirical evaluation.

From the results presented in figure 2, we can notice that the activities and procedures specific to the process areas were always adequate for most of the participants. Moreover, more than 90% of the participants recognized that the **Taba Workstation** significantly reduced the effort for executing most of the process activities. Although nearly 85% of the participants stated that there was adequate sensitization in the companies concerning the importance of the use of the processes, almost 65% of the participants noticed resistance to the deployment of such processes. In order to cope with this divergence, the high-level management demonstrated strong support for the processes deployment and stimulated the participants to develop the projects according to the defined process. As a result, we can observe in figure 2 that most of the projects were always developed according to the defined processes, and the team members recognized that such processes were actually adequate to the projects.

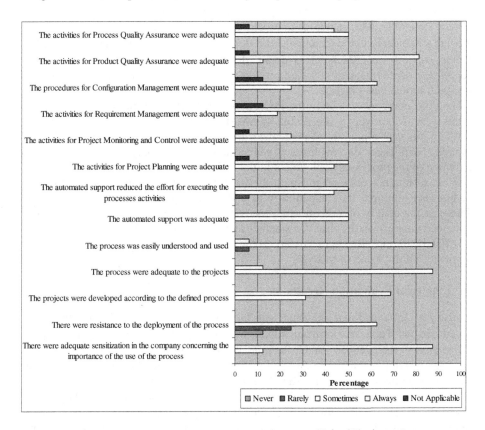

Fig. 2. Empirical evaluation results of the processes and the **Taba Workstation** support

The participants of the experiment also identified that both the processes and the **Taba Workstation** facilitated the dissemination of best practices from the project planning until the post–mortem analyses. Moreover, the centralization of information and knowledge related to processes execution also supported decision-making situations, because project managers could easily consult information about similar projects. The institutionalization of the processes with **Taba Workstation** also facilitated the communication among the project team members and diminished the occurrences of misunderstandings along the project concerning the procedures and activities to be executed and the artifacts to be produced.

6   Lessons Learned

Some lessons were learned from the results of the experience of the MR mps Br deployment: (i) a generic and comprehensive model is very important to allow a great variety of deployment processes that depends on particularities and size of the companies involved; (ii) the cooperative deployment in a group of companies has been demonstrating adequate and capable of satisfying the reality of small and medium size companies, because it allows the deployment of the model within a more feasible cost and maintaining the good quality; (iii) the experience and consultants background level, and the existence of a companies group coordination that drives the groups actions in an adequate way are fundamental aspects for success of the deployment of the MR mps Br; (iv) the work with a group of companies demands a high number of consultants in order to give the necessary attention at the moment the companies need it the most; (v) the participation in a group demonstrated not to be adequate for companies with a high level of specificity or that already has a defined and institutionalized process; in such cases, individual deployment is more suitable; (vi) the training activities for developers, system analysts and project managers have been positively evaluated and we intend to increase their comprehensiveness in the next trainings; and (vii) the **Taba Workstation** supporting tools demonstrated to be adequate to facilitate the processes use and deployment, reducing time and effort for the institutionalization of such processes within the companies.

7   Conclusion

This paper presented the mps Br Project. The project has been achieving a high level of adherence by private companies and governmental organizations. The search for a solution that really satisfies the characteristics of Brazilian companies has been involving a great discussion and an effort of a large team represented by professionals from different regions of Brazil.

The mps Br Project has seven differentials that characterize it: (i) seven maturity levels that allow a gradual deployment, and is adequate to small and medium size companies, and that allow the increase of visibility of both the processes and the improvements; (ii) compatibility to ISO/IEC 12207, ISO/IEC 15504 (SPICE) and CMMI; (iii) developed to the reality of Brazilian companies; (iv) software process deployment cost feasibility; (v) periodic appraisals (from 2 and 2 years); (vi) great potential to be replicated in Brazil and other countries; and, (vii) defined and deployed with a great industry-university cooperation constituting a catalyser of business and technology developments.

This paper also presented a pilot experience concerning the deployment of the presented approach in Brazilian software companies, and the main functionalities of the Taba Workstation SDE. Practical results from MR mps Br deployment in small and medium size Brazilian companies, and the empirical evaluation results were presented and analyzed aiming to identify the benefits of the presented approach and future directions for the project.

Acknowledgements

The authors thank all the participants of the mps Br Project, the professionals and companies that participated in this experience in Rio de Janeiro, Márcio P. Amaral, Benito Diaz, coordinators of the RioSoft – Núcleo Softex do Rio de Janeiro and specially Kival Weber and Eratóstenes Araújo, coordinators of the mps Br Project.

References

1. Fuggetta, A.: Software Process: A Roadmap, in Finkelstein, A. (ed.) The Future of Software Engineering, ACM Press, (2002)
2. Weber, K. C., Pinheiro, M.: Software Quality in Brazil, In.: Quality World Magazine, The Institute of Quality Assurance (IQA), London, UK, Vol. 21, Issue 1.1, Nov. (1995)
3. Weber, K. C., Rocha, A. R. C., Nascimento, C. J.: Qualidade e Produtividade em Software, 4a edição renovada. São Paulo, Makron Books, (2001)
4. Veloso, F., Botelho, A. J. J., Tschang, T., Amsden, A.: Slicing the Knowledge-based Economy in Brazil, China and India: A Tale of 3 Software Industries, In.: Report. Massachusetts Institute of Technology (MIT), Sep. (2003)
5. ISO 9001:2000 - Quality management systems - Requirements, (2000)
6. Weber, K. C., Almeida, R.A.R., Amaral, H.G., Gunther, P. S., Xavier, J.H.F., Loures, R.: ISO 9001/TickIT Certification in Brazilian Software Companies, In.: 5th Int. Conf. on Software Quality Management (SQM'97), Bath, UK, Mar. (1997)
7. ISO/IEC 12207:2000 - Information technology –software process life cycle, (2000)
8. ISO/IEC 15504 –1 Information Technology – Process Assessment, - Part 1: Concepts and Vocabulary, (2003)
9. Chrissis, M. B., Konrad, M, Shrum, S.: CMMI: Guidelines for Process Integration and Product Improvement, Addison-Wesley, (2003)
10. Montoni, M., Miranda, R., Rocha, A. R., Travassos, G. H.: Knowledge Acquisition and Communities of Practice: an Approach to Convert Individual Knowledge into Multi-Organizational Knowledge, In: Lecture Notes in Computer Science (LNCS), ISBN 3-540-22192-1, 6th Int. Workshop on Learning Software Organizations (LSO'2004), Banff, Canada, Jun. (2004) 110-121
11. Santos, G., Montoni, M., Rocha, A. R., Figueiredo, S., Mafra, S., Albuquerque, A., Paret, B. D., Amaral, M.: Using a Software Development Environment with Knowledge Management to Support Deploying Software Processes in Small and Medium Size Companies, In.: 3rd Conf. Professional Knowledge Management Experiences and Visions, Kaiserslautern, Germany, April 10-13 (2005), 72-76

12. Montoni, M., Santos, G., Villela, K., Miranda, R., Rocha, A.R., Travassos, G.H., Figueiredo, S., Mafra, S.: Knowledge Management in an Enterprise-Oriented Software Development Environment, In: Proc. of the 5th Int. Conf of Practical Aspects of Knowledge Management, Vienna, Austria, (2004) 117–128
13. Farias, L., Travassos, G. H., Rocha, A. R. C.: Knowledge Management of Software Risks, In: J. of Universal Computer Science, Vol. 9, No 7 (2003), 670- 681
14. Montoni, M., Santos, G., Villela, K., Rocha, A. R., Travassos, G. H., Figueiredo, S., Mafra, S., Albuquerque, A., Mian, P.: Enterprise-Oriented Software Development Environments to Support Software Products and Processes Quality Improvement, Lecture Notes of Computer Science (LNCS), to be presented at the 6th International Conference on Product Focused Software Process Improvement, Oulu, Finland, June, (2005)
15. Ferreira, A., Cerqueira, R., Rocha, A. R., Santos, G., Montoni, M., Mafra, S.,: Software Process Deployment in BL Informática: A Success Case, In: Brazilian Software Quality Symposium, Brasilia, Brazil, Jun. (2005)
16. Natali, A., Duarte, E., Silva, R., Rocha, A. R., Santos, G.: An Approach to Software Process Deployment with ISO 9001 and CMMI, In: Brazilian Software Quality Symposium, Brasilia, Brazil, Jun. (2005)

Using Rational Unified Process in an SME – A Case Study

Geir Kjetil Hanssen[1], Hans Westerheim[1], and Finn Olav Bjørnson[2]

[1]SINTEF ICT, N-7465 Trondheim, Norway
{geir.kjetil.hanssen, hans.westerheim}@sintef.no
[2]Norwegian University of Science and Technology, N-7491 Trondheim, Norway
bjornson@idi.ntnu.no

Abstract. The Rational Unified Process (RUP) is a comprehensive software development process framework emphasizing use-cases, architecture focus and an iterative approach. RUP is widely known and many organizations have tried to adopt it. Being a framework, RUP has to, in some way, be tailored to the specific context of use, no software development project is alike. This paper presents a case study of a Norwegian SME that tried to adopt RUP in the simplest way, by introducing the methodology by providing comprehensive documentation and some simple training. Our study shows that the use of RUP had some positive effects but also that the use has been scattered. Interviews with users of RUP show that there is a great need of better training and practical support in getting most value out of RUP. The key message is that if you consider taking RUP into use you have to invest resources in it. Training and support are key success factors.

1 Introduction

The Rational Unified Process (RUP) is a software development process framework consisting of a more or less complete set of process elements for software development projects [1]. RUP defines a software development project as a set of disciplines, e.g. requirements handling, implementation etc., running from start to end through the whole project life cycle divided in a set of project phases. A project is performed by a group of actors, each having one or more well defined roles. Each role participates in one or more activities producing one or more artifacts. A discipline can run in iterations, that is, repetitions within a phase. Activities, roles and artifacts are the basic process elements of RUP. RUP is a prescriptive and plan driven methodology. As RUP is a comprehensive framework covering most aspects of a software development process it means that it in some way must be adapted to the situation of use, either ad-hoc for each project or in advance to produce a company wide standard.

In this paper we present a case study that describes the use of RUP in a company where no restrictions or guidelines were put on the use of RUP. The project managers and senior developers were given courses in RUP, and RUP Online (an electronic process guide on web) was purchased and installed. No common guidance for the use of RUP in projects was given. The company had no defined goals for introducing

I. Richardson et al. (Eds.): EuroSPI 2005, LNCS 3792, pp. 142–150, 2005.

RUP; it was basically based on a belief that RUP would increase the professionalism in the company. The study has been conducted within a smaller Norwegian software development company. Three researchers have followed the company during a period of three years. This paper describes the experience from using RUP and derives some key conclusions that may be of use for others considering the use of RUP.

The paper has the following structure:

- The research method is described (collection of empirical data and data analysis).
- The research context of the case study, that is, the company, is described.
- The results part documents information and data collected. This includes descriptions of the usage of RUP as well as elements laying the ground for the forthcoming tailoring of RUP. Further on the results from the analysis of four projects and five interviews are documented.
- A discussion trying to clarify the key points from the analysis and giving a conclusion.

2 Research Method

2.1 Data Collection

The study has taken the form of a case study [2]. The research has been conducted by three external researchers mainly using project managers and software developers from the company as a source for data.

The first set of data was collected by interviewing project managers representing four projects. Prior to this series of interviews, the researchers prepared a spreadsheet that had a row for each role, activity and artifact described by RUP, grouped by the disciplines defined by RUP. A column was allocated to each project. The researcher conducting the interview asked the project manager about the use of every single role, activity and artifact in the actual project. If the element was used in the project as described by RUP, the actual cell was colored. If the item was used as described by RUP, but changed or replaced by a tailored element, the cell was colored and a comment was written about the change from the original item description in RUP. If the element was not used at all in the project, the cell was left blank.

The second set of data was collected by the means of semi-structured interviews with five other employees (each having experience with RUP from several various projects). The respondents had the following main responsibilities: 1) developer, 2) developer/project manager, 3) developer/project manager/test manager, 4) project manager/requirements engineer and 5) customer contact. Prior to the interviews, the researchers developed an interview guide. The guide consisted of questions with focus on their personal experience with using RUP across multiple projects to document a broader experience. The guide was open, allowing the respondents to freely discuss their experience.

These interviews were recorded and transcribed by the researchers. The transcriptions were reviewed by the interviewed objects, and possible corrections and clarifications were made.

2.2 Data Analysis

The spreadsheet documenting the use of RUP and the transcribed interviews were basis for the data analysis. From the beginning it was clear that the researchers were to use qualitative data analysis methods due to the nature of the data collected [3, 4].

Analysis of the spreadsheet. The spreadsheet was printed in 25% size of its actual size. This was done to get an *overview* of the RUP usage. The overview gave a clear visual picture of what parts of RUP which were really used. The comments in the spreadsheet were read through. The researchers tried to match comments with the non-use, to see if there might be some statements supporting the lack of usage. The RUP usage for the projects were also compared to the project definition, the scope of the project and the type of customer as a starting point for an understanding of the actual use and non-use of RUP elements.

Analysis of the interviews. The researchers used the constant comparison method [3] to identify the factors affecting the use of RUP among the project managers and senior developers. All the transcriptions were printed out, and each of the researchers got one copy each. The single transcriptions were read individually, and the researcher tagged statements in the documents which said something about use or non-use of RUP, reasons for using or not using RUP, and also positive and negative aspects with RUP itself. Then the researchers had a common work shop where the individual tagging were put onto a white board, and then compared. The comparison was the basis for a common summary of the interviews.

The main motivation for selecting this approach to data collection and data analysis was that the researchers did not have any pre-information about the use of RUP, and therefore no assumptions or hypothesis to test, thus a qualitative approach seemed appropriate. This motivation was supported by the relative low number of data points available from such a small company.

3 Research Context

The company described in this case is today a Norwegian software consultancy company with 50 employees, located in two different geographic offices.

They are mainly developing software systems with heavy back-end logic and often with a web front-end, typically portals. However, they also develop lighter solutions with most emphasis on the front-end.

The company acts as an independent software supplier, though there are close relationships to the biggest customers. Of the 50 employees today, 35 are working as software developers. Java and J2EE are used as the main development platform. The domain of which the company develops software is mainly for the banking and finance sector, as well as for public sector. The company has run 50 development projects within the bank and finance sector the last twelve years, and about 30-40 projects within the public sector the last 15 years.

Four employees are certified RUP-mentors acting as advisors in other SW-organizations, in addition to this they also used to run training courses in RUP as part of their partnership with Rational (now IBM Rational).

During the work described in this paper the company was declared bankrupt, and then restarted with new owners, but with the same employees. The data collection (using the spreadsheet) took place before the bankruptcy; the interviews took place about six months after the company was restarted.

4 Results

4.1 Interview Round 1: Documenting the Use of RUP

The four projects investigated had a scattered use of RUP. Interviewing the project leaders we documented the projects per phase to see which process elements were used and which were not and the corresponding reasons for that. In the following we present a summary per phase for each project (named project A to D).

The business modeling discipline
Project A was about porting functionality, no new functionality was introduced, thus not needing business modeling. For project B the customer had provided a business use case that was sufficient. Project C was developing software to be integrated with other systems. The business modeling discipline was used to clarify these interfaces. Project D had a business modeling discipline although it was not performed exactly as described by RUP.

The requirements discipline
Project A used the discipline partly to specify requirements for how to join the user interface of several systems. The other three projects used the requirements discipline quite extensively.

The analysis and design discipline
The elements in the discipline were partly used for all four projects. However there was a lot of adoption to the project context.

The implementation discipline
The use of the process elements in the implementation discipline was scattered. Although all four projects used it, project A used it briefly, project C and D used it extensively.

The test discipline
Project B and D had an extensive use of the process elements in the test discipline while the two other projects did not follow RUP for testing.

The deployment discipline
Project A had deployment activities but these were not done according to RUP. Project B had at the time of the interview not got to this. The deployment in project C

was done partly by the customer that had responsibility for most of the activities. Project D did utilize most elements from RUP.

The configuration and change management discipline
Project A did not follow RUP at all; this was however done using a specialized system guiding the process of configuration and change management. Project B and C did use RUP pretty extensively for this discipline. For project D the customer handled this responsibility following other procedures than described by RUP.

The project management discipline
Project A did not follow RUP except for the use of the software architect role. Project B and C did use most of the process elements from RUP. In the case of project D the customer had the project management responsibility themselves.

The environment discipline
Project A had merely no use of this discipline. Project B used most process elements. Project C used only a few but project D used several.

By mapping the use of process elements for the four projects we made a visual map documenting the use of each process element in RUP, ordered by the eight disciplines that RUP describes (see fig. 1).

4.2   Interview Round 2: Experiences with Using RUP

Five project participants with experience from several projects were interviewed to document positive and negative experiences from their use of RUP as well as any improvement suggestions. Note that these interviews are not related to the interviews in round one.

Some of the respondents had experience with more than one role and project type. The five persons interviewed had the following background:

- Respondent 1: Roles: Developer, project manager and test manager. Project types: Web applications with backend logic.
- Respondent 2: Roles: Developer, project manager and test manager (often combined). Project types: Web applications.
- Respondent 3: Roles: Project manager, requirements manager. Project types: Publication systems, banking systems.
- Respondent 4: Roles: Developer. Project types: Mostly system maintenance.
- Respondent 5: Roles: Key account manager. Project types: Secure systems.

Of the five respondents three defined their RUP knowledge as 'good', one as 'medium' and one as 'little'. Following is a summary of common statements from the interview transcriptions showing which respondents having which statements.

Fig. 1. Usage map

Table 1. Interviews summary

+/-	Nodes from interview coding	1	2	3	4	5
Positive experience	The RUP training was good				x	
	Roles defined by RUP	x	x			
	Important to have a supporting process				x	
	Used inception and elaboration [with success]				x	
	SW maintenance projects uses RUPs guidelines for transition between phases/milestones	x				
	Templates and role definitions are good checklists	x				
	Want to be better at using RUP	x	x	x	x	x
	Reasonable division in phases and iterations	x				
Negative experience	To extensive for small projects	x	x	x	x	
	Too document-driven				x	
	Too much focus on just the development					x
	Missing roles for customer contact prior to and past the development project					x
	Requires good knowledge [of RUP]					x
	Missing a common standard of use		x	x		
	Does not fit a software maintenance processes	x				
	Miss adaptation to extreme programming	x				
	We do not evaluate our use of RUP	x				
	Continues with old practice				x	
	We have not changed our practice after RUP was introduced		x			
	I have no progress [as a software professional]	x			x	
	Missing follow-up during projects		x	x		
	Hard to understand RUP		x			

Note that this list is a collection of all statements found relevant to the use of RUP. Some are clear and can be generalized; others are specific to a single project. The definition of the nodes is based on an interpretation of the interviews (due to the constant comparison method).

Besides this overview of experience using RUP, the respondents also had improvement suggestions:

- RUP should be used in a regular manner through the whole project (avoiding deep focus in only parts of the project)
- Projects must be guided in the use of RUP
- Web-projects need more specialized support than RUP can offer
- Establish a project manager forum (for learning and experience exchange)
- Avoid the use of RUP in the case of software maintenance
- Offer support in using and adapting RUP

5 Discussion and Conclusion

Offering RUP out-of-the-box leaves all the responsibility of tuning RUP to each individual project. This may cost both time and resources. Good knowledge on RUP is also needed. As the results from interview round one show, the use of RUP is scattered and deviates partly from the RUP guidelines. Project participants seems to end up using some RUP elements mixed with old practice, not as a consequence of deliberate decisions but as a consequence of low knowledge of RUP and how to adapt it.

The phases (and disciplines) of RUP covers the complete lifecycle of a software development project. However, in a real context, as the interviews show, the customer often has done some part of the job initially following an internal process. This may affect the use of RUP later on in the project.

Looking at the results from interview round two we see that most respondents support the idea (in general) of having a guiding process that includes role descriptions and regulates the work in disciplines, phases and iterations. However, all of the respondents feel that they need to and want to be better at using RUP. The reason for this may be that RUP is extremely comprehensive and that the task of fitting this framework to a project may be overwhelming. We also see that four of the respondents find RUP too comprehensive for small projects. This indicates a definitively need for tailoring of RUP in advance of use in projects. Two respondents also miss a common practice for the use of RUP, also indicating the need of a general tailoring of RUP.

In general, the interview results show that providing RUP just in the form of the full documentation (in this case RUP Online – right out of the box) have negative effects, at least not as good effects as one would believe in advance. It is perceived as too comprehensive and the users have problems finding the parts that would benefit their project. The consequence may be avoidance of use or even worse, wrong use. Two respondents claim that they have not changed their practice of developing software after RUP became available. This resembles with known acceptance models[5]; the methodology must be perceived as useful (will using RUP enhance the job performance?) and it must be perceived as easy to use (will using RUP require low effort?).

Besides doing a thorough adaptation in advance to increase usefulness and ease of use, projects also need practical guidance throughout the project; two respondents miss this type of support, this is also on the list of improvement suggestions. Introducing guidance and mentoring would both improve the degree of use and the effect of use of RUP as well as it would serve as a experience transfer mechanism.

Conclusion: The basic learning from this case study is that a methodology or framework (such as RUP) can not be provided "as is" without experiencing low/wrong use. The users of the methodology need to keep their focus on doing their job (developing software), not struggling to understand the theory. This is actually what the RUP documentation says, but that many unfortunately forget. Introducing a methodology such as RUP is an investment beyond the license fee. In this case the outcome could have been better if the introduction of RUP was carefully managed and not left as an autonomous effort in each project.

A comment: The learning from this study made the company decide to initiate a RUP adaptation process to provide their employees with better process support. This work is described in [6].

6 Further Research

The research reported in this paper, and also in other papers has put emphasis on the challenges in implementing and tailoring RUP for use in an organization [6-8]. Implementing a process framework like RUP can be looked upon as implementation of a new technology in an organization. It would therefore be of interest to study such implementations in spite of technology acceptance models [5] and investigate the success factors of tailoring and introduction of methodologies.

Acknowledgements

The authors would like to thank the participants from the case company. We would also like to thank the SPIKE-project (funded by the Research Council of Norway) for funding and support.

References

1. Krutchen, P., *The Rational Unified Process: An Introduction*. 2nd ed. 2000: Addison-Wesley. 298.
2. Yin, R.K., *Case Study Research - Design and Methods*. Applied Social Research Methods Series, ed. D.S. Foster. 1994: SAGE Publications.
3. Seaman, C., *Qualitative methods in empirical studies in software engineering*. IEEE Transactions on Software Engineering, 1999. **25**(4): p. 557-572.
4. Avison, D., et al., *Action Research*. Communications of the ACM, 1999. **42**(1): p. 94-97.
5. Riemenschneider, C.K.H., et al., *Explaining software developer acceptance of methodologies: a comparison of five theoretical models*. Software Engineering, IEEE Transactions on, 2002. **28**(12): p. 1135-1145.
6. Westerheim, H. and Hanssen, G.K., *The Introduction and Use of a Tailored Unified - A Case Study*. in *31st EUROMICRO CONFERENCE on Software Engineering and Advanced Applications (SEAA)*. 2005. Porto, Portugal: IEEE.
7. Bergström, S., Råberg, L., *Adopting the Rational Unified Process*. 2004, Addison-Wesley. p. 165-182.
8. Hanssen, G.K., et al., *Tailoring RUP to a defined project type: A case study*. in *6th International Conference on Product Focused Software Process Improvement, PROFES*. 2005. Oulo, Finland: Springer.

Goal-Driven Requirements Engineering
for Supporting the ISO 15504 Assessment Process

André Rifaut

Centre de Recherche Public Henrit Tudor, 29, Avenue John F. Kennedy,
L-1855 Luxembourg-Kirchberg, Luxembourg
Andre.Rifaut@tudor.lu
http://www.tudor.lu

Abstract. It is advocated to use the ISO/IEC 15504 standard into new domains not related to Information Technology (IT), giving a powerful enterprise-wide assessment tool for quality managers. Outside quality management, ISO/IEC 15504 assessments are becoming used for assessing conformance to regulations. Two examples of this occur with the process models "SPICE for SPACE" and "Operational Risk Management" in financial institutions. This success could result in the emergence of many ISO/IEC 15504 process models for the same or different domains. How to give support for ensuring their quality, their adequacy to the business domains they address, their compatibility across overlapping domains? Goal-driven Requirements Engineering (RE) methods give an effective support to answer to those questions. Within the setting of three case studies, this paper presents goal-driven RE activities and models that help to increase the agreement on domain specific process models and to enhance the compatibility of process models.

1 Introduction

The ISO/IEC 15504 standard gives opportunities for assessing processes of business domains not limited to Information Technologies (IT), bringing new opportunities for improving the quality of the actual practices related to those domains. This is mainly due to two aspects of the standard. First, it allows defining process models[1] tailored to any business domain. Second it defines a clear, rigorous and internationally recognized process assessment method. It is expected that this standard will be more and more used with core business domains not concerned with IT-related processes, or IT-related domains.

Quality Managers and Regulators. Quality managers (or consultants) are expected to be the main actors interested in using this standard. In order to align business criti-

---

[1] The term "process model", instead of *model*, will be used for a *Process Assessment Model* and the *Process Reference Models* it relates to. All along the paper (except for section 2.2), the *Italic* font style is used for the terms defined in the part 1 of the ISO/IEC 15504 standard or used in part 2 (normative parts of the standard) [10], [11]. That style is not used for all occurrences of these terms, but only when necessary to ease the understanding of the paper. However, knowledge of the ISO/IEC 15504 standard is still a prerequisite.

I. Richardson et al. (Eds.): EuroSPI 2005, LNCS 3792, pp. 151 – 162, 2005.

cal activities with the organizations' strategic goals, those activities are often defined, analyzed and optimized with business process models.

However, regulators (e.g. governments and their governmental agencies, international regulatory organizations) are also interested in increasing the quality of the organizations' processes for ensuring socio-economic quality factors, such as population healthiness and economic stability. Because systems (technical, industrial, financial, ...) become too complex, regulators pay attention to not introduce any implementation details into the process models they define in order to allow the creation of better business processes. However the process models described in regulations must be sufficiently precise to enforce rigorous and objective assessments.

The ISO/IEC 15504 standard is an appropriate tool for regulators. This is the case for the two process models "SPICE for SPACE"[4] and the "Operational Risk Management" in financial institutions [3]. This latter, which is one of our three case studies, has been defined in close cooperation with the Luxembourg financial institutions regulators.

Challenges. The expected widespread use of the ISO/IEC 15504 standard raises the challenge of reaching a consensus about process models within the same domain. There is a need for systematic methods for reaching the consensus of domain experts for *process reference models*.

Another challenge arises with the incompatibility between *process models* across overlapping domains. For instance, in the same organization the following domains overlap: operational risk management, security management, and supply chain management. For the quality manager, it is important that the different *process models* lead to consistent process assessment results on the overlapping areas. This consistent overlap of regulatory *process models* with business *process models* will also ease the work to be done for conformance to regulations.

Table 1. This table shows for each artifact the activities that are well supported by a goal-driven RE method

Artifact	Design & Validation	Conformance	Tailo-ring
Process purpose	X	X	
Process outcome	X	X	
Assessment indicator	X	X	
Assessment instrument	X		X
Organization's business goals	X		X
Organizational unit's processes	X		X

In this paper it will be shown that goal-driven RE methods can give an answer to those challenges. The paper will focus on the ISO/IEC 15504 artifacts and on the support of the three kinds of activities presented in Table 1. Only three RE activities will be detailed. The first activity is the design of process models (including their validation). The second one is the verification of the conformance to ISO/IEC 15504 requirements. The last column is about the activities related to the effective use of the process models during assessments: mainly the tailoring[2] to the target *organizational units* made during preparation of assessments.

The paper recalls the benefits of RE methods in section 2. That section presents a goal-driven method that fit our purpose. Next, section 3 describes the goal-driven models that are appropriate for each aforementioned ISO/IEC 15504 artifacts. Then in section 4, their use is presented in the context of different case studies. Lastly, the conclusion and future works are presented in section 5.

2 Requirements Engineering and Goal-Driven Methods

For many years, the Software Engineering community has been recognized the importance of RE methods. Most of the causes of failures or partial failures of software projects (identified in, e.g. [7]) can be addressed with RE methods leading to more successful projects. In particular, one aim of RE methods is to reach an agreement between stakeholders concerned by the specifications (goals, requirements and constraints) of a system. For this, techniques used are elicitation, modeling, and validation of those specifications in order to build specifications that are correct, unambiguous, complete, consistent, verifiable, modifiable, traceable, ... [8].

2.1 From Functionalities to Business Goals

At the beginning, RE was mostly concerned with the description of functional and non-functional aspects of software systems. Nowadays, it is used for system engineering. Its scope includes human-machine interface, organizational constraints, and also business processes and goals.[1] Due to the nature of system engineering, the requirements can range from very detailed low-level constraints about hardware, to precise high-level organizational or business goals. The former is described by using more prescriptive languages, whereas the latter uses more declaratives languages.

This paper will focus on the latter, especially goal-driven requirements, because the ISO/IEC 15504 standard requires that *process models* may not be prescriptive about the process' implementation. The declarative and high-level nature of the goal-driven languages fits well this requirement. The language used in this paper is a variant of the *i** language [12] because it is more appropriate for defining organizational processes and business goals.

2.2 A Goal-Driven Method Based on *i** in Support of ISO/IEC 15504

The RE method *i** has been created to be used in very different contexts. From high-level business and organizational requirements to formal specifications of software systems. This method advocates also a goal-driven analysis of requirements. In this work, the *i** notation (see Figure 1) has been adapted in order to better fit the needs of the ISO/IEC 15504 standard.

---

[2] This term has not the same meaning as the term *tailoring guidelines* defined in the ISO/IEC 15504 attribute PA3.1.

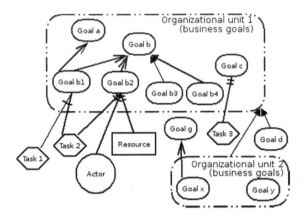

Fig. 1. The concepts of the *i** model adapted to support ISO/IEC 15504 process models

The concepts of *goals*, *tasks*, *resources* and *actors* can be modeled, as shown in the Figure 1. A task represents any kind of activity made by actors. Actors are humans, software tools or systems.

Goals can be *refined* into sub-goals. For instance the goal *b* is refined into the conjunction of the goals *b3* and *b4* (see the plain arrow). The informal meaning of a goal is just a (logical) statement that should be fulfilled. (Due to lack of place, no distinction will be made between goals and requirements or constraints. They will all be modeled with goals.) The meaning of the refinements is that the conjunction of the sub-goals participating in this refinement implies the goal: for instance "*b3* and *b4* implies *b*". The plain arrow indicates a *full refinement*:"*b3* and *b4* is fully equivalent to *b*". The simple arrow models a *partial refinement*: the goal *a* is partially refined into the goal *b1*, which means that *b1* implies *a*, but *a* is not equivalent to *b1*.

Some goals can refine two or more goals. For example the goal *b1* participates into the refinement of goal *a* and goal *b*.

Sometimes stakeholders cannot immediately agree on a model. In that case, one can model the *alternatives* for the goal refinement. For instance, the goal *b* is alternatively refined into the goals *b1* and *b2*. At some moment one of the two alternatives will be agreed upon, and only that one will be kept in the model.

When aspects of how to implement goals must be described, the *decomposition* link is used (lines with a double cross for *full decompositions*, and lines with a simple cross for *partial decompositions*). For instance the goal *b1* is decomposed into the *task 1* and the *task 2*, meaning that the successful tasks performance ensures the goal fulfillment. In goal-driven methods, when the focus of the analysis does not require too many details, a task can be reduced to the task's goal. For instance, the *tasks 3* can be summarized with the goal *c*. (This is indicated with the double crossed line defining a full decomposition of the goal *c* into that only *tasks 3*.) Similarly, resources and actors can be reduced to goals. Recall that this is just a means to abstract details from models of tasks, resources and actors.

Tasks can also be further decomposed into sub-tasks. (Not shown on the figure.) Goal (or task) can be decomposed into other tasks, resources and actors.

Goals can be collected into *sets of goals* (with a dotted rounded box). The meaning is just the conjunction of all goals of the set. The figure shows that business goals of the organizational unit 2 participate in the refinement of the first organizational unit's business goals. This notation is used when it is not important to show explicitly the individual contributions to the refinements. Actually, one cannot say exactly which are the individual contributions. However, in the example, the full refinement symbol shows that each goal of the first organizational unit is fully refined by one or more goals of the second organizational unit or by the goal *d*.

The refinements and decomposition links are rich traceability links [13] that can be used to automatically produce the traceability matrix and powerful checks can be defined on those links.

3   Goal-Driven Requirement Engineering Models of ISO/IEC 15504 Assessments Artifacts

In this section, a goal-driven RE model will be given for each of the main assessments artifacts that are listed in table 1. Section 4 explains how these models can be used in support of ISO/IEC 15504 assessments.

3.1 Process Purpose

Together with the *process outcomes*, it is the basis of the definition of process reference models. The ISO/IEC 15504 standard makes an explicit link between the *process purpose* of a process and the set of objectives expected to be fulfilled when performing that process.[11 sec. 6.2.4] So, it is adequate to model a process purpose with a goal and this goal being fully refined into an equivalent collection of sub-goals. The top part of the Figure 1 summarizes their graphical representation.

Explicitly decomposing the purpose into sub-goals makes easier to validate each main aspect of the purpose than with a text paragraph. Moreover, the relationships between processes belonging to the same process reference model can be more precisely identified onto specific sub-goals of the process purposes. The Figure 2 shows that refinements can be included into the collection of sub-goals, in order to represents the structure of the domain into those sub-goals.

3.2 Process Outcome

The achievement of a *process purpose* must be demonstrated by the collection of outcomes. Each outcome can be described with a goal (which can be detailed by refining them). The ISO/IEC 15504 gives three types of outcomes: the fulfillment of a specified goal (or requirement, or constraint), a change of state, or the production of an artifact (which, formally, can be represented as a kind of change of state described with only one artifact).

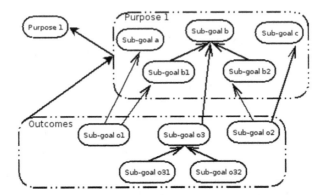

Fig. 2. The purpose is decomposed into an equivalent collection of sub-goals. The outcomes are related to that collection of sub-goals. Sub-goals of purposes and outcomes can be refined.

The main difference between the full refinement of the purpose into a collection of sub-goals, and its full refinement into the collection of outcomes, is that the outcomes must be observable. This is why it is expected that the sub-goals refining the purpose are less detailed than the goals representing the outcomes. It is important to note that the part of the (goal-driven) domain knowledge model that must be added to obtain the proof of any full refinement is not shown in this paper by lack of place. Refinement links explicitly show the relationship between each outcome and a number of the sub-goals refining the purpose, easing the validation of outcomes. A check can be defined to ensure that the collection of outcomes is a full refinement of the purpose.

3.3 Assessment Indicator

Although they are not mandatory, the definition of *assessment indicators* can increase the quality of the assessments because they enhance the rigorous observation of the fulfillment of the outcomes and the purposes. The ISO/IEC 15504 gives the example of three kinds of indicators: *practices*, *work products* and *resources* needed for the performance of the process. Those kinds of indicators are easily mapped into the goal-driven concepts of task (for *practices*), *i**-resources (for *work products* and *resources*) and actors (for *resources*). The section 2 explained that goals can be decomposed into tasks and *i**-resources ; this is also the case for tasks. The relationship between indicators and outcomes or sub-goals of purposes can be made explicit. Recall that goal-driven models allow summarizing a task into the task goal, so *practices* can also be summarized by goals. This eases detailing the relationship between practices and the two first kinds of outcomes (the fulfillment of a specified goal, and a state change). To check a full cover of the outcomes by the indicators, their goals can be compared.

Attribute indicators related to *attributes of level* greater than 1, can be linked to the goal-driven description of those attributes. Indeed, for a specific *process reference model*, the attributes of level greater than 1 can be described with goal-driven models. This gives the same support than the one brought by the goal-driven model of the purposes and outcomes. The lack of place prevents us to detail this.

3.4 Assessment Instrument

These are used to help the assessors to collect a complete set of evidences concerning the fulfillment of the purposes and outcomes. The usual examples of assessment instruments are checklists and questionnaires.

With goal-driven method, when indicators have been given their goal-driven definition, it is easier to set the focus of the corresponding questions through a goal. Indeed, a goal representing a question can be seen as a refinement of its corresponding indicator. This has the advantage to strongly link the question with the indicator. More importantly, goals give the main focus of each question that can be referred to by assessors when preparing an assessment or during an assessment when the assessment context is unusual.

Goal-driven methods have been used to build such kind of instruments. An example is the Goals-Questions-Metrics method (GQM) which has been used in the field of quality improvement.[14] Just like here, in the GQM method the design of questionnaires starts with the definition of goals and organizational unit's processes.

3.5 Organization's Business Goals and Organizational Unit's Processes

The ISO/IEC 15504 standard stresses the importance of the *organizational unit* where the assessment will take place. Although compliant process models must be independent of any specific *business needs* (or business goals) and current practices, those process model must be adequate for all *organizational units* that would be interested in using those process models for an assessment.

In order to build the most adequate process models, some knowledge about the business needs and about the current practices of *organizational units* is necessary. This knowledge can be found in reference documents, such as standards or regulations, or in experts' knowledge. In all cases, a goal-driven model of the basics of this knowledge can be obtained quite easily and will be valuable for process models design and validation purposes. For instance, after having collected a sample set of business goals, if some refinement member of a process purpose (or process outcomes) is never useful for any of those business goals, one should make a deeper analysis of this member. Similarly, after having collected a sample set of current practices, if some refinement member of a process purpose, outcome, assessment indicator or instrument cannot be related to any current practice, one should go further into the design and validation of the process model. This kind of check were made during the design of the "Operational Risk Management" process model.[3] This might have helped the design of the "SPICE for SPACE" process model.

The figure 3 illustrates the fact that elements of process reference models should refine business goals and that current practices should relates to elements of process models. The four levels: business, purpose and outcomes (used in process assessment model), indicators (used in process reference model), and organizational units' processes (specific implementations of processes). The relationships between two cases studies are shown in goal refinements. Purposes *1* and *2* (left side) belong to the operational risk management model [3] and purposes *a* and *b* (right side) belong to service management model [2]. A first relationship is the business goal "business impact of incidents reduced" shared with the purpose *1* and the purpose *a*. Quite naturally, service management (SM) should improve the operational risk management (ORM), which means that some goals of the SM should contribute to some goals of ORM. The model indicates that the outcome "incidents tracked and recorded" of purpose *a* of SM contributes to the indicator goal "risk probabilities assessed" of ORM. This is a second relationship between ORM and SM. A third one is the contribution of the business goal "problem trends identified" of SM (top right) to the goal "risk indicators defined" (bottom left). [3] This confirms the idea that some part of the implemented processes for SM contributes to ORM. By finding the relationships between goals of the process models one can show the compatibility between different process models.

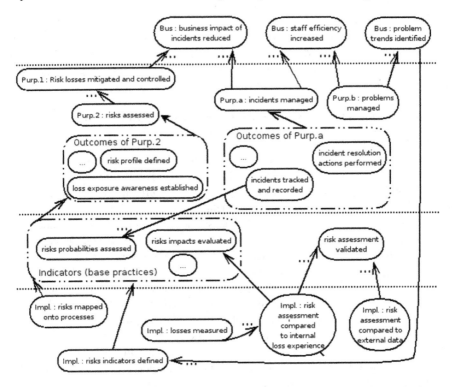

Fig. 3. The organizational unit goals and current practices are related to the process model elements. The dotted goals and arrows show that many refinements are missing on this figure. Usually, a number of small diagrams are drawn, where missing links can be spotted easily.

The next section gives concrete case studies where this business model was an important factor to reach stakeholders' consensus and quality of the process model.

---

[3] This latter refinement could have targeted the rounded box of indicators of purpose 2. Just for illustration purposes it points to an implementation goal to indicate precisely the contribution of the business goal "problem trends identified".

4 Goal-Driven Requirement Engineering Activities for Supporting ISO/IEC 15504 Assessments

4.1 Design and Validation Activities

Recall that RE validation activities are appropriate for dealing with process model artifacts due to the high-level declarative nature of those artifacts. Instead of presenting these activities in a lifecycle, they will be presented in relation to the requirements found in the ISO/IEC 15504 standard.

Validation for Reaching Consensus. The ISO/IEC 15504 requirement to make a statement about the consensus reached by the community of interest shows that this consensus is important for acceptance of the process model: "The Process Reference Model shall document the community of interest of the model and the actions taken to achieve consensus within that community of interest" [11, sec. 6.2.3.2]. Well-known RE techniques and also the high-level nature of goal-driven models are in favor of reaching this consensus.

The case study concerning the domain of knowledge management is illustrative in this respect. In order to reach agreement and acceptation of the process model, meetings were organized between experts, users interested in the process model and solution providers in knowledge management. A goal-driven method was used to collect the users' business goals, the solution providers' process implementation models and the expert knowledge about goals, solutions and knowledge management models. Process models were extracted from the goal-driven models and submitted for validation. Each stakeholder could validate the process model against its business goals and current practices, so that the process model may be useful for each of them. Actually, a set of diagrams integrating business goals, purposes, outcomes and organizational units' current practices (like the diagrams shown in Figure 3) where used to reach this agreement.

Domain and Process Engineering. The ISO/IEC 15504 standard requires that the processes of the process reference model will be described within their domain. It requires also that the relationships between the processes are defined.[11, sec. 6.2.3.1]

The RE methods share also this concern about the importance of the description of the domain context and the analysis of the relationships between model elements.[15] The example on Figure 4 represents a part of the Acquisition Process of the Software Engineering PAM[9]. The indicators (from bottom to top) BP1, BP2 and BP4 form a hierarchy of refinements. Notice that the upper right goal belongs to the textual description of BP4, raising a question to domain experts: is it a sub-goal of BP4, a benefit of BP4, or a benefit of ACQ4?

In the case study concerning the operational risk management [3], in order to design the process assessment model, it has been necessary to complete the regulation reference documents with other regulatory documents describing current recommended practices. In another case study, the IT service management process model based on ITIL reference documents [2], an important work has been done in order to link the process model with the business goals (called "benefits" in the ITIL documents) and the best practices recommended in the ITIL reference documents.

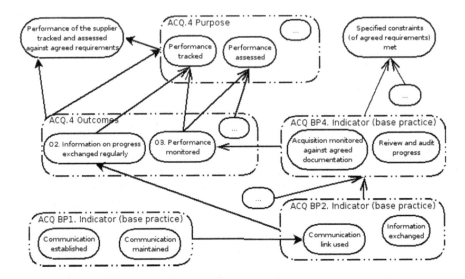

Fig. 4. The Acquisition process of the ISO 12207[9] process assessment model exemplar (found in ISO/IEC 15504) is partially shown here

4.2 Conformance Verification Activities

The ISO/IEC 15504 standard gives requirements on the conformance of the process models (in particular, see sections 6.2, 6.3 and 7.2 of [11]). These conformance verification activities can occur in parallel with the design and validation activities, or after the completion of those activities. However, in both cases, the goal-driven methods can give an effective support to those activities, as explained in this section.

Let us recall the conformance requirements already addressed in the Section 3 where it has been shown how goal-driven models could help for conformance verification. First expressing the processes purposes and outcomes in terms of goals ease the verification of a description that concerns high-level objectives of the processes. Second, the fact that the processes outcomes are necessary and sufficient conditions of the processes purposes is addressed through the verification the refinement of the purpose into outcomes is complete. Third, the required link between the assessment indicators and the process purpose and outcomes is explicitly given in goal-driven models through the refinement relationship. These are checks that can be systematically done through the analysis of the refinement links.

It is also required that the process reference model does not contain, nor implies any condition pertaining to the *measurement framework* (i.e. attributes of levels greater than 1). This can be checked through inspections of goals describing the process reference model and goals describing the attributes of levels greater than 1. As said in Section 3.3, with a goal-driven description of generic attributes, based on the simple understanding of the basic logical relationships, it is easier to check against those logical dependencies such as "implying", "being implied", or "containing" and "being contained" which are mentioned in the ISO/IEC 15504 standard when requiring no overlap between the process reference model and the generic attributes.

However, most importantly, the ISO/IEC 15504 standard requires that evidence to conformity requirements will be obtained and documented. The rich traceability links contained in the goal-driven models allows to automatically extracting the structured set of evidences to conformity. Because those links are explicit and have a simple natural meaning it is easier to document those evidences and track their changes.

For instance, in the case study concerning the operational risk management [3], this traceability was used for both verifying the conformance to the ISO/IEC 15504 requirements on process reference models and process assessment models, and for the conformance to the regulations concerning the operational risk management in financial institutions. The completeness of the conformance checks, even when process model modifications occurred during late validations activities, was ensured. The traceability matrix obtained from those traceability links allowed spotting weaknesses in the regulatory documents. In particular, the regulators agreed that the requirements implied by the attributes of level PA2.1, PA2.2 and PA3.2 were applicable although not explicitly present in the regulatory documents.(The attribute PA3.1 is well represented in the regulatory requirements that details, for instance, the content of strategies, the involvement of managers, and the documentation needs.)

4.3 Tailoring for Assessment Activities

The ISO/IEC 15504 standard has been designed for allowing the best adaptation of assessments to organizational units. The goal-driven models are the basis of a knowledgebase of organizational units' business goals and current processes. Using the traceability links, an assessor can modify the assessment instruments to make them more appropriate to the domain of a specific organizational unit. Moreover, during assessments, new kinds of base practices are discovered, and their goal model are stored in the knowledge base.

5 Conclusions and Future Works

To the best of our knowledge, most of the support given to the ISO/IEC 15504 standard are software tools that can be used for recording process models, navigating through them and tools for supporting the assessors' activities.[6]

The work presented in this paper aims to give a simple but effective set of techniques supporting analysis activities during the life cycle of ISO/IEC 15504 process models. Goal-driven RE methods provides a good basis for this set of techniques: in addition to the usual benefits of RE methods, the goal-driven style ensures a high-level declarative expression together with rich traceability links which are important aspects for analyzing and verifying process models.

Another benefit of this basis is to put forward the challenges that should be addressed by ISO/IEC 15504 experts, such as, the analysis of relationships between processes reference models, and also the use of assessments in the context of conformance to regulations.

The future work of the author focuses towards better guidance and software tool support. First, it is important to give a more extensive set of checks on the goal-driven models that could help to uncover weaknesses in the process models. Refinement links can be used for discovering those weaknesses (such as the set of sub-goals partially cover a set of goals, or sub-goals that are always used in the same refinements, ...). Second, for our process model a knowledgebase must be created with business goals and current practices concerning the process models used in the case studies.

A prototype based on the Semantic Hypertext Object Repository Framework [16] allows extracting the traceability matrix from the refinements links and define checks on those links. In addition, support to the design of process models, the knowledgebase management, and the export of the knowledgebase into the assessor tool (under development) for assessment instruments tailoring will be implemented in the future.

References

1. B. A. Nuseibeh and S. M. Easterbrook, "Requirements Engineering: A Roadmap", In A. C. W. Finkelstein (ed) "The Future of Software Engineering ". (Companion to the proceedings of the 22nd Int. Conf. on Software Engineering, ICSE'00). IEEE Computer Society Press.
2. B. Di Renzo, B. Barafort, V. Lejeune, S. Prime, J-M. Simon, "ITIL Based Service Management Measurement and ISO/IEC 15504 Process Assessment: A Win-Win Opportunity", International Conference SPiCE 2005.
3. B. Di Renzo, M. Hillairet, M. Picard, A. Rifaut, C. Bernard, D. Hagen, P. Maar, D. Reinard, "Operational Risk management in Financial Institutions: Process Assessment in Concordance with Basel II", International Conference SPiCE 2005.
4. A. Cass, C. Volcker, L. Winzer, J.M. Carranza, A. Dorling, "SPiCE for SPACE : A Process Assessment and Improvement Method for Space Software Development", ESA, Bulletin 107, August 2001, pp. 112-119.
5. R. Hunter and G. Robinson and I. Woodman, "Tool support for software process assessment and improvement", Software Process: Improvement and Practice, vol. 3, n. 4, 1997.
6. Compita Ltd, Software Innovation Centre, Livingston, UK. (http://www.compita.com/)
7. Standish Group "Chaos: A Recipe for Success", Standish Group International, 1999.
8. IEEE Std 830-1984, "IEEE Guide to Software Requirements Specifications".
9. ISO/IEC 12207:1995, "Information Technology – Software Life-cycles Processes".
10. ISO/IEC 15504-1:2004, "Information Technology – Process assessment – Part 1: Concepts and vocabulary"
11. ISO/IEC 15504-2:2003, "Information Technology – Process assessment – Part 2: Performing an assessment"
12. E. Yu, "Strategic Modelling for Enterprise Integration," Proceedings of the 14th World Congress of International Federation of Automatic Control (IFAC'99), 1999, Beijing.
13. Jeremy Dick "Rich Traceability for interrelating requirements," Telelogic, Sweden 2000
14. Van Solingen, "The Goal/Question/Metric Method: A Practical Guide For Quality Improvement of Software Development", McGraw-Hill, Jan. 1999, ISBN-0077095537
15. R.S. Pressman, "Software Engineering: A Practitioner's Approach," McGraw-Hill, 2005
16. B. Zündorf, H. Schulz, Dr. K. Mayr "SHORE – A Hypertext Repository in the XML World," 2000, SD&M Corporation, Southfield, MI 48075, USA

Improving the Software Inspection Process

Tor Stålhane and Tanveer Husain Awan

Norwegian University of Science and Technology
stalhane@idi.ntnu.no
BEKK Consulting, Oslo, Norway
Tanveer.Awan@bekk.no

Abstract. In this paper we look at the results from three experiments. We discuss the results and combine them into advices for code inspection. The main observations are that 1) it is beneficial to use large inspection groups in order to have access to a large amount of diverse experience and knowledge, 2) hands-on experience is more important than general knowledge and experience and 3) if left on their own, large groups tend to use a voting-like mechanism when deciding which defects to report after the group meeting.

1 Introduction

Code reading and code inspections is a hot topic in software development. We already know that the number of defects found during inspection varies greatly – the problem is why they do so and what we should do about it. Following the TQM philosophy, we see this variation as an opportunity – some persons find many defects. Thus, we know it is possible. How can we repeat their successes? We also know that many persons find quite few defects. Thus, we know there is a danger. How can we avoid it? The same questions apply to inspection meetings – some work well while some do not contribute in the defect detection process at all. What can we learn here?

The discussions and results presented in this paper are based on a set of code inspection experiments done by one of the authors during his sabbatical stay at the CSE, UNSW [1] plus two experiments run at NTNU by the other author as part of his master degree in software engineering [2], [3].

The rest of this paper is organized as follows: First we present a summary of earlier code inspection experiments. We then give a short description of the UNSW experiment and a detailed description of the experiments done at NTNU. We go on to present the data analyses and the main results before presenting our conclusions and some ideas for further work.

2 Related Work

Code reading and code inspection has been a popular field for experiments. There are several reasons for this – for instance that the technique is important and that the results from the experiments are easy to analyze using simple statistical methods.

I. Richardson et al. (Eds.): EuroSPI 2005, LNCS 3792, pp. 163 – 174, 2005.

Already in 1978, Meyers run an experiment at the IBM Systems Research Institute where he compared testing and inspections [4]. The experiment showed no significant differences between the methods when it comes to error detection efficiency but testing showed a higher variability than inspection.

In 1987, Basili presented an experiment where he compared code inspection to two testing methods [5]. While code reading came out on top among professional developers, the results varied quite a lot for the students participating in the experiment. Porter and Votta ran an experiment in 1994 where they compared scenario-based inspection to checklist-based inspection [6]. The experiment used both individual inspections and a following inspection group meeting. For the defects touched by the scenarios, the scenario-based inspection was the most effective. For the other defects, no significant difference was observed. A related method – perspective-based code reading, was used in an experiment by Laitenberg in 1999 [7] where he found that this method outperformed checklist-based inspection.

Basili, Porter and Votta have later run several related experiments, Basili in 1996 [8] and in 2001 [9] and Porter and Votta in 1997 [10]. Votta found that the inspection effectiveness was not affected by team size and there was a great variation between the groups in the number of defects found. The same was observed by Kelly [11].

The reported works have made a lot of observations and some interesting conclusions. What is missing is a thorough analysis of the causes for the variations and how they can be used in an SPI process to improve inspection. Our contribution is to add this perspective.

3   Code Reading, Variation and SPI Opportunities

The statistical control view of improvement insists that we must first reduce the variation, then understand the cause – effect relationship and then improve the process. The main argument behind this approach is that a great variation will mask any possible effect of an improvement action.

There is, however, another way to look at variations – they tell you how good or bad things might turn out. One of the first to raise this issue was E. Auråen [12]. Following his idea, we can use the results from the inspection experiments as follows: Some inspections or inspection groups find more defects than the rest. We should learn how to repeat their success. Some inspections or inspection groups find fewer defects than the rest. We should learn how to avoid their failures.

In the same way, we have observed that several organizations, including large organizations like Sun Microsystems, have skipped the inspection meeting since they, on the average, do not contribute to the number of defects identified. Again we have a case where an activity sometimes helps and sometime has no beneficial effect whatsoever. Again the SPI opportunity has been missed – why does the inspection meeting sometimes work, while at other occasions it has turned out to be counterproductive?

If we do not grab the SPI opportunities offered by the experiments and experience but instead build our decisions on discussions around average values, we will miss an important opportunity to achieve substantial improvements.

4 The Experiments in Detail

4.1 The UNSW Experiments

One of the foci for these experiments was to see if the group meeting had a beneficial effect on the number of defects found. The three experiments were all run in the same way - the participants (120 students) were given a piece of code with a set of seeded defects. They inspected the code and reported the defects found before meeting as a group to decide on the final inspection report. In each experiment, all participants inspected the same code containing the same seeded defects.

In order to study the effects of the inspection meetings we introduce the two terms nominal group (NG) and real group (RG). The nominal group contains the number of defects identified by the group members *before* the inspection meeting – NG = |Union of defects found by each group member| - while the real group contains the number of defects reported by the group after the inspection meeting.

The difference between the number of defects found by the nominal group (NG) and the defects found by the real group (RG) is a measure of the effect of the group meeting. The NG - RG distribution for each experiment is shown in figure 1 below.

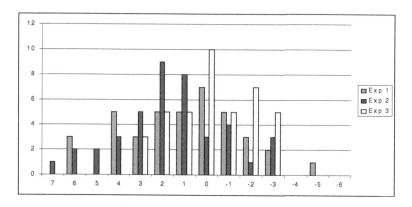

Fig. 1. The distribution of the difference between nominal and real groups, NG - RG

The differences between the numbers of defects found in the nominal group and in the real group from all three experiments yielded the same standard deviation. The mean value of the differences changed, however, significantly from experiment 2 with a mean of 1.6 to experiment 3 with a mean of 0.3. This difference is significant at the 1.4% level and it seems that the gain / loss value moves towards a symmetrical distribution.

The most surprising info from the data shown in figure 1 is the size of the variation - SD = 2.5. In some real groups they find much more defects – up till five defects more and thus have a process gain – while in some real groups they find much fewer defects – up till seven defects less and thus have a process loss. If we pool all the data shown in figure 1 together, we find a probability of 53% for process loss (64/120) and a probability of 30% for process gain (36/120).

The picture becomes much clearer if we make a table showing the number of defects reported from the group meeting (RG) and the number of group members that identified each defect during their individual inspections.

Table 1. How many persons in a group identified each defect?

		Number of persons who found a defect during individual inspection			
	Experiment	0	1	2	More than 2
Defects reported by real group	1	138	134	82	54
	2	109	145	48	8
	3	90	87	32	17
Defects *not* reported by real group	1	896	149	26	3
	2	1070	160	16	2
	3	454	69	10	1

Based on the data shown in table 1 we can estimate P(in RG | found by n in NG). The result is shown in the graph below.

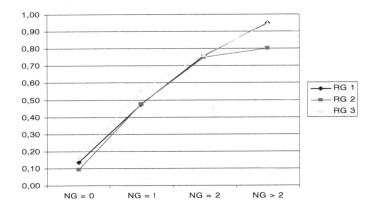

Fig. 2. The probability of reporting a defect as a function of persons that found it

Even though all persons participating in the inspection were instructed to include all defects in the final report, it seems that they ignored this instruction.

If nobody in the nominal group had found the defect during individual inspection, there was a 10% probability that the group would find it during the meeting. If only one person in the group found the defect there was a 50% probability that the group would report it. If more than two persons found the defect – mostly meaning all in the group – the probability of reporting the defect rose to between 80 and 95%. The group does not necessarily use a voting process – group pressure would give the same effect.

We can use these data in two ways – the standard solution is to skip the final inspection meeting since there is a 53% probability of process loss as opposed to only a 30% probability of process gain. The other, more productive way of using the results, is to ask the question – how can we assure a process gain in the inspection meeting? We already know that it is possible.

If we take a closer look at the data, an interesting pattern is revealed. The diagram below show three percentages from the group process: defects not found during individual inspections but identified during the inspection meeting – denoted New – the defects found during individual inspections and reported from the meeting – denoted Retained - and the defects found during individual inspections but not included in the inspection report – denoted Removed.

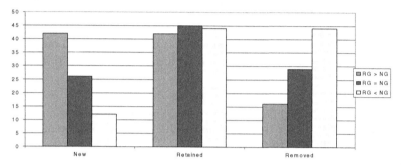

Fig. 3. New, Retained and Removed defects in experiment 3

The three columns show the data for three categories of groups – the real group performed significantly better than the nominal group – RG > NG - the real group and the nominal group were about equal – RG = NG – and the real group performed significantly worse than the nominal group – RG < NG. We see that the three categories keep about the same percentage of the defects from the nominal group – 44% on the average. What make the difference, however, is that on the average, in groups were we experience process

- Loss, we find few new defects (12%) but remove many old ones (44%).
- Gain, we find a lot of new defects (42%) and reject few of the old (16%).
- Stability, we find some new defects (26%) but remove approximately the same amount of the old ones (28%).

We thus have two important mechanisms that must be understood in order to improve code inspections – why are already identified defects removed and why do they find so few new ones? In our opinion, both effects can be satisfactory explained by the mechanism shown in figure 2 – the voting-like mechanism. Strong tendencies to use this mechanism in the group process will both make it easy to throw out already identified defects and make it difficult to include new ones.

4.2   NTNU Experiment 1

The first NTNU experiment [2] was concerned with two issues – group size and the use of checklists. Checklists have been heavily used in inspection experiments and, as should be expected, the results vary. The experiments were run with 20 NTNU students and had two phases – one where the student inspected the code alone and one where the students got together in groups to construct a final list of defects, just as in the UNSW experiment. Ten students used a tailor-made checklist and ten students used an ad-hoc approach. The code they inspected was 130 lines of Java code with 13 seeded defects.

We used a t-test to compare the results from the students using checklist and the students that used an ad-hoc approach. As expected, the groups that used the check-lists did significantly better – the checklist group found on the average 8.4 defects while the ad-hoc group found on the average 6.7 defects. The difference is significant at the 1.4% level.

In order to check that we have enough participants we use the standard relationship between the sample size, effect size and the probabilities for a type I or type II error – commonly denoted α and β respectively. If we use $\alpha = 0.05$ and $\beta = 0.20$, we have

$$N = \frac{32}{ES^2} \tag{1}$$

N is the sample size and ES is the effect size. Since we already have used the t-test, we will compute the effect size based on t is the t-statistics and the degrees of free-dom for the test - df. See [18]:

$$ES = \frac{2t}{\sqrt{df}} \tag{2}$$

In our case, we have t = 2.42 and df = 16. Thus ES = 1.21 and we have that N > 21. We have just 20 participants and we should thus be a little careful when concluding on this experiment.

What is more interesting, however, is the effect of the size of the groups that pro-duced the final list of defects. We used groups of size two, three and five. We will focus on the groups with two and five persons in order to get as great a contrast as possible. The data are organized as shown in table 2 below. We have used the stan-dard experimental design notation – see for instance [13].

Table 2. Two-factor experiment table

Group size A	Use of checklists B	A X B	Number of defects reported
-	-	+	7
-	+	-	9
+	-	-	13
+	+	+	11

We can now estimate the effects of each factor and interaction in the usual way – see for instance [13]. We find

- Group size effect = [(11 + 13) – (9 + 7)] / 2 = 4
- Checklist effect = [(9 + 11) – (13 + 7)] / 2 = 0
- Interaction effect = [(7 + 11) – (13 + 9)] / 2 = -2

In order to conclude, we need the standard deviation of the effects. This is usually estimated based on the assumption that the higher order interactions – order of three or more – equal zero. Since we have two factors and thus only one interaction, this approach can not be used here. Instead we have used the standard deviation value for the pooled data of all individual inspections, which is 1.7. Two standard deviations – 3.4 – give us an approximate confidence level of 5% which means that we will reject both the checklist effect and the effect of the checklist – size interaction, and only accept the size effect as significant.

Since the checklist has a significant effect on single person inspections, it seems that the checklist is used as an ersatz for diverse experiences – albeit an inferior one.

4.3 NTNU Experiment 2

The second NTNU experiment [3] was performed to study the influence of experience and the effect on three common types of defects – wrong code, missing code and extra code. In this experiment, we used only individual inspections. In order to increase the available experience, we supplied a checklist. As observed in NTNU experiment 1, using a checklist will have a beneficial effect for small groups.

We had 21 persons with high experience and 21 persons with low experience. A simple graph shows the effect of experience on the probability of detecting the tree defect types, depending on the level of experience:

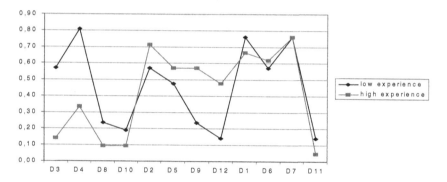

Fig. 4. Defect types, experience level and the probability of defect detection

The four first defects are missing code; the next four defects are extra code while the four last defects are wrong code. See appendix A for a description of each defect. The first important question is – did those with more experience find more defects? The rather surprising observation is that the persons with low experience found more defects than did the personnel with high experience – 5.5 versus 5.1. The difference is, however, not significant. Thus, it seems like we cannot improve the code inspections by including more experienced personnel; at least not personnel with more general software engineering and development experience.

If we, instead of looking at the overall data, look at the data from each defect category, we find that personnel with

- Low experience is better at finding missing code. The difference is statistically significant – p < 0.01.
- High experience is better at finding extra code statement. The difference is statistically significant with p = 0.01

- Low – or high – experience are no better than the others in finding wrong code statements since p = 0.38.

The results are consistent with the results reported by V. Basili [9]. Now that we know this, how can we use it to improve code inspections? First we have to look beyond the rather broad word "experience". The main difference in experience between the high level and the low level participants was general experience. The participants in the high experience groups were PhD students, while the participants in the low experience groups were third and fourth year students. A closer look at the entry questionnaire for the two groups shows that the low experience group had more recent hands-on experience in writing and debugging Java code than the high experience group.

The data indicates that the high experience subjects focused more on the overall functionality of the software and did not really read all the code. Thus, they missed simple but low level defects like the missing keyword "static" – D3 – which anyone that has ever coded Java *must* know is a defect. Trivial missing code defects were not even considered, while they found defects related to extra code.

What should worry us most are the two missing statement defects D8 and D10 and the wrong statement defect D11. These defects were found by few persons in both experience categories and are the defects most likely to be missed. The difference between the number participants finding these three defects and finding the rest of the defects is statistically significant with $p < 0.01$.

An explanation to this effect can be deduced from the way the checklist is organized. The checklist has 47 questions all in all, spread over 12 sections, covering two full pages. No question in the checklist is related to D11 and the questions related to defects D8 and D10 are in the last section of the checklist. The observed effect is most properly named the fatigue effect and seems to occur if we have long checklists or large amount of code.

5 Threats to Validity

Since all the three experiments reported here were student experiments run at a university, we will discuss the threats to validity for all three experiments together. Most of the following discussion is taken from [3].

5.1 Conclusion Validity

The conclusion validity is concerned with to what extent the conclusions are statistically valid. From equations (1, 2), we see that we need 22 participants or more given our chosen probabilities for type I and type II errors. Since we have only 20 participants, we feel that the conclusion validity in this case is medium. Threats related to our selection of subjects are taken care of since both groups – high and low experience – were homogenous with respect to education and relevant experiences.

5.2 Internal Validity

The internal validity is concerned with whether we are able to show a cause – effect relationship in our experiment. It is, in general impossible to prove a cause - effect relationship by means of statistical analysis alone. It is likewise impossible to show this by a discussion. What we can show is that we have taken reasonable precautions concerning some of the dangers that an experiment meets when trying to observe an effect of a treatment and have chosen to focus on selection, and instrumentations.

The groups in the NTNU 1 experiment were made homogeneous by using the participants' profiles. For the NTNU 2 experiment we had a set of subjects that were quite homogeneous from the start, except for the amount of experience. For the UNSW experiment we had no control over the experience and knowledge profile of the group other that they all belonged to the same course. On the other hand – the fact that they had the same amount of software engineering education makes them a quite homogeneous group from the start.   Thus, in all three cases we feel confident that the groups were reasonable homogeneous.

The instrumentation threat to validity arises out of differences in the way we perform pre- and post-measurements. Since this experiment is only concerned with counting defects found, this threat can only arise if we define or count defects in different ways. We hade defined the defects before the experiment started and registered the seeded defects from the forms turned in by the subjects. The code base has been used for quite some time and no defects other than the seeded defects have been observed.

5.3 Construction Validity

Construction validity is concerned with the extent to which we measure the data relevant to our hypotheses. Our main concerns are whether the metrics we used captured the attributes of interest – the ability to identify defects in a piece of code. The metric used – number of faults found – will measure the participants' ability to find defects and is thus considered to be reliable. Threats like hypothesis guessing, researcher expectancy and evaluation apprehension are not relevant for our experiments.

5.4 External Validity

External validity is concerned with one of the most important validities – can the results be generalized? The largest threat to generalization is that all three experiments used students as subjects. Students with low experience may not be representative for professional software developers. The students with high experience, on the other hand, have quite a lot of industrial experience through the jobs they have had during their summer vacations or through part-time jobs.

All in all, the choice of persons to participate in the experiment is the largest threat to validity. This problem is discussed in several papers - see for instance [15], [16] and the interested reader should consult these papers. The main conclusion is worth repeating here: the main difference is not related to professionals versus students but to the amount of knowledge and experience. People with knowledge and experience in a certain area will perform better than those without this knowledge and experience. Thus, a student with recent hands-on experience with Java programming will perform better at code inspection than a highly experienced project leader who has not coded for years.

The code used in the experiment may not be representative for real-world software code when it comes to size and complexity. The code used is 130 lines of Java. On the other hand, the time used was only one hour and there is thus a reasonable relation between time used and code size. Fagan suggested 125 LOC per hour [17] and this is the same as we have used. Even large pieces of code are broken down into smaller pieces for inspection and thus, our choice of code size and time used is well within the limits that one should expect to find in an industrial setting.

6 SPI Opportunities

This chapter sums up our most important advices for how to do inspections.

Hands-on experience is important. As we have seen, the class of defects detected depends on the reviewers' experience. There seems to be little need for general experience - what we need is theme-specific experience. Thus, when constructing an inspection team, we need to consider the relationship between the participants' experience and the type of defects we are trying to detect.

Large groups do better than small groups. This is not in agreement with what Votta found in [10]. His reason for stating that there is no difference between small and large inspection teams is the possibility of process loss – see chapter 4.1 above – and a low return from extra time spent in inspection meetings. We have shown that an inspection meeting can give process gain as well as process loss but the main reason why we get a different result from the one published by Votta et al. [10] is in our opinion that on the average, a large group contains a larger amount of experience and knowledge. The first NTNU experiment shows that large groups in general perform better than small groups, even if the small groups use a checklist. If we can put together a group that is diverse enough to cover all important topics, we will find more defects.

A review must be understood as a social process. Even though we can lay down rules for how to perform an inspection, the group will, in general, behave as they like. Thus, we need to build a spirit of trust and cooperation in the inspection teams. It is for instance important that all defects identified are reported. As the UNSW experiment shows, this might not always be the case.

The ordering of items in a checklist is important. There are some indications that many of the subjects used the checklist in a sequential way. Defects pertaining to topics mentioned towards the end of the checklist were found by significantly fewer subjects – for instance D8 and D10.

Long checklists should be split up into smaller checklists covering each area of concern – the fatigue effect. The new, shorter checklists should be distributed among the participants according to their experience and goal for the review. In this way, each reviewer can use both his experience and the checklist to focus on the topics where he should be able to identify the most defects.

7 Further Work

The most important questions raised by the experiments are why people ignore or are unable to detect specific classes of defects and why an inspection group seems to report defects after a voting process instead of reporting any defect found by at least one member. In order to understand these effects it is not enough to conduct the type of experiments described in the experiments reported above – we need to observe the groups in action and conduct post-experiment interviews.

Since specific experience and knowledge is an important factor for the result of an inspection, it might be possible to tune an inspection team and the checklists used to a defect profile – what kinds of defects are usually found in our code?

Lastly – we might improve our inspection process by using defects that are found later, for instance during testing and operation, and do a focused post mortem asking "Why didn't we find this defect during inspection and how can we improve our inspection process so that we are more efficient the next time?"

We plan to perform experiments pertaining to these three problem areas during the autumn 2005 and spring 2006.

References

1. Stålhane, T. et al., Teaching the Process of Code Review, ASWEC 2004, Melbourne, Australia, April 13 – 16, 2004
2. Awan, T.H., Sources of variation in software inspections; An empirical and explorative study. TDT 4735, Software Engineering, NTNU, Norway, 2003.
3. Awan, T.H., Sources of variation in software inspections: An empirical research project. Master thesis, NTNU, Norway, 2004.
4. Meyers, G.J., Experiment in Program Testing and Code Walkthrough/Inspection, IBM Systems Research Institute, 1978
5. Basili, V.R and Selby, R.W., Comparing the Effectiveness of Software testing Strategies, IEEE Transactions on Software Engineering, SE-12 (7), Dec. 1987.
6. Porter, A.A. and Votta, L.G., An experiment to assess different defect detection methods for software requirements inspection. NASA research paper, 1994.
7. Laitenberg, O., et al., An Experimental Comparison of Reading Techniques for Defect detection in UML Design Documents. National research Council Canada, 1999.
8. Basili, V.R. et al., The Empirical Investigation of Perspective-Based Reading, 1996.
9. Basili, V.R et al., Investigating the effect of Process Experience on Inspection Effectiveness. University of Maryland, Institute for Advanced Computer Studies, 2001
10. Votta, L.G. et al., An Experiment to Assess the Cost – Benefits of Code Inspection in Large Scale Software Development. IEEE Transactions on Software Engineering, SE 23 (6), 1997.
11. Kelly, D. and Shepard, T., Task-Directed Software Inspection Technique: An Experiment and case Study, Royal Military College of Canada, 1997.
12. Auråen, E. Manufacturing World Commodities at the '94 Internet Conference – Dynamic Leadership through project management. Oslo, Norway, June 9 – 11.
13. Box, G.E.P. et al., Statistics for Experimenters. John Wiley and Sons, Inc., 1978.
14. Wohlin, C. et al., Experimentation in Software Engineering. An Introduction, Kluwer Academic Publishers, 2000.

15. Sølvberg A. et al.: Evaluating the quality of information models. Empirical testing of a conceptual model quality framework, Proceedings of ICS, 2003, Portland, Oregon
16. Arisholm, E. and Sjøberg, D.I.K.: Evaluating the Effect of a Delegated versus Centralized Control Style on the Maintainability of Object-oriented Software, IEEE Transaction on Software Engineering, vol. 30, no. 8, August 2004.
17. Fagan, M.E., Design and code inspection to reduce errors in program development. IBM Systems Journal, no. 15, 1976.
18. Rosenthal, R. & Rosnow, R. L. (1991). Essentials of behavioral research: Methods and data analysis (2nd ed.). New York: McGraw Hill.

Appendix A – Seeded Defects

D1: wrong statement – wrong port number
D2: extra statement – unused variable
D3: missing statement – main method is missing the keyword "static"
D4: missing statement – no closing of out-stream
D5: extra statement – unused variable
D6: wrong statement – sends wrong parameter value
D7: wrong statement – wrong parameter value
D8: missing statement – no exception handling
D9: extra statement – unnecessary parameter
D10: missing statement - no closing of output file
D11: wrong statement – wrong parameter value
D12: extra statement – code not needed

Project Web and Electronic Process Guide as Software Process Improvement

Nils Brede Moe[1], Torgeir Dingsøyr[1],
Ken Rune Nilsen[2], and Nils Jakob Villmones[2]

[1]
SINTEF ICT, NO-7465 Trondheim, Norway
{nils.b.moe, torgeir.dingsoyr}@sintef.no
[2]
Kongsberg Spacetec AS, NO-9292 Tromsø, Norway
{kenrn, nils}@spacetec.no

Abstract. Software companies have to identify and manage numerous linked processes to function effectively. We describe how a medium-sized software company improved their software development methodology through implementing an electronic process guide. We discuss how involvement in creating an electronic process guide through process workshops influences the use of the guide over time. We have found that the workshop participators were more positive, and had a higher degree of use. Processes developed by the stakeholders themselves seem to be a perfect starting point when introducing a process guide. An evolutionary introduction of the guide created a high and continuous focus on software process improvement in the whole organization. We also found that integrating the existing administrative systems and tools supporting project work with the process guide increased its usefulness.

1 Introduction

Software development is a complex process involving a number of stakeholders, and activities. Software companies have to identify and manage numerous linked processes to function effectively. Process participants need effective guidance when process conformance is important, when a process changes frequently, and when new personnel join a project.

Traditionally, this has been the realm of large organizations, and the way of describing and communicating processes has focused on printed standards and handbooks. However, such handbooks are often of limited use as Software Process Improvement (SPI) facilitators, and especially so in small and medium-sized companies.

1.1 Electronic Process Guides

An electronic process guide (EPG) can be seen as a structured, workflow-oriented, reference document for a particular process, and exists to support participants in carrying out the intended process [1]. The potential of an EPG can only be realized

I. Richardson et al. (Eds.): EuroSPI 2005, LNCS 3792, pp. 175 – 186, 2005.

when key capabilities are not only adopted, but also infused across the organization. This is complicated by the fact that there is considerable skepticism among software developers to learn from and adhere to prescribed process models, which are often perceived as overly "structured" or implying too much "control" [2]. Therefore, we cannot expect infusion of an EPG unless it is perceived as useful and easy to use in daily practice and consistent with the existing values, past experience, and needs of the software developers [2],[3]. Dybå, Moe and Mikkelsen [4] found that perceived usefulness is a fundamental driver of both usage and use intentions and, thus, that the prospects for successfully infusing EPGs will be severely undermined if they are not regarded as useful by the developers.

1.2 Process Workshops

One initiative to increase the use and benefit of an EPG is to involve the users in creating it. Participation has been one of the most important foundations of organization development and change [5].

Within the context of software development, the software developers and their first-line managers are the main experts on the realities of the company's business with respect to the day-to-day details of particular technologies, products, and markets. Therefore, it is important to involve all those who are part of the software process, and have decisions regarding the development of EPGs made by those who are closest to the problem.

Consequently, and in order to get realistic descriptions with accurate detail as well as company commitment in an efficient manner, all relevant employee groups should be involved in defining processes by using the process workshops [6] as a tool to reach consensus on work practice.

The process workshop can last from half a day to several days, depending of the complexity of the process, and the number of participants. It makes people discuss how they work – which fosters learning even before the process guide is available in the company. It also assures quality – the process guide is developed by people who know how to do the work; it does not describe how consultants or senior staff imagine the development processes to be like. More on how the process workshops described below were organized can be found in [5].

1.3 Kongsberg Spacetec

Kongsberg Spacetec AS ("Spacetec") of Norway is one of the leading producers of receiving stations for data from meteorological and Earth observation satellites. Since the company was founded in 1984 its products has been delivered to a number of clients around the world, with a current export share of 85%. Spacetec has expertise in electronics, software development and applications. 80% of the 62 employees in the company have a master's degree in physics or computing science.

At the start in 1984 the main task of the company was engineering through customer specific projects, and the main customer was the European Space Agency [7]. Because of this the ESA PSS-05 [7] software engineering standards were adopted. The standard follows the traditional "waterfall approach". During the 1990s the market situation changed, and a new kind of customer became increasingly important. These customers were not interested in how the product was developed or how the quality assurance was performed. Instead of providing detailed requirements specifications they expected off-the-shelf products that could be delivered at short notice. In return for lack of uniqueness the customer expected a much lower price, so it became impossible to charge enough for a product to cover the complete development costs. This made it necessary to develop generic products through internally financed and managed projects [8].

1.4 Motivation

The work described in this paper is motivated by a research question as well as the needs for Spacetec to change their development strategy.

The motivation for the research was to understand how involvement in creating an EPG through process workshops influences the use of the EPG among project participants in a medium-sized software company. The core research question is:

How does the involvement in process workshops influence the use of electronic process guides over time?

In answering this question we focus on finding out if there is a difference over time among those participating in the process workshop and those who did not. The research question is described and discussed in detail in [9]. In particular, we are interested in examining if process workshop participants use the electronic process guide more in what we later will define as three stages of introduction at Spacetec.

To meet the requirements from the new market, Spacetec found that using their old engineering standard suited for large projects was perceived as cumbersome and did not emphasize aspects such as incremental and component development. In order to further strengthen the quality assurance focus, Spacetec became ISO-9001 certified in 1998. The paper based, document-heavy and highly manual quality system came under increasing pressure. It became impossible to follow the standards and even more impossible to do effective quality assurance on all projects.

The need for improvement became obvious. The new ISO-9001:2000 [10] standard demands a process oriented quality system, and to keep the ISO certificate, a process oriented system had to be implemented before December 2003. Spacetec decided to define a whole new system for the entire company [11].

2 Research Method

To investigate our research question and to achieve the improvement goals of the company, we used the participative research method *action research* [12] We have organized the research according to the five principles suggested by Davison et al. [13]. As for the first principle of researcher-client agreement, this research is done in a general project on software process improvement, where the company writes an improvement plan and the researchers write a research plan. The research plan gives an overview of what data was to be collected during the study, which included semi-structured interviews of users of the process guide and project web, usage logs and minutes from discussion meetings between the company representatives and the researchers.

We followed the action research model (principle two) proposed by Susman and Evered [14] in discussing the situation of the company, planning action, taking action, evaluating action, and finally specifying for learning. We went through three "evolutionary" cycles, one with the main focus on introducing an electronic process guide, one for constructing the project web, and a final cycle for integrating the project web with existing databases in the company, see Fig. 1.

The third principle of theory is satisfied in our research question, inspired by previous work on electronic process guides and the technology acceptance model. We analyzed the qualitative interview material using principles from grounded theory, in the tool Nvivo.

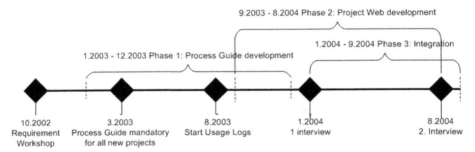

Fig. 1. Project timeline

The fourth principle of change through action is satisfied because of the actions taken prior to each of our cycles, with thorough assessments of the outcome of each cycle – through participation in six process workshops, gathering interview material, analyzing logs and discussing the usage of the web-based tool.

The fifth principle of action research deals with learning through reflection. This was ensured in the project through project meetings where researchers and company representatives discussed actions that were taken and analyses made by the researchers. For example, after the process workshops, we asked participants to comment on the way the workshop was organized, which led to changes in subsequent workshops.

3   Phase 1: The Electronic Process Guide

3.1   Diagnosing

Spacetec needed to improve and document their development methodology. This was important to meet the requirements from the new market, and to keep the ISO-9001:2000 [10] certificate. ISO 9001:2000 requires that processes are documented. Spacetec decided to develop and implement an EPG.

3.2   Action Planning and Action Taking

To get a flying start in planning the EPG, the software company Firm was invited to present their EPG for the quality department and representatives from the management. Firm had involved their own developers in defining the process descriptions and developing the EPG software [15]. Inspired by Firm's experiences the following tasks were planned:

- An initial workshop defining existing project types, and to decide the format and most important requirements for the EPG
- A series of process workshops involving the employees
- A strategy for implementing the EPG on the company's intranet.
- Dates for interviewing the EPG users and a plan for usage logging.

Spacetec defined four main project types, and they chose "Product Development" - the most common one - as a starting point for the following process workshops. Product development projects were typically 1000-4000 work hours. Other project types were customer controlled development projects, delivery projects, maintenance projects, and studies [6]. After defining the project types, Spacetec defined the most important EPG requirements. In addition to easy access, ease of use, easy to maintain, and up to date, the process guide should provide:

- Descriptions of tasks for the most important roles in a project.
- Checklists for each main process.
- Templates for all documents to be produced.
- Descriptions of best practice.
- Access to project tools (e.g. a requirement and a bug tracking system).

In the first process workshop, "Product Development" was divided into four sub processes: "Specification", "Elaboration", "Component Construction" and "System Integration". "Initiation" was the focus for the second workshop. This process was defined to include "Offer", "Follow-up" and "Blast off". As the initiation of projects is an interface between different parts of the organization, it was important to bring together people from marketing, quality assurance and the development department.

After the two main processes were defined, Spacetec released the first version of the EPG. This is described in detail in [6]. While implementing and releasing the process guide, Spacetec completed 6 more process-workshops.

The workshops usually lasted half a day, had 4-6 participants (researchers not included), and over 20 persons (1/3 of the employees) from Spacetec participated in one or more workshops. The researchers acted as moderators and secretaries.

3.3 Evaluating

The development and infusion of the EPG was evaluated through feedback from users to the quality department, discussions in the project management forum, and through the ISO revision. The researchers got feedback from participating in the process workshops, studying EPG usage logs over 13 months, interviewing the users, and from discussing with the quality department.

The enthusiasm was high after the workshops. Spacetec found it important to give the workshop participants feedback through a running system, even if it was not complete, fearing that waiting would kill the enthusiasm. The early release also resulted in complaints on the user interface and how the information was structured.

Some users never gave feedback on the EPG. This could be because they did not have time or a suitable forum for discussing the EPG.

Studying the usage logs (Fig. 2) we found that the persons participating in the workshops showed a higher use of the process guide than those not participating. We logged the usage of all the 25 persons in the software development department. These 25 were divided into two groups:

1. Participants in one or more process workshops (8 persons).
2. Not participating in any workshop (17 persons)

50% of the persons in each group were project leaders in addition to software developers. Fig. 2 shows the average number of hits for each month per person. In phase 1 (month 1-4) the workshop participants had an average use of 15 hits per person per month, and the rest had only 2 hits. For the whole period the workshop participants had an average of 20 hits per person per month, and the rest had 5 hits.

The results from the interviews confirm that the workshop participants show a higher degree of usage over time and express more advantages with the EPG [9].

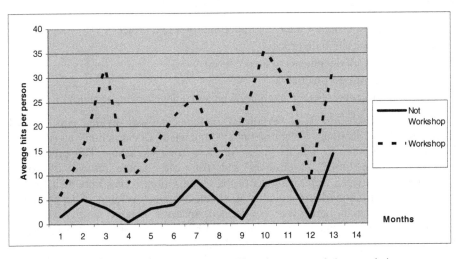

Fig. 2. Usage of process model. First phase = month 1 – month 4.

3.4 Specifying Learning

We found that the workshop participants had a higher degree of usage of the electronic process guide than the ones that did not participate in the workshops. The process workshops were also found to be efficient in terms of resources spent to design the process guide [6].

In [4] we tested the importance of organizational support and four factors on the perceived attributes of using the EPG for its infusion. We found that perceived usefulness is the fundamental driver in explaining current system usage and future use intentions, and furthermore, that perceived compatibility, perceived ease of use, and organizational support were the key determinants of perceived usefulness. Focusing on the early releases at Spacetec may have resulted in too little focus on organizational support, and that the system may have been difficult to use since it was only partly finished. Several of those not participating in any workshops reported they missed training. The EPG users gave a very positive feedback on the few project tools implemented in this phase. This motivated for the next phase.

4 Phase 2: Project web

4.1 Diagnosing

One of the important requirements from phase one, was the ability to access tools from the EPG. Examples of such tools were: requirements and bug databases, action lists, and work package planning [11]. The tools were never the main purpose of the process guide, rather they where added because they where easy to make and they fitted naturally with the process guide. The popularity of these process independent tools came as a surprise, and they were regarded as one of the major benefits of using the process guide. In addition to the tools mentioned, functionality was requested for tailoring the process of each project, showing project-progress, and organizing the project archive. Implementing these features would make the EPG a complete workbench for the project managers and project members. This workbench was called the Project Web (PW). This was the process guide in practice.

4.2 Action Planning and Action Taking

Loads of suggestions for new tools were received, and a strategy of rapid incremental development and deployment was chosen. It was decided to implement one tool at a time starting with the obvious tools. This strategy made it possible to quickly provide increased benefit to the projects, but it could also result in the most valuable tools not being developed first. It might also lead to early design choices that could cause problems later, e.g. choosing a storage format without knowing all the needed interfaces. The disadvantages of premature design choices were considered manageable, and the order of tools was considered less important as long as the tools were useful and helped boost the productivity. The following project planning and management tools were implemented:

- Work package planning - budget and remaining estimates, progress reports.
- Action-tracking
  - Automatic alerts via e-mail when due-date is reached.
  - Between customer and company.
- Risk planning and tracking
- Payment plan - planning and keeping track on payment milestones
- Project "front page" - documenting key economic and other information.
- Project "end-page" - summarizing the final project status schedule.
- Inventory - tracking equipment purchased, consumed and sent.
- Resource planning – whom and at what time.
- Deliverable list - planning and documenting HW/SW components.
- Archive - Project and contracts archive, links to related projects.
- Statistics - showing changes in the estimated remaining effort over time.

The following tools were implemented to support process activities:

- Requirements tool for writing requirements according to the company standard.
- A use-case documentation tool - a standard way of describing use-cases.

4.3 Evaluating

Analysis of the usages logs (Fig. 3 and Fig. 2) shows that the project web was more frequently accessed than the process guide in phase 2 (month 4-12). Tools were accessed more than six times as frequently as process descriptions (18 000 PW hits and 3000 EPG hits for the whole period), and the workshop participants used the PW three times as much as the other group. These results were also confirmed by the interviews. In addition to a higher degree of usage over time, we found that the workshop participants took a larger number of functions in use [9]. Also the ISO9001:2000 revision of 2004 was conducted with great success, and there were no non-conformances.

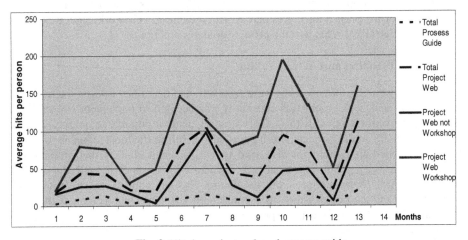

Fig. 3. Hits in project web and process guide

From the logs and dates of new tools being released, not surprisingly we found that new tools increased the number of hits on the Project Web, and this lead to more hits on the Process Guide. We believe tools are one major reason for the popularity of the EPG. Since the tools are integrated closely with the processes they encourage the use of the process descriptions.

4.4 Specifying Learning

We found that the workshop participants had a higher usage level of the Project Web than those not participating in any workshop. Workshop participants are also using new functionality to a higher degree. Involvement and initial use seem to have an effect over time.

With all the tools in place, the Project Web became a workbench for all the projects at Spacetec. The concept of integrating tools with the EPG to get the PW as well as the tools themselves has been well received by the users, and it was also obvious that people got more enthusiastic from discussing tools than process descriptions. The major advantages of the integration were:

- Interfacing to the project process and the everyday tools via one web page encourages people to check up on the process more frequently.
- All project information stored in the same system eases information sharing between projects and swapping between projects. A new project member knows by default where and how to retrieve all vital project information.
- The system becomes an experience database.

There have also been some negative feedback/experiences:

- Many of the new tools tend to compete with the use of already established tools such as MS-Word, MS-excel, MS-project and miscellaneous design tools.
- It is important with more training before introducing new tools. Some project managers and developers kept on using their old tools as well as using the new tools. They complained about double work, and were therefore more negative towards the PW.

It is not easy to decide whether to integrate an existing tool instead of making a new one. The disadvantage of integrating existing tools is that it is hard to achieve a common look and feel. The integration of tools was a huge success. A clear requirement in the ISO 9001:2000 is "processifying" the quality system, which is very well fulfilled through the Project Web implementation. It became obvious that the next step would be to integrate the project web and the tools with the rest of the company administrative infrastructure, making the Project Web and EPG a complete single interface for project work. The first obvious case was integrating the work package list with the hour accounting system. Already the work package tool showed budget and remaining estimate per work-package, it only lacked a column showing actually spent effort per package.

5   Phase 3: Integration

5.1 Diagnosing

With the implementation of tools and realisation of the project web in phase 2 the project management process had become easier and consistently integrated with the EPG. Even though this helped in generating and maintaining the project plans as well as reporting status, a substantial manual task of collecting and organising data remained. In order to have complete control of the project it is also necessary to know how many hours have been spent, the status of invoicing and payments, the status of equipment orders and tracking of correspondence. To get even larger benefits from the PW, it was clearly desirable to integrate with the other company administrative systems. In addition to the benefit of easy access to vital project data, automation has the potential of increasing accuracy and keeping project status up-to-date at all times.

5.2 Action Planning and Action Taking

When planning the integration focus was placed on:

- Technical feasibility of integration - cost and possibility of integration.
- What kind of integration gives the best value for the project manager?

The following administrative and economical systems were integrated:

- The financial/economic system - project costs such as purchases, travels, sub contractors and other expenses
- The hour accounting system
- The vendor database - containing all approved software, hardware suppliers
- The mail journal system - registers all incoming and outgoing paper mail
- The module, component and product software databases
- The bug database - errors in software during formal testing
- Document database - all documents produced in the last five years

After integrating these systems, each project member should easily find what job or work packages he or she was supposed to perform; how many of the estimated hours were used and how the total engagement was for the next 5-6 months. From the progress indicators it was now very easy to see who had not delivered progress reports, what projects run financially badly or well, and which schedules and milestones to monitor.

5.3 Evaluating

It was not possible to measure the exact use level of the integrated systems. These integrated systems have all been included in the tools developed in phase two, and do not have separate web-pages on the intranet. But from comparing the dates when new systems were integrated with the usage logs (Fig. 3) we have seen that this has increased the number of hits on the EPG. The QA department also reported that the integration phase significantly improved the reporting from the projects. Earlier the progress reporting task was mostly concerned with collecting data and performing calculations, but now it had been transformed into reviewing facts and planning ahead, as it should be.

5.4 Specifying Learning

The cost of the integration phase per system has only been from a couple of hours to a week, which is considered "cheap" compared with the benefits gained. The integration has improved the quality of the project reports and decreased the time for making them, and made it easier to get an overview of the status in all the projects.

With continually increasing functionality and provision of new services the enthusiasm was still high after 13 months, which was confirmed by the interviews.

6 Conclusion and Further Work

We have learned that it is indeed possible to find solutions that satisfy all stakeholders – from top management down to project members. A process guide with processes developed by the stakeholders themselves is a perfect starting point. Next the development of tools and "views" can be done evolutionary, with frequent feedback from the stakeholders. The evolutionary approach resulted in a continuous focus on software process improvement in the whole organization. The high degree of involvement is probably the reason why the project web is considered a success. The strategy of focusing on tools and integration made the whole system more useful. The Process guide and Project web also made it possible to keep the ISO 9001:2000 certificate.

The results show that usage of the Process Guide and Project Web differs between the groups who participated in the workshops and those who did not participate in the workshops. The workshop participators were more positive, and had a higher degree of use through all three phases, of both process descriptions and tools. The implication of these findings is that users of a process guide should be involved in developing it.

6.1 Further Work

In the future, we will continue to follow the evolution of the electronic process guide and project web through several other data sources such as quantitative surveys of process guide use over time, and project inspection to find out more on the use level.

Acknowledgement

This work was supported by the SPIKE project, partially funded by the Research Council of Norway.

References

1. Kellner, M.I., et al. Process Guides: Effective Guidance for Process Participants. in Proceedings of the Fifth International Conference on the Software Process: Computer Supported Organizational Work. 1998. Lisle, Illinois, USA.
2. Conradi, R. and T. Dybå. An Empirical Study on the Attitudes to Formal Routines to Transfer Knowledge and Experience. in Proceedings of the Norwegian Computer Science Conference (NIK). 2001. Tromsø, Norway.
3. Venkatesh, V. and F.D. Davis, A theoretical extension of the Technology Acceptance Model: Four longitudinal field studies. Management Science, 2000. 46(2): p. 186-204.
4. Dybå, T., N.B. Moe, and E.M. Mikkelsen. An Empirical Investigation on Factors Affecting Software Developer Acceptance and Utilization of Electronic Process Guides. in Proceedings of the International Software Metrics Symposium (METRICS). 2004. Chicago, Illinois, USA.

5. Dingsøyr, T., et al., A workshop-oriented approach for defining electronic process guides - A case study, in Software Process Modelling, S.T. Acuña and N. Juristo, Editors. 2004, Kluwer Academic Publishers: Boston. p. 187-205.

6. Dingsøyr, T. and N.B. Moe, The Process Workshop - A Tool to Define Electronic Process Guides in Small Companies, in Proceedings of the Australian Software Engineering Conference (ASWEC), Melbourne, Australia. 2004, IEEE Press.

7. ESA, ESA software engineering standard. 1991, European Space Agency.

8. Villmones, N.J. Project manager's guide to the Galaxy - The ultimate tool for running software development projects? in Proceedings of the industry track of EuroSPI 2004. 2004. Trondheim, Norway.

9. Moe, N.B. and T. Dingsøyr. The Impact of Process Workshop Involvement on the Use of an Electronic Process Guide: A Case Study. in EuroMicro. 2005. Porto, Portugal.

10. ISO, ISO 9001:2000 Quality management systems -- Requirements, ISO, Editor. 2000.

11. Nilsen, K.R. Process improvement through development of an extended electronic process guide - from electronic process guide to integrated work tool. in Proceedings of the industry track of EuroSPI 2004. 2004. Trondheim, Norway.

12. Avison, D., et al., Action research. Communications of the ACM, 1999. **42**(1): p. 94-97.

13. Davison, R., M.G. Martinsons, and N. Kock, Principles of canonical action research. Information Systems Journal, 2004. **14**(1): p. 65-86.

14. Susman, G. and R. Evered, An assessment of the scientific merits of action research. Administrative Science Quarterly, 1978. **23**(4): p. 582-603.

15. Moe, N.B., et al. Process Guides as Software Process Improvement in a Small Company. in Proceedings of the European Software Process Improvement Conference (EuroSPI). 2002. Nürnberg, Germany.

16. Moe, N.B. and T. Dybå. The Adoption of an Electronic Process Guide in a Company with Voluntary Use. in Proceedings of the European Software Process Improvement Conference (EuroSPI). 2004. Trondheim, Norway: Springer-Verlag.

Forces Affecting Offshore Software Development

Miklós Biró and Péter Fehér

Corvinus University of Budapest, Deparment of Information Systems,
1053 Budapest, Veres Pálné u. 36
{miklos.biro, pfeher}@informatika.uni-corvinus.hu
http://informatika.uni-corvinus.hu

Abstract. This paper identifies the forces affecting offshore software
development based on a knowledge management perspective. The identified
four major forces act along the dimensions of finance, individual education,
organizational maturity, and culture. The analysis is validated on cases of
European offshoring practice exhibited in the database of the EuroSPI
(European Software Process Improvement) series of conferences.

1 Introduction

Contrary to the commonly joint use of the words "offshore outsourcing", offshoring is
not a special case of outsourcing whose most concise definition is "**contracting of
work to another company**"[1]. Offshoring can be defined on the other hand as the
relocation of work to another country. By consequent, the relationship of
offshoring and outsourcing can be depicted as two sets whose intersection consists of
offshore outsourcing:

The distinction of the above cases is important because of their different business
significance.

Recent as it may seem, outsourcing is one of the oldest process reengineering
activities of humanity, formerly called "**specialization**" or "**division of labour**"[1].
The recent outburst of interest in this approach is due to the globally **increasing share
of services and intellectual content** in products which opens new levels of
outsourcing opportunities **onshore, nearshore, and offshore** depending on the
factors discussed below.

It is the spread of **Information Society Technologies** which gave the most recent
boost to offshoring whether through the establishment of **offshore development**

I. Richardson et al. (Eds.): EuroSPI 2005, LNCS 3792, pp. 187–201, 2005.
© Springer-Verlag Berlin Heidelberg 2005

centers fully controled by the mother company, or through **offshore outsourcing** to companies in the other country. In fact, in addition to being highly enabling, **Internet services are themselves inherently outsourced offshore**, since we definitely have to rely on services operated in other countries because of its fundamentally distributed nature.

Similarly to outsourcing, offshoring is also a new expression for an old business approach. Beyond technology, it is enabled by globalization whose history just goes back to the times of **Chandragupta Maurya** founder of the first Indian empire (321 B.C.) and **Alexander the Great** whose troops were the first to open the route from Europe to Asia called **Silk Road** later. The significance of globalization is clearly recognized by **Adam Smith** back in the 18th century[2]: "But if in any of those distant employments, which in ordinary cases are less advantageous to the country, the profit should happen to rise somewhat higher than what is sufficient to balance the natural preference which is given to nearer employments, this superiority of profit will draw stock from those nearer employments…".

And we are at the heart of the issue. What are the opportunities and threats raised by offshore software development? The fact is that all opportunities are challenged by threats both of which are dialectically present in all business decisions (yin-yang).

Here are the generalised dimensions which were identified as a result of our literature review, and which were analysed in our research:

1. **Financial dimension:** Low salaries vs. labour market forces having an increasing effect on salaries (see Adam Smith[2] quotation above)

2. **Individual education dimension:** Workforce benefiting of traditionally high quality professional education vs. disadvantaged by traditionally undervalued but improving management education and practice.[3][4][5]

3. **Organizational maturity dimension:** Organizations leapfrogging to high maturity levels avoiding resistance to change vs. missing motivated gradual process improvement.[6][7]
   In the more general terms terms of knowledge transfer, the issue underlying this dimension   is   the   following:
   The transfer to another company of an intellectual asset like a mature process has the advantage of time savings and the avoidance of the necessity of unfreezing. It has on the other hand the potential disadvantage of the lack of the individual internalization and of the socialization process at the receiving company.[8]

4. **Cultural dimension:** National cultures and value systems are becoming increasingly visible across the globe due to the Internet facilitating the comprehension of the way of thinking of people in distant locations. This comprehension will hopefully turn into the recognition that the variety of cultures can be beneficial for progress in a variety of ways. National cultures on the other hand determine strongly implanted value systems whose clash may result in serious conflicts even in case of apparently minor differences. [13]

The research directions were expanded on the basis of case-studies, and the research model was built on the identified driving forces of offshoring (Figure 1). This model is analysed and explained in the paper.

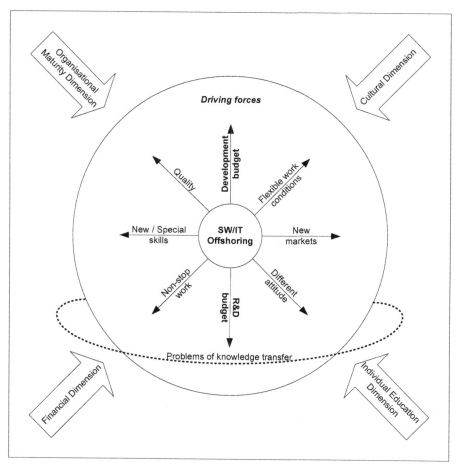

Fig. 1. Driving factors and influence challenges of offshoring

2 Research Methodology

This study is part of a research that analyses the relationship of software process improvement practices, maturity models, and offshoring, focusing on European practice exhibited in the database of the EuroSPI (European Software Process Improvement) series of conferences. A total of 80 cases - software development organisations and software/IT consulting companies – were analysed. The results are based on both the reports of the organisations (from the EuroSPI database) and personal interviews.

In order to explore the deep relationships and details, a qualitative and explorative research approach was selected. Since the relationship of software process improvement and offshoring, concerning intellectual capital, is a rarely explored area, the results are not matured, and this area is a frontier of more than one scientific fields, a qualitative approach is required.

In qualitative research, there is the possibility to explore the thoughts, definitions and assumptions of the researched persons and organisation – the context of the research. In this complex field, researchers have more possibilities to explore new, unexpected results that are relevant to the research   [31]. In qualitative research, analysis of numerical data is also possible, but the main emphasis is on the deep exploration and understanding of relationships of the research area [32].

Among the tools of the qualitative research approache, the case study based research method is the most suitable, because it provides the possibility of deep understanding. Based on Yin, case study based research should be used when the field of research is wide and complex. The research can answer the questions of why...? and how...?, but the questions should be posed by the researcher. Case study based research is suitable for testing, developing and competing theories [30]. Therefore the addressed research questions were analysed through the cases, and based on the analysis, further factors were identified (Figure 1).

Because of the research approach (explorative, qualitative, case-based), the phenomena that were identified during the research are illustrated with living examples of the analysed organisations, as short cases. Inasmuch as these case studies are presenting some problems and difficulties of companies, the names of the organisations are presented in the form of a three-character anonymous code. The cases were used as the basis of the analysis of the addressed phenomenon to explore more the research questions in detail.

3 The Financial Dimension

Undoubtedly, the major driving force behind offshoring is financial leverage (see Adam Smith2 quotation above) resulting from reduced labour costs. But financial leverage for whom and for how long time? The challenging questions relate to the **interests of stakeholders** and to the **balancing effect of labour market forces**.

The primary stakeholders of offshoring are of course the capital-owners who must benefit, otherwise would not do it. The other stakeholders are the workers of both the capital exporting country and the offshore service provider country, supplier industries, and the government of the offshore service provider country collecting taxes.

Table 1. Share of the gain by stakeholders in the US and India from 1 Dollar spent offshore

	US	India	Total
Capital-owners and customers	.62		
Extra revenue from additional exports	.05		
Profits retained		.10	
Central and State Government		.04	
Suppliers		.09	
Workers	.47	.10	
Country economy	1.14	.33	1.47

The McKinsey Global Institute (MGI) published studies in 2003 and 2004 showing statistics about the benefits of offshoring to stakeholders in the US, India[9], and Germany[10]. The aggregated summary (table 1) shows the share of the gain by the stakeholders from 1 Dollar or Euro spent offshore according to the MGI studies. The benefits include the net cost savings due to offshoring instead of spendig at home.

The numbers indicate that the offhore service provider country and the investors clearly win, while the 47 cents going back to the workers from new jobs generated is 25 cents less than the 72 cents of wage they lose according to the same study. The savings realized by lower wages are actually moderated by additional costs of telecommunication and management.

The study regarding Germany shows the numbers summarized in Table 2.

Table 2. Share of the gain by stakeholders in Germany from 1 Euro spent offshore

	Germany
Capital-owners and customers	.48
Extra revenue from additional exports	.03
Workers	.29
Country economy	.80

According to the study, the difference in capital-owners' and customers' gain between the US and Germany is due to higher coordinating costs resulting from differences in language and culture. Offshoring investors still win in Germany, the overall economy is however loosing because of the unflexible labour market.

In summary, offshoring means definite financial leverage for capital-owners, while labour market forces exercise increasing pressure on wages in capital exporting countries. On the other hand, wages are naturally increasing in the offshore service provider countries including Eastern Europe. As a consequence, time will make offshoring less attractive on the long run.

Because of the above, and many other reasons, a very recent study by Deloitte Consulting[11] states regarding general outsourcing, that "In today's economy and labor market, organizations looking for differentiated growth solutions should avoid outsourcing when based solely on cost savings."

Nevertheless, lower costs in the offshore service provider countries have also an indirect beneficial effect on the capital exporting countries and their workers on the long run. Lower costs allow for more flexibility in experimenting with innovative products and services[12] which leads to competitive advantage and eventually more highly qualified jobs in the capital exporting countries. It has to be mentioned that in the case of Germany, experimentation is also enabled by the less uncertainty avoiding culture of the offshore service provider country, as well as the higher flexibility of the labour market.

4 The Individual Education Dimension

It is generally recognized that the educational systems of offshoring target countries releases graduates with a high quality professional education. This characteristic is mainly due to the traditionally high respect for intellect and wisdom in these countries as compared to the business and management abilities. Whether the observation of these priorities originates from the political system or the national culture, globalization made it visible that it cannot secure a competitive position alone.

As the need became imminent, business and management education started to spread based on practices proven in other countries. There are however natural obstacles to the transfer of best practices even within developed countries, one of which is the resistance to change, while the other one is the difference in cultural value systems.

The issue of the resistance to change was clearly experienced by trainers from Western Europe invited to Eastern Europe for example. "Management development in Eastern Europe needs to emphasize the skills associated with diagnosing the environment, reacting to it in the appropriate manner and negotiating adequate political power to initiate and maintain the change" [5]. The above author also recognized however that this problem is only amplified in the fast changing Eastern European business environment and in fact, there is a global need to "abandon the traditional model of management education". And this is again the result of Information Society Technologies whose message is that "education is no longer a matter of content but rather an attitude of mind with a 'tool-box' of developed skills, chief of which must be diagnosing the environment and managing change".

The impact of the differences in cultural value systems on the potential of the penetration of individual management skills is highlighted by the following example of a senior Indian executive with a Ph.D. from the U.S. [13]:

–   "What is most important for me and my department is not what I do or achieve for the company, but whether the Master's favor is bestowed on me. ... This I have achieved by saying "yes" to everything the Master says or does. ... To contradict him is to look for another job. ... I left my freedom of thought in Boston."

5   The Organizational Maturity Dimension - Problems of Transferring Organisational Maturity

Analysing the offshoring practice of organisations, several typical problem areas were identified. One of the major problems of offshoring is the transfer of knowledge, transfer of intellectual capital related to the organisational processes, standardisation, quality, control – in summary: the maturity of the organisation.

The basic problem is that knowledge that should be transferred is mostly tacit, and therefore it is hard to formalise, hard to codify [14], furthermore, it is embedded in the minds of the employees, and in organisational processes. Transferring this intellectual capital can give rise to the following problems:

•   **Codification problem:** A task of the codification process is to transform organisational knowledge into a form that makes it accessible to the members of the offshore company. Therefore, the knowledge should be organised, converted into explicated, formalised and portable form that is easy to understand. In this process, the loss of the tacit parts is the most important challenge. For capturing tacit knowledge stories, detailed case descriptions are necessary, but the most useable solution of transferring tacit knowledge is the transfer of the employees themselves [15].

- **Absorption capacity problem:** In order to use the transferred knowledge, users should have the required experience, perquisite knowledge and skills so that they understand and accept knowledge [16]. If the users have different views about the world, the internal workings of the company that is included in the transferred knowledge, users will question this knowledge [17]. In this case, the use of the transferred knowledge may be either blocked, or may require further validation. In this case, knowledge transfer does not make sense, since the time and cost of this process will dramatically raise. In order to avoid the absorption capacity problem, it is necessary to recur to the right level of formalisation that can be different in different situations and contexts. Employees in similar environments, with similar tasks and in similar culture do not need a detailed explanation or background for new knowledge, for an unknown person however, at least a full overview is required. Therefore, every situation requires different abstraction levels. The highest abstraction level is the level of self knowledge sharing (e.g. personal notes or diary), that can hardly or not at all be understood by other persons. Higher abstraction level requires higher perquisite knowledge, while knowledge on lower abstraction level is understandable for more people, but the costs of formalisation are high. In the case of knowledge transfer, the optimal zone is required, in which neither abstraction level nor costs (and time requirement) are high.[18]

- **Trust problem:** It is widely investigated and accepted, that the basic condition of knowledge friendly culture is the confidence towards those, to whom employees give the knowledge, or from whom they accept it [19]. Confidence helps to form human relationships, which make possible communicational and knowledge changes. As Huemer et al [20] make a point, confidence is the main condition of knowledge changing, combination and also its development. Controversial or incomplete communication, non-defined expectations and secret-mongering of management can lead to losing the confidence [21].

- **Support problem:** Another common success factor is the right environment, support for sharing knowledge. Based on a codification approach [21], the transfer process should be supported by information technology solutions. The problem is that this approach neglects the importance of tacit knowledge. Therefore, organisational support factors, other communication solutions are necessary. In order to develop a conscious support environment, it is necessary to develop knowledge management practices, that include a well-grounded knowledge management strategy (that covers the possible goals and tools), technological tools (systems, infrastructure), and organisational solutions (HRM, culture, learning processes, structure, processes, and leadership). The continous assessment of the practice is also required (for further details: [23]).

Offshore companies are subsidiaries of existing organisations, therefore in most cases they are newly founded. But practising at the same level as the mother organisation does is not any easy process. The transferable methods, processes, culture can be identified as intellectual capital. The intellectual capital, that is required for the same practice is often tacit, hard to formalise and transfer. The national environment, culture, the behaviour of the new employees could be a barrier of using the same methods and processes that are quite common in the mother organisation. In order to transfer the existing intellectual capital and provide the same practice level, the following methods were identified.

The simplest and most common case, when the offshore subsidiary of newly founded, and the practice is based on the methods and the processes of the mother organisation. In this case, new employees should accept the methods, processes and culture of the organisation, the perquisite employment is acceptation. Employees are using this intellectual capital without questioning it, but the problem is that employees probably do not understand the reasons of this practice. In addition, the experience that is required for understanding the reasons is embedded in the mind of the employees of the mother organisation, it is tacit and therefore hard to transfer. The danger with this solution is that employees only mechanically repeating the instructions, without the possibility of improving it, and they often believe, that these requirements are only company requirements without deeper meaning. This phenomenon can lead to half-hearted work, or sabotage of the processes.

Case Studies of transferring organisational maturity and knowledge

WMA was founded in 1994 with around 10 employees as a subsidiary of a German company. Since 1994 – despite of the economical problems – the organisation dynamically grows. At the beginning, the organisation has a family-like working environment with 2-3 groups of employees. Every worker knew everything about all of the projects, methods, processes and all of the colleagues. They had all competencies which were required to solve the problems. Everybody had the possibility to know the outcomes of every project, and it was easy to ask details from the colleagues. By 2000 the number of the employees has durative exceeded 100.

Selecting a new employee was always a very important and critical task. The organisation hired not only fresh graduates but also experts in the area of IT and management. New employees should be flexible, open-, logically thinking and talent, should accept the organisational culture, methods and processes. Acceptance is not the only criteria: the personality of new employees should fit to the existing organisational culture. Even in the case of a talent expert does not pass the test (because the personality is radically different, or cannot accept the requirements), this applicant can not be hired. This approach effects the very slowly change of the organisational culture, but the acceptance and usability of the required processes and methods are high.

Over the years of successful working, new problems arisen: because employees did not understand the reasons why processes are regulated by very strict ISO specifications, the continuous use became occasionally: several documentation of report task were performed only when it was really necessary, and the practice became to abrade. Another problem was, that rules, policies, processes were good for a small company are not suit the requirements of a bigger one, therefore new locally arisen problems should be solved for what the original methods are not useable.

To avoid these problems of understanding, companies let their subsidiaries to develop themselves, to gain experience, and the employees to understand the requirements of standardization and quality orientation. The introduction of the methods and processes of the mother organization can be performed as a radical change, or as a step-by-step way.

RER initiated a project to improve its software engineering processes, this improvement required however a more formalised documentation of employees during their work. As could have been expected, the resistance to change was very strong, since employees did not know why the changes were necessary, and what the benefits of the project were. This negative attitude was overcome by formal training activities which involved the employees for whom the advantages of the new requirements were clarified. This change in the behaviour of employees resulted in their acceptance of the new methods and empowered them with personal experience, which means knowledge development. As a positive side-effect of the project, personal knowledge sharing and team-work were intensified.

CTO is the Hungarian office of an international company that has a major practice in IT consulting and system development area. The office was opened in 1989, similarly to other international organizations. The organisation has high quality standards, and it was one of the first few companies who have realised the importance of knowledge as a resource, already in the early '90s. In 1996 the company headquarter decided to apply standardized processes and methods to control the organisational practice. The new processes were introduced with certain incentives to the employees, in order to motivate acceptation.

After a few years, the management of the subsidiary were able to proudly present the success of the change management project: employees accepted and use the newly introduced processes and methods, they document their activities, and the whole practice is monitorable. But after many years of use, it is visible, that the culture of the headquarter can not impact the culture of the subsidiary any more. The turnover of the employees are very high: the expected employment of a fresh graduate is around 3 years. Therefore new employees do not feel that they should support expected processes of *CTO*.

The headquarter realized the problems, and decided changes: The incentives were cancelled, and it was believed, that the existing culture and habits will vitalise the system. It was expected that starting from that moment, the impact of the culture will be strong enough, that employees will use the expected processes for their usefulness, and not for the incentives. The outcome was a total failure: the number of the submitted items is almost dropped to zero, and the usage is lower than before.

Although in the case of *CTO*, the organization had the experience, in order to know, why the standard processes, documentation and measurability is important, this culture cannot be strong enough, because it was controlled by the mother company. To avoid these problem, it is suggested, that based on its experience, the subsidiary should realize the necessity of standardization, documentation and related activities, and with the help and advices of the mother organization, they should step forward in maturity, in their own speed. This process is more successful, but the introduction and development is much more longer than in other cases.

To summarise these experiences, it is visible, that the direct and immediate transfer of intellectual capital for methods and processes can be successful for new organisation, but problems can arise after years. For developing companies the introduction can be successful, if it is not a radical change, the changes build into the culture and the daily life of the organisations. Therefore conscious change management is required.

Table 3. Comparing organisational types related to maturity

Phenomena	Advantages	Disadvantages / Problems
New organisations with accepted methods e.g.: WMA	- Easy introduction - Fast acceptation	- Tacit knowledge is hard to transfer - Employees do not understand the reasons - Risk of sabotage - Neglecting local requirements
Experienced organisations e.g.: CTO	- Existing experience	- Unstable introduction - Required CHM - Sabotage
Developing organisations	- Stable introduction - Existing experience	- Different results - Long time of success

6 The Cultural Dimension

It was already mentioned in the introduction that Information Society Technologies enable people to easily get in touch with other cultures facilitating the comprehension of the way of thinking of people in distant locations, and that this comprehension will hopefully turn into the recognition that the variety of cultures can be beneficial for progress in a variety of ways.

The above mentioned comprehension and recognition are especially critical in the software and services industry where the capability of identifying itself with the customer's value system is of utmost importance.

It was the seminal work of Hofstede[24] which identified the generic factors, which characterize value systems in different national cultures, including those of software and systems developers', applying statistical cluster analysis. The analysis was based on questionnaires from more than 50 countries. Each of the countries could be given an index score for each of the following dimensions of national cultures:

− Power distance
− Individualism versus collectivism
− Masculinity versus femininity
− Uncertainty avoidance
− Long-term versus short-term orientation or Confucian dynamism

From the point of view of offshoring, uncertainty avoidance is particularly interesting, since it characterizes people's attitude towards ambiguous or unknown situations. Innovation usually involves a lot of uncertainty; it is by consequence easier in weak uncertainty avoiding cultures. A strong uncertainty avoiding culture like the German one, creates high anxiety in people who usually like to work hard and like establishing and following rules. The actual implementation of the results of innovation is an activity, which exactly requires this attitude.

The above discussion is a proof of the existance of different benefits that different cultures can bring to progress.

It was also mentioned that national cultures determine strongly implanted value systems whose clash may result in serious conflicts even in case of apparently minor differences. In order to highlight the impact of cultural differences[25] on the management of offshore businesses, a few examples will be described which also prove that this issue is not only relevant between distant cultures but between otherwise close ones as well.

- **Example: USA and Finland**
Atwong and Lange [26] give account of a virtual classroom experiment with students of the California State University-Fullerton and Lappeenranta University of Technology, Finland. The subject of the experiment was a marketing research project, which is irrelevant in our context. The important is that "the project combined the American and Finnish students into one virtual classroom with cross-national teams. Students used the Internet extensively for data collection… and conducted Internet chat with foreign team members when necessary." The message of the story can be summarized with the opinion of a Finnish student:
- "It was interesting to see the effect of cultural differences, even in a relatively simple project like this. When we first established contact with our American teammates, they wanted first to introduce themselves and chat about their interests and hobbies, which we thought was strange. Later we realized that this was their way to establish rapport with small talk. The Finns are used to getting immediately down to business. In the oral presentations, the American students seemed to emphasize presentation technologies more than us. However, in my opinion the quality of the work was roughly equal."

It is noteworthy that even these two otherwise close cultures may find each other ridiculous, strange, shocking or even hateful.

- **Example: France, Germany, England**
Hofstede[19] describes the results of an organizational behavior course examination reported by Owen James Stevens, an American professor at INSEAD business school in Fontainebleau, France. A mixture of French, German, and British students received a case study where they had to resolve a conflict between two department heads within a company. A sales and a manufacturing manager for example have usually conflicts since sales tries to satisfy changing customer demands, while manufacturing is more efficient if batches are larger and changes are less frequent. "The results were striking."
- "The solution preferred by the French was for the opponents to take the conflict to their common boss, who would issue orders for settling such dilemmas in the future."
- "The solution preferred by the Germans was the establishment of procedures."
- The British solution was the registration of both department heads to a management course to develop their negotiation skills.

In summary, the French with large power distance and strong uncertainty avoidance prefer to concentrate the authority and structure the activities, the Germans with strong uncertainty avoidance but smaller power distance want to structure the activities without concentrating the authority, while the British with small power distance and weak uncertainty avoidance believe in resolving conflicts ad hoc.

Case Studies related to the Cultural Dimension

To illustrate the problems of cultural differences, the example of a Polish offshore company is presented: *ITP* is a subsidiary of a German company. In the mother organisation, the standardisation of processes and methods, as well as continuous evaluation is very strong, and it is the basis of the organisational culture (that is very well suited to the national culture). In the subsidiary, this kind of approach was strange, and the risk emerged that the activities connected to the individual processes can lead to the measurement of the individual or team performance (that is embedded in the national culture, and it was new for an Eastern-European country). So e.g. the use of the system registering the defects and failures can reflect on the developers. Therefore, instead of documenting, they chose informal channels (telephone, notes). This process can compromise the quality of the processes and products on the long run. Therefore, ITP sharply separated the performance evaluation from the development processes, i.e. the information about the development processes cannot be applied for evaluating the individual or team performance. The human research management department does these evaluations in the frame of a separate process.

In another case, *DIS* can maintain an open, communication supporting culture. The company has 30 employees, therefore knowledge sharing is mainly based on personal interaction, that is even tacit knowledge can be transferred. Because of the openness of the culture, it allows fast acceptance of new ideas, and higher quality level based on direct knowledge exchange and feedback.

7 Conclusion

The goal of this paper was to identify the forces affecting offshoring. Based on the analysed cases, the following phenomena were identified in the practice of offshore software development organisations and software/IT consulting companies (Figure 1):

The most important reason for offshoring is cost reduction. The cost of the software development companies consists of two parts: development costs and research costs. The costs of these activities are concurrent, but because of the high level of competition, a general decrease of costs is required. In most cases, an offshore solution can release 20% of the budget for innovation goals [27]. In addition, this cost reduction effects, these offshore companies can have a higher budget, and they can handle more tasks, than the mother organisation. This can lead to the effect that offshore organisations are leading the competition for quality products.

In offshore countries, the company can not only use the skills (and probably the different professional views) of the new employees, and integrate them into the global practice of the organisation, but these countries can be a new, developing market of the products and services. Most of the time, in offshore countries, software development companies can find unique and special knowledge. *"We outsourced, because we had skills over there we couldn't find [here]"* says Vivek Wadhwa, CEO of Relativity Technologies, a Cary, North Carolina [28].

Beside the costs, and business perspective, offshore countries have most of the time flexible policies for work conditions and practice, and these developing countries with skilled employees gladly welcome any new investment.

Sean Chou, CTO of Fieldglass mentioned the reason for offshoring that with several offshore organisations around the world, they can stay on-line 24 hours a day, and they can satisfy the requirement of their customers very quickly [28].

Of course, there are more reasons for offshoring, but these are the main driving forces supporting a decision to found an offshore organisation. Although, there are these factors, there are some problems, challenges for these activities, which were presented in this paper. The success of every offshore organisation is very highly dependent on the success of the transfer of intellectual capital, knowledge and experience of the mother organisation. At least the transfer of core knowledge is required, that is the minimal scope and level for becoming part in the competition [29].Organisations have to deal with the challenges of codification, absorption capacity, trust, and knowledge management support factors. The challenge of the transfer of intellectual capital is a problem for every offshore organisation.

A solution for knowledge transfer is also required, when organisational processes, maturity should be shared, but it is not only a challenge for knowledge transfer, it is also a cultural change, acceptance and understanding (organisational maturity dimension, cultural dimension): employees should understand and accept the processes, policies and ideas of the mother organisation, in order to use them. Organisations should decide between a centralised solution (full standardisation for every company), and the half-independence of offshore organisation (standard policies, but freedom for realisation).

As it was seen, offshoring is a complex process, which is driven by several factors, and which is influenced by other challenges. Organisations that want to achieve success in offshoring should consciously analyse the possibilities and satisfy the requirements.

References

[1] www.tecc.com.au/tecc/guide/glossary.asp
[2] Adam Smith: An Inquiry into the Nature And Causes of the Wealth of Nations. 1776
[3] Biró,M. IT Market and Software Industry in Hungary. Documentation of the European Software Institute (ESI) 1997 Members' Forum
[4] Biró,M. (moderator); Gorski,J.; Stoyan,Yu.G.; Loyko,M.V.; Novozhilova,M.V.; Socol,I.; Bichir,D.; Vajde Horvat,R.; Rozman,I.; Györkös,J. Software Process Improvement in Central and Eastern Europe. Software Process Newsletter (IEEE Computer Society) no.12, Spring 1998, pp.19-21. < http://members.iif.hu/birom/spn_no12.pdf >
[5] Shaw,J. Management training in Eastern Europe and the Implications for Managing Change in a Changing Context. The Higher Education Academy in Business, Management and Accountancy (2001) <http://www.business.heacademy.ac.uk/resources/reflect/conf/2001/shaw/index.html >
[6] Biró,M. 10 years of SPI in Hungary (2004). < http://members.iif.hu/birom/BIRO-10-years-of-SPI-in-Hungary.ppt >

[7] Biró,M.; Ivanyos,J.; Messnarz,R. Pioneering Process Improvement Experiment in Hungary. Software Process: Improvement and Practice (John Wiley & Sons, Ltd.) Volume 5, Issue 4, 2000. Pages: 213-229. < http://www3.interscience.wiley.com/cgi-bin/abstract/76503384/START >

[8] Biró,M; Balla,K; Ivanyos,J; Messnarz,R. Stages of Software Process Improvement Based on 10 Year Case Studies. In: EuroSPI'2004 Industrial Proceedings (ed. by R.Messnarz, M.Christiansen, S.Konig). (Norvegian Technical University) (ISSN-NO 1503-416X) pp.I2-B.7—I2-B.18.

[9] Vivek Agrawal and Diana Farrell, "Offshoring: Is it a Win-Win Game?", McKinsey Global Institute, August 2003.

[10] Diana Farrell, "Can Germany Win from Offshoring?", McKinsey Global Institute, July 2004.

[11] Calling a Change in the Outsourcing Market, Deloitte Consulting, April 2005.

[12] Lael Brainard and Robert L. Litan, "Offshoring" Service Jobs: Bane or Boon – and What to Do? The Brookings Institution Policy Brief #132, April 2004.

[13] Negandhi, A.R., Prasad, S.B. (1971). Comparative Management. Appleton-Century-Crofts, New York, 1971.

[14] Polányi M. (1966) The Tacit Dimension, Routledge & Kegan Paul, London

[15] Davenport, T.H. – Prusak, L. (1999) Working Knowledge - How Organisations Manage What They Know, Harvard Business School Press, Boston

[16] Szulanski, G. (1996) Exploring internal stickiness: Impediments to the transfer of best practice within the firm, in: Strategic Management Journal, Vol. 17, Winter Special Issue, pp. 27-43.

[17] Child, J. – Foulker, D. (1998) Strategies of Co-operation, Managing Alliances, Networks and Joint Ventures, Oxford University Press

[18] Snowden, D. (2002) Complex Acts of Knowing: Paradox and Descriptive Self-awareness, in: Journal of Knowledge Management, Vol. 6, No. 2, pp. 100-111.

[19] Boussaouara, M. – Deakins, D. (2000) Trust and the acquisition of knowledge from non-executive directors by high technology etrepreneurs, in: International Journal of Entrepreneurial Behaviour & Research, Vol. 6. No. 4, pp. 204-226.

[20] Huemer, L. – von Krogh, G. – Roos, J. (1998) Knowledge and the concept of trust, in: Knowing in Firms (von Krogh, G. – Roos, J. – Kleine, D., eds.), Sage Publications, Newbury Park, pp. 123-145.

[21] Galford, R. - Drapeau, A.S. (2003) The Enemies of Trust, in: Harvard Business Review, February, pp. 88-95.

[22] Hansen, M. – Nohria, N. – Tierney, T. (1999) What's Your Strategy for Managing Knowledge? in: Harvard Business Review, Mar-Apr, pp. 106-116.

[23] Fehér, P. (2005) A technológiák szerepe a tudásmenedzsment folyamatok támogatásában (Role of technologies in supporting knowledge management processes), in: Vezetéstudomány (Budapest Management Review), Vol. 36. No.4., pp. 11-22. (Hungarian) – Fehér, P. (2004) Combining Knowledge and Change Management at Consultancies, in: Electronic Journal of Knowledge Management, Vol. 2. No. 1, pp. 19-32.

[24] Hofstede, G. (1994). Cultures and Organizations, Software of the Mind: Intercultural Cooperation and its Importance for Survival, McGraw-Hill, London, 1994.

[25] Biró,M; Messnarz,R; Davison,A.G. The Impact of National Cultural Factors on the Effectiveness of Process Improvement Methods: The Third Dimension. Software Quality Professional (ASQ~American Society for Quality) Vol.4, Issue 4 (September 2002) pp.34-41. (http://www.asq.org/pub/sqp/past/vol4_issue4/biro.html)

[26] Atwong, C.T., Lange, I.L. (1996). How collaborative learning spans the globe, Marketing News, 8/12/1996, Vol.30 Issue 17, pp16-17.

[27] Gilbert, G. – Sood, R. (2003) Outsourcing's offshore myth, December 15, 2003, http://news.com.com/2010-1022-5121783.html

[28] Hoffman, A.: CIOs on Offshoring, Monster, http://technology.monster.com/articles/offshore/

[29] Zack, M.H. (1999) Developing a Knowledge Strategy, in: California Management Review, Vol. 41, No. 3, pp. 125-145.

[30] Yin, R.K. (1994) Case Study Research: Design and methods (2nd edition), Sage Publishing, Beverly Hills, CA

[31] Oakley, A. (1999) People's way of knowing: gender and methodology, in: Critical Issues in Social Research (Hood, S., Mayall, B., Oliver, S., eds.), Open University Press, Buckingham, pp. 154-177.

[32] Blaxter, L. – Hughes, C. – Tight, M. (2001) How to research, Open University Press, Buckingham

A Framework for Improving Soft Factors in Software Development

Harald Svensson

The Royal Institute of Technology,
Forum 100, SE-164 40 Kista, Sweden
haralds@dsv.su.se

Abstract. The purpose of this research is to investigate the meaningfulness to develop process improvement support at an individual level for soft factors in software development. Soft factors are non-technical activities that are hard to measure which is problematic when developing support for these activities, as improvements are achieved by collecting and analyzing process data. The Business Process Analyst, BPA, works mainly with soft factors in software development projects. The BPA leads and coordinates analysis and modelling of businesses. The BPA was chosen to receive support for improving soft factors. The support was provided in form of a framework for collecting and analyzing qualitative data. The framework is based on interviews and assessments with BPAs from industry. The results indicate that soft factors at an individual level can be supported in software development. This is positive since more roles than the BPA work with soft factors and thus may receive support.

1 Introduction

As software development is growing increasingly more complex new areas and roles are introduced that help contribute to the software development activity. As a result, there exist roles that do not address traditional programming-related tasks such as design, code and test activities. These non-technical areas address, to a larger extent than programming-related areas, management of so called soft factors. Chakrapani [2] provides one definition of a soft factor

> *"Soft factors are used as a collective term for factors that are difficult to quantify exactly, i.e. non-technical aspects."*

Following the reasoning in the statement made by DeMarco [8] "You cannot control what you cannot measure", it may be a challenging task to provide process improvement support for soft factors, since these issues tend to be difficult to quantify by objective means. Soft factors cover a broad spectrum of activities and concepts for example including group dynamics and motivation of people. Although often difficult to quantify, there exists improvement support for these kind of issues in areas such as project and change management,

I. Richardson et al. (Eds.): EuroSPI 2005, LNCS 3792, pp. 202–213, 2005.

provided for instance by Lientz and Rea [10] and Johansson [3]. However, the underlying assumption for this study is that it is more difficult to provide support for soft factors in software development environments. This assumption is based on three factors. First, software development is a complex activity where teams often consist of people with specialized competence areas such as programming, testing, project management and so forth. This aspect can hinder communication as people may have difficulties of understanding each other, which makes it difficult to know what or how to improve a soft factor. Second, there is often a lot of changes in software development, not only in requirements but also for instance in team constellations and use of technology. This may have a negative impact when improving soft factors such as team work or motivation of team members, as unknown parameters are introduced which may reduce personal commitment to a project. Further, these changes may make it difficult to realize in which contexts or situations the support for soft factors should be provided for. Third, software development projects are often under severe time pressure. Thus, the collection and analysis of qualitative data, which is not automatic, requires time which may not be affordable. These factors or characteristics of software development is mentioned by Brooks [20] where he argues that progress in software engineering will not be substantial due to among other things the complexity and changeability inherent in software development which may create tight schedules, misunderstandings and disorientation how to develop software.

To investigate the meaningfulness of supporting soft factors in software development, support was developed for a role in software development who worked with soft factors. The reason for developing support for managing soft factors to a role was based on the relative success with PSP. PSP is a process at an individual level which provides support for the software engineer role. Although it has been difficult to transfer PSP into industrial usage, as mentioned by Humphrey [14], there has been a number of studies for instance by Ferguson et al. [21] which shows that PSP may be an efficient way to develop software. This motivates development of support for other roles, which may help improve the individual performances when applying the roles. The BPA role was chosen to receive process improvement support since it is a role who to a large extent works with soft factors in software development and it had not, prior to this study, received any process improvement support. The BPA includes tasks that are quantifiable, but the main part of the tasks concern soft factors. The BPA role is important since it identifies business requirements and transforms them into software development requirements. Further, it is a communication channel between the organization and the software developers which helps develop software that is meaningful to the organization. A more complete description of the BPA's role in software development projects is provided in Chapter 3. The purpose of the research is to investigate the meaningfulness of providing support at an individual level to soft factors in software development. Thus, although the BPA role was chosen to illustrate how soft factors can be supported in software development, other roles that handle similar soft factors may benefit from using the framework.

The outline of the paper is as follows. Chapter 2 contains related work and Chapter 3 includes a description of the BPA. Chapter 4 presents the research methodology. Chapter 5 provides an overview of the framework. Chapter 6 presents the research results and Chapter 7 presents the conclusions from the study.

2   Related Work

An important but often overlooked issue in software development is the role soft factors play in software development and how these factors may be controlled. This view is shared by McConnell [22] where he states that although programmers have the same amount of experience, can their productivity differ tenfold. This can of course partly be explained by different use of applications and so forth which address the technical side of software development. However, as argued by McConnell it is the personnel human-oriented factors that have the largest impact on productivity and quality of the delivered software. McConnell identifies motivation and the availability of senior staff as the main factors that contribute most to enhanced software development performance. The ability to motivate personnel leads to even more committed people as they tend to recognize their own increased performance which makes them eager to perform better in future projects. Further, senior staff provides a substantial amount of experience (both technical and social) to a software development project which has a positive effect on the rest of the project participants.

Wohlin et al. [23] present an approach how to control soft factors in order to reduce the time to market for a software product. The approach is based on analyzing 12 projects, where 10 soft factors have been graded in each project on a scale from 1 to 5 where the hypothesis is that high values result in fast projects. By analyzing the data, correlations between the soft factors and the completion of a project (i.e. the time to market) could be identified. Further, Wohlin et al. emphasize that the understanding and knowledge of soft factors help improve planning and control of software development projects. Thus, the study shows that controlling soft factors may improve specific activities in software development, such as planning and delivery of software as addressed in this study.

3   The Business Process Analyst

In software development projects, the BPA has a wide variety of responsibilities. They may include translating business requirements into software requirements, developing training material for software tools or specifying and executing test plans in collaboration with involved parties in an organization. The BPA is a multifaceted role, that is its work issues range from areas such as motivating people to modelling business processes. Thus, not everything the BPA does is related to software development. For instance, the BPA should be familiar with techniques for organizational design, process improvement, technology assimilation, organizational change and process modelling. The role should identify opportunities for improving business processes, organizational design and corporate culture. Thus, many of its tasks are not related to software development activities. However, the purpose of the SPI support is to provide means for improving software-related tasks that concern soft factors. As a consequence, the BPA role is supported to improve soft factors in software development.

A BPA involved in software development is defined by Kruchten [16] as:

> "The business-process analyst leads and coordinates business use-case modelling, by outlining and delimiting the organization being modelled. For example, establishing what business actors and business use cases exist and how they interact."

This definition only describes high level goals for the BPA. For instance, it mentions that the BPA must be able to work in groups of people and lead teams, but leaves it at that. To define an SPI framework which provides meaningful support to the BPA's role in software development, a more complete and detailed picture of the BPA's working situation and personal qualities should be obtained. This detailed picture was obtained through interviews conducted with BPAs from the business world.

4   Research Methodology

The research approach for developing the BPA framework is divided into a number of steps which address the development and validity aspects of the BPA framework. The study consisted of the following main steps. First, a number of BPAs from the business world were interviewed to realize important goals in their work. After determining these goals a literature survey was conducted on related works before defining the framework contents, where interrelations between the framework contents and the identified goals were made. The BPA framework was then assessed by BPAs from the business world. Finally, the BPAs were interviewed. The interviews provided more information regarding the meaningfulness of a process improvement framework for the BPA, involved in software development. After evaluating the results, an assessment of the framework's meaningfulness was made. The research question addresses the meaningfulness to develop SPI support at an individual level for software-related tasks that concern soft factors. The research question is formulated as

> To what extent is it meaningful to develop SPI support at an individual level for software-related tasks that concern soft factors?

The support was provided in form of an SPI framework for the BPA role in software development.

4.1   Selection of Subjects

Due to time and budget constraints, no sophisticated random sampling technique was applied when choosing BPAs to interview. Instead, available BPAs were interviewed in the local region. This approach could be summarized as convenience sampling described by Wohlin et al. in [4]. To ensure that the chosen BPAs were representative of the target population, they were subjectively assessed through interviews before participating in the study. Although the study participants were few (seven in total) they had different backgrounds and experiences which indicate a wide variety in the sample data thus increasing the likelihood that the sample data is representative of the target population.

4.2   The First Round of Interviews

The purpose of the first round of interviews was to gain information from BPAs in the business world, and identify important goals in their work. The interviews were prepared by studying RUP's definition of a BPA. This way, the questions were based on relevant material. The interviews were of the type open-guided interviews described by Lantz in [9]. Open-guided interviews allow a vague formulation of the research question, which is suitable when there is limited knowledge of the actual research area. Thus, the interviewees can respond with open answers to the questions, open in the sense that they may respond to the actual problem at a broader level.

4.3   Developing the Framework

The first round of interviews provided work goals for the BPA. Based on these goals contents of the framework, i.e. guidelines, metrics and templates were defined. The Goal Question Metric, GQM, technique, for instance described by Berghout and Solingen [17] was applied when developing the framework. For instance, one goal was to make people motivated to participate in business improvement work. To reach this goal it is important to know the current status of the team members' motivation, thus the question *How motivated are the team members?* was constructed. To address this question two metrics were defined. The metric *Commitment Indicator* is a subjective metric that is defined as the level of commitment of a team member for a certain time period, decided by the BPA. The metric *Complaint Metric* is defined as the number of received complaints from a team member for a certain time period, of how the BPA is leading the change analysis work.

4.4   The Assessments

The study participants assessed the framework based on its usefulness for supporting the BPA to improve soft factors in software development. Their assessments were based on how they perceived it would help them in software development, as they had not applied it in real situations. A questionnaire was used in the assessments. Each assessment was graded with five alternatives. The ordinal and absolute scale types were used on the questionnaire, because in the ordinal scale type an ordering among classes exists. Further, the absolute scale was chosen since it was important to count how many times each alternative was chosen.

4.5   The Second Round of Interviews

The purpose of the second round of interviews, was to gain additional information about the framework's support to soft factors in software development. The assessments provided raw data. The interviews provided more information that the study participants could not express in the assessments. The questions for the second round of interviews were based on the assessments. That way, a deeper understanding of the BPAs perception of how the framework would support them in their work was gained, as it was possible to follow up on issues encountered from the results of the assessment.

4.6   Validity

It was the same people that were interviewed as did the assessments. Thus, it is possible that a different result would have been obtained if it was not the same BPAs who were interviewed as did the assessments. However, due to time and economical constraints this option was not feasible. Further, the study participants were only seven in total which may affect the validity of the results. Although this is not a quantitative study where it is important to have a lot of data, a larger number of study participants would have increased the likelihood that the sample was representative of the population.

5   Framework Overview

The purpose of the framework is to help the BPA improve his work routines in software development. The framework helps the BPA focus on important aspects in software development that relate to the areas the BPA is involved in. Further, the framework provides means for the BPA to collect and analyze process data regarding his performance which help realize opportunities for improvement. For instance, the framework helps the BPA improve his/her modelling activity by providing a questionnaire which contains questions that address important modelling aspects to consider in software development organizations. As stated above, the SPI support is provided in form of a framework. In our work, a framework is defined as an environment defined for a purpose which supports activities in that environment. An alternative would have been to provide the support in form of guidelines, but a limitation with guidelines is that they only provide suggestions without really stating when to apply these suggestions. Further, guidelines are no means for collecting and analyzing data, which is a vital aspect in SPI. These limitations do not apply to an SPI framework. Thus, a framework may include both guidelines and instructions when to apply them and means for collecting and analyzing data. The defined framework consists of guidelines, metrics and templates. While the underlying principles of the framework such as guidelines for improving team work and so forth are useful, the use of a framework provides more support. The framework provides the BPA with means for improving his software development efforts by answering the questions what, why, when and how to apply the process improvement support. These questions are not answered when only applying the underlying principles. The framework consists of both unique material and support from other sources which have been adapted to fit the BPA in a software development context.

The framework is based on literature such as Lientz and Rea [10] on measuring and managing soft factors. The material was reviewed from a software development point of view. The chosen material was then adapted to support the BPA in software development. The intention of the BPA framework is to assist the BPA realize his work progress, analyze and model business processes, determine the impact of process changes and lead a team working with improving business processes. An overview of the framework, consisting of guidelines, metrics and templates are presented below in the contexts where they should be applied.

Analysis and Modelling. This work area contains a *model review checklist* which helps the BPA to verify that a business process model covers relevant aspects when modelling software development activities. *The guidelines* contain advice when analyzing or modelling, such as choosing suitable notation when modelling.

Motivation of People. This work area includes a *motivation assessment template* which helps the BPA understand how his behavior affects the motivation of the rest of the team. The team members assess the BPA on a number of factors that affect their motivation. *The guidelines* contain advice how to motivate people, such as creating a vision for the team to work towards or making sure that the software project has enough resources so that the team perceive their work as important.

Team Work. The *issue resolvement chart* helps the BPA to monitor resolved and unfinished issues. The *issue management form* is a way for the BPA to define the characteristics of an issue such as who is assigned the issue, when it was solved and how. This provides control and structure when dealing with soft factors which often are vaguely described and complex. *The guidelines* concern issues how the BPA should act to maximize the effects from team work.

Process Improvement. This work area includes *the task and schedule planning templates*. These templates help the BPA to keep track of how his actual task and time schedules relate to his planned schedules. The templates offer a good overview when prioritizing between tasks, which is important as changes are common in software development. *The guidelines* cover issues such as advice on establishing peer networks.

The BPA works with many people and in different contexts which change the purpose and goal of his work regularly. This advocates use of different parts of the framework depending on the actual situation the BPA is involved in. This condition does not suit the use of maturity levels used for instance by PSP where parts of the framework are introduced gradually in a determined way, since it is not possible to know when the BPA needs certain SPI support. Instead, the structure of the framework is based on the 4 areas mentioned previously in this chapter where each area consists of a number of goals which are important for the BPA to fulfill in order to be successful in software development projects. The framework provides an overview of the 4 areas and their associate goals, where the BPA can use parts of the framework as regarded appropriate depending on the current needs. This approach may be classified as a context-dependent framework structure where the initiative to choose framework elements is transferred to the user, instead of the contrary as with PSP. The structure (i.e. areas and goals) of the framework is presented in Figure 1.

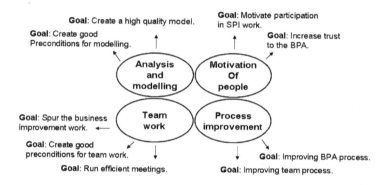

Fig. 1. The structure of the BPA framework

A more detailed description of the actual framework elements is provided at our web site [1]. It should be mentioned that although the maturity level approach was not used, the notion of gradually introducing the framework elements still applies as the BPA only uses those elements that are valid for the actual situation. In the BPA framework, guidelines outnumbers metrics. The reason for this may be that soft issues are hard to develop metrics for, due to their abstract nature. PSP, which supports the software engineer in design, coding and testing has equal number of guidelines and metrics. Thus, it seems easier to develop meaningful metrics for tasks that do not concern soft issues.

6   Results

In addition to the developed contents of the framework the results also contain an assessment from the study participants, regarding how they perceived that the framework would help improve their software development activities. The average grade on the framework's applicability consists of their assessments of the framework and answers from the second round of interviews. The results from the assessments are presented in section 6.1, and the results from the interviews are presented in section 6.2.

---

[1] http://www.dsv.su.se/ haralds/

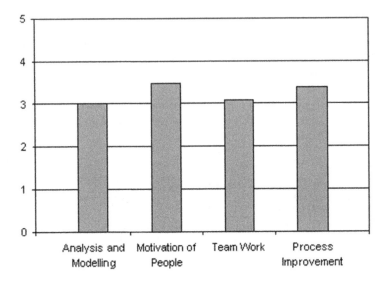

Fig. 2. The assessment results

6.1   Assessment Results

The BPAs assessed the framework's support for the BPA to fulfill identified goals in the work areas. Figure 2 presents the assessment results. It presents an aggregated view where the columns refer to the work areas. A value of five indicates maximum support from the framework. A value of one indicates minimal support.

Column one refers to the work area Analysis and Modelling. Column two refers to the work area Motivation. Column three concerns the work area Team Work. Column four refers to the work area Process Improvement.

The total average value from the BPAs was 3.3 out of 5, regarding the framework's support for a BPA involved in software development. Thus, the BPAs perceived that the framework would probably help them perform better in software development projects. The goals that received the lowest grades were goals in the area Analysis and Modelling, and the goal *Run Efficient Meetings* in the area Team Work. The goals that received the highest grades were goals in the area Motivation of People and the goal *Constantly improving the work process of the group* in the area Process Improvement. As Figure 1 shows, the BPAs assessed that the work areas received similar amount of process improvement support.

6.2   Interview Results

A summary of the answers is presented to provide an understanding how the BPAs perceived the framework. The first two questions concern improvement support from the existing framework. The last two questions concern unattended aspects that the BPAs perceived would improve the framework's level of support.

Are there some elements that you would apply in your work?

The BPAs perceived that they would apply the main part of the framework's contents, especially the elements in the work areas Team Work and Process Improvement. They were deemed as particularly useful as they addressed project progress issues and continuous improvement of team members.

Are there some elements that you would not apply in your work?

The BPAs perceived that the elements in the work area Analysis and Modelling were not so useful as they assume use of formal models, whereas the BPAs many times work with informal models, where it is more important to communicate ideas and concepts than to develop consistent formal models.

The next two questions address unattended aspects that the BPAs perceived would improve the framework's level of support.

The average assessment grade was 3.3 out of 5. What do you think it would have taken to raise the value to 4-5?

The BPAs were of the opinion that to increase the level of support the framework should provide support when dealing with political forces in an organization. Further, the BPA should know when to apply the contents of the framework.

Are there some work areas or goals of the BPA that have not received process improvement support?

The BPAs were of the opinion that a BPA needs to understand an organization's vision or view on future actions. That issue is not addressed by the framework.

Overall comments from the BPAs regarding the framework's support for soft factors were that it seems to be difficult to define meaningful metrics for soft factors. Further, the framework assumes that the BPA can spend time on analyzing collected data, which may not be the case. Further, some of the material assume that the BPA is active during a long period of time in order to improve soft factors. This may not either be the case as the BPA may participate shortly in, and move between, different software projects.

7   Conclusions

The BPAs' overall assessment of the framework's support was 3.3 out of 5. Thus, they perceived that the BPA framework would likely help them perform better in software development projects. The interviews made it clear that the framework in the work area Analysis and Modelling focused too much on a system approach, whereas it should focus more on analyzing and modelling an organization, i.e. a social phenomenon. Regarding the work area Motivation of People, the BPAs appreciated the templates for evaluating the team's relation to the BPA and the guidelines pointed out important motivation aspects. The BPAs perceived that an experienced BPA would not likely achieve major improvements in his work as a new BPA probably would, since it provides support to several work areas of the BPA which he may be unfamiliar with. This conclusion is based on opinions from the interviewed BPAs. Thus, an important contribution from the interviews was an improved understanding of what parts of the framework that provide versus do not provide process improvement support. Further, another insight gained from the interviews was that the framework should support the BPA to manage political issues in an organization, as this is seen as an important part of the BPA's work, by the interviewed BPAs.

The result from this study indicate that it is meaningful to develop SPI support at an individual level, for software-related tasks that address soft factors. A concern though mentioned in the second round of interviews is that the BPA is often involved in many activities and may not find the necessary time to collect and analyze process data, in order to identify and implement improvement initiatives. This factor was one of the reasons for conducting this study. The assumption was that time pressure would hinder the support to soft factors, who consist of qualitative data which may be more time-consuming and difficult to analyze than quantitative data. This assumption is supported by the study results. Hence, tight time schedules in software projects seem to have a negative impact on support for soft factors in software development.

Although the results indicate that soft factors can be supported in software development, further evidence is needed. As the framework has not yet been evaluated in practical use, future research includes introducing the framework into industrial organizations where it can be evaluated in real environments.

Acknowledgements

The author would like to thank Professor Harald Kjellin for comments that greatly improved this paper.

References

1. Gilbert, S.: Wearing Two Hats: Analyst-Managers for Small Software Projects. IT Professional, July/Aug, (2004) 34–39
2. Chakrapani, C.: How to Measure Service Quality & Customer Satisfaction. Technical report, ISBN 0-87757-267-4, (1988)
3. Johansson, S.: Verksamhetsbedömning i mjuka organisationer (in Swedish). Department of Business Administration, Gothenburg University, (1992)
4. Wohlin, C., Runeson, P., Höst, M., Ohlsson, M., Regnell, B., Wesslèn, A.: Experimentation in Software Engineering – An Introduction. Lund University, (2000)
5. Humphrey, W. S.: A Discipline for Software Engineering. Addison-Wesley Publishing Company, (1997)
6. Humphrey, W. S.: Introduction to the Team Software Process. Addison-Wesley Publishing Company, (2000)
7. Fenton, N. E., Pfleeger, S. L.: Software Metrics: A Rigorous and Practical Approach, second edition. International Thomson Publishing Inc, (1997)

8. DeMarco, T.: Software Metrics: Controlling Software Projects. Yourden Press, (1982)

9. Lantz, A.: Interjumetodik - Den professionellt genomförda intervjun (in Swedish). Studentlitteratur, (1993)

10. Lientz, B. P., Rea, K. P.: Professional's Guide to Process Improvement – Maximizing Profit, Efficiency, and Growth. Harcourt Professional Publishing, (2001)

11. Masaaki, I.: Kaizen - the Key to Japan's Competitive Success. Random House Trade, (1986)

12. Tague, N. R.: The Quality Toolbox, Second Edition. ASQ Quality Press, (2004)

13. Humphrey, W. S., Khajenoori, S., Macke, S., Matvya, A.: Results of Apply the Personal Software Process. IEEE Computer, May, (1997) 24–31

14. Humphrey, W. S.: The Personal Software Process: Status and Trends. IEEE Software, November/December, (2000) 71–75

15. Basili, V., Weiss, D.: A Methodology for Collecting Valid Software Engineering Data. IEEE Transactions on Software Engineering, November, (1984) 728–738

16. Kruchten, P.: The Rational Unified Process: an introduction. Addison-Wesley Publishing Company, (1998)

17. Solingen, R., Berghout, E.: The Goal/Question/Metric Method. McGraw-Hill, (1999)

18. Robson, C.: Real World Research, second edition. Blackwell Publishing Ltd, (2002)

19. Paulk, M. C., Weber, C. W., Curtis, B., Chrissis, M. B.: The Capability Maturity Model – Guidelines for Improving the Software Process. Addison-Wesley Professional, (1995)

20. Brooks, F.: No silver bullet: essence and accidents of software engineering. IEEE Computer, April, (1987) 10–19

21. Ferguson, P., Humphrey, W. S., Khajenoori, S., Macke, S. and Matvya, A.: Results of Applying the Personal Software Process. IEEE Software, May, (1997) 24–31

22. McConnell, C.: Quantifying Soft Factors. IEEE Software, November/December, (2001)

23. Wohlin, C., Xie, M. and Ahlgren, M.: Reducing Time to Market through Optimization with Respect to Soft Factors. The Engineering Management Conference, June, (1995) 116–121

Author Index

Lecture Notes in Computer Science

For information about Vols. 1–3691

please contact your bookseller or Springer

Vol. 3744: T. Magedanz, A. Karmouch, S. Pierre, I. Venieris (Eds.), Mobility Aware Technologies and Applications. XIV, 418 pages. 2005.

Vol. 3740: T. Srikanthan, J. Xue, C.-H. Chang (Eds.), Advances in Computer Systems Architecture. XVII, 833 pages. 2005.

Vol. 3739: W. Fan, Z.-h. Wu, J. Yang (Eds.), Advances in Web-Age Information Management. XXIV, 930 pages. 2005.

Vol. 3738: V.R. Syrotiuk, E. Chávez (Eds.), Ad-Hoc, Mobile, and Wireless Networks. XI, 360 pages. 2005.

Vol. 3735: A. Hoffmann, H. Motoda, T. Scheffer (Eds.), Discovery Science. XVI, 400 pages. 2005. (Subseries LNAI).

Vol. 3734: S. Jain, H.U. Simon, E. Tomita (Eds.), Algorithmic Learning Theory. XII, 490 pages. 2005. (Subseries LNAI).

Vol. 3733: P. Yolum, T. Güngör, F. Gürgen, C. Özturan (Eds.), Computer and Information Sciences - ISCIS 2005. XXI, 973 pages. 2005.

Vol. 3731: F. Wang (Ed.), Formal Techniques for Networked and Distributed Systems - FORTE 2005. XII, 558 pages. 2005.

Vol. 3729: Y. Gil, E. Motta, V. R. Benjamins, M.A. Musen (Eds.), The Semantic Web – ISWC 2005. XXIII, 1073 pages. 2005.

Vol. 3728: V. Paliouras, J. Vounckx, D. Verkest (Eds.), Integrated Circuit and System Design. XV, 753 pages. 2005.

Vol. 3726: L.T. Yang, O.F. Rana, B. Di Martino, J. Dongarra (Eds.), High Performance Computing and Communications. XXVI, 1116 pages. 2005.

Vol. 3725: D. Borrione, W. Paul (Eds.), Correct Hardware Design and Verification Methods. XII, 412 pages. 2005.

Vol. 3724: P. Fraigniaud (Ed.), Distributed Computing. XIV, 520 pages. 2005.

Vol. 3723: W. Zhao, S. Gong, X. Tang (Eds.), Analysis and Modelling of Faces and Gestures. XI, 4234 pages. 2005.

Vol. 3722: D. Van Hung, M. Wirsing (Eds.), Theoretical Aspects of Computing – ICTAC 2005. XIV, 614 pages. 2005.

Vol. 3721: A. Jorge, L. Torgo, P.B. Brazdil, R. Camacho, J. Gama (Eds.), Knowledge Discovery in Databases: PKDD 2005. XXIII, 719 pages. 2005. (Subseries LNAI).

Vol. 3720: J. Gama, R. Camacho, P.B. Brazdil, A. Jorge, L. Torgo (Eds.), Machine Learning: ECML 2005. XXIII, 769 pages. 2005. (Subseries LNAI).

Vol. 3719: M. Hobbs, A.M. Goscinski, W. Zhou (Eds.), Distributed and Parallel Computing. XI, 448 pages. 2005.

Vol. 3718: V.G. Ganzha, E.W. Mayr, E.V. Vorozhtsov (Eds.), Computer Algebra in Scientific Computing. XII, 502 pages. 2005.

Vol. 3717: B. Gramlich (Ed.), Frontiers of Combining Systems. X, 321 pages. 2005. (Subseries LNAI).

Vol. 3716: L. Delcambre, C. Kop, H.C. Mayr, J. Mylopoulos, Ó. Pastor (Eds.), Conceptual Modeling – ER 2005. XVI, 498 pages. 2005.

Vol. 3715: E. Dawson, S. Vaudenay (Eds.), Progress in Cryptology – Mycrypt 2005. XI, 329 pages. 2005.

Vol. 3714: H. Obbink, K. Pohl (Eds.), Software Product Lines. XIII, 235 pages. 2005.

Vol. 3713: L.C. Briand, C. Williams (Eds.), Model Driven Engineering Languages and Systems. XV, 722 pages. 2005.

Vol. 3712: R. Reussner, J. Mayer, J.A. Stafford, S. Overhage, S. Becker, P.J. Schroeder (Eds.), Quality of Software Architectures and Software Quality. XIII, 289 pages. 2005.

Vol. 3711: F. Kishino, Y. Kitamura, H. Kato, N. Nagata (Eds.), Entertainment Computing - ICEC 2005. XXIV, 540 pages. 2005.

Vol. 3710: M. Barni, I. Cox, T. Kalker, H.J. Kim (Eds.), Digital Watermarking. XII, 485 pages. 2005.

Vol. 3709: P. van Beek (Ed.), Principles and Practice of Constraint Programming - CP 2005. XX, 887 pages. 2005.

Vol. 3708: J. Blanc-Talon, W. Philips, D.C. Popescu, P. Scheunders (Eds.), Advanced Concepts for Intelligent Vision Systems. XXII, 725 pages. 2005.

Vol. 3707: D.A. Peled, Y.-K. Tsay (Eds.), Automated Technology for Verification and Analysis. XII, 506 pages. 2005.

Vol. 3706: H. Fukś, S. Lukosch, A.C. Salgado (Eds.), Groupware: Design, Implementation, and Use. XII, 378 pages. 2005.

Vol. 3704: M. De Gregorio, V. Di Maio, M. Frucci, C. Musio (Eds.), Brain, Vision, and Artificial Intelligence. XV, 556 pages. 2005.

Vol. 3703: F. Fages, S. Soliman (Eds.), Principles and Practice of Semantic Web Reasoning. VIII, 163 pages. 2005.

Vol. 3702: B. Beckert (Ed.), Automated Reasoning with Analytic Tableaux and Related Methods. XIII, 343 pages. 2005. (Subseries LNAI).

Vol. 3701: M. Coppo, E. Lodi, G. M. Pinna (Eds.), Theoretical Computer Science. XI, 411 pages. 2005.

Vol. 3700: J.F. Peters, A. Skowron (Eds.), Transactions on Rough Sets IV. X, 375 pages. 2005.

Vol. 3699: C.S. Calude, M.J. Dinneen, G. Păun, M. J. Pérez-Jiménez, G. Rozenberg (Eds.), Unconventional Computation. XI, 267 pages. 2005.

Vol. 3698: U. Furbach (Ed.), KI 2005: Advances in Artificial Intelligence. XIII, 409 pages. 2005. (Subseries LNAI).

Vol. 3697: W. Duch, J. Kacprzyk, E. Oja, S. Zadrożny (Eds.), Artificial Neural Networks: Formal Models and Their Applications – ICANN 2005, Part II. XXXII, 1045 pages. 2005.

Vol. 3696: W. Duch, J. Kacprzyk, E. Oja, S. Zadrożny (Eds.), Artificial Neural Networks: Biological Inspirations – ICANN 2005, Part I. XXXI, 703 pages. 2005.

Vol. 3695: M.R. Berthold, R.C. Glen, K. Diederichs, O. Kohlbacher, I. Fischer (Eds.), Computational Life Sciences. XI, 277 pages. 2005. (Subseries LNBI).

Vol. 3694: M. Malek, E. Nett, N. Suri (Eds.), Service Availability. VIII, 213 pages. 2005.

Vol. 3693: A.G. Cohn, D.M. Mark (Eds.), Spatial Information Theory. XII, 493 pages. 2005.

Vol. 3692: R. Casadio, G. Myers (Eds.), Algorithms in Bioinformatics. X, 436 pages. 2005. (Subseries LNBI).